War Over Kosovo

Politics and Strategy in a Global Age

Edited by
Andrew J. Bacevich and Eliot A. Cohen

COLUMBIA UNIVERSITY PRESS   NEW YORK

COLUMBIA UNIVERSITY PRESS
Publishers Since 1893
New York   Chichester, West Sussex
Copyright © 2001 Columbia University Press
All rights reserved

Library of Congress Cataloging-in-Publication Data

War over Kosovo : politics and strategy in a global age /
edited by Andrew J. Bacevich and Eliot A. Cohen.
     p. cm.
   Includes bibliographical references and index.
   ISBN 0-231-12482-1 (cloth : alk. paper) — ISBN 0-231-12483-X
    (pbk. : alk. paper)
   1. Kosovo (Serbia)—History—Civil War, 1998– 2. United States—Military
policy. I. Bacevich, A.J. II. Cohen, Eliot A.

   DR2087 .W37 2001
   949.7103—dc21   2001042269

∞

Casebound editions of Columbia University Press books
are printed on permanent and durable acid-free paper.
Printed in the United States of America

c 10 9 8 7 6 5 4 3 2 1
p 10 9 8 7 6 5 4 3 2 1

War Over Kosovo

Contents

To Owen Harries

Acknowledgments

This volume was made possible by a generous grant from the Smith Richardson Foundation. The editors would like to thank the trustees and governors of the Foundation and especially Dr. Marin Strmecki, vice president and director of programs.

We would also like to thank James Warren, our editor at Columbia University Press, for taking this project on. We are grateful to Nicholas Frankovich and Plaegian Alexander of the Press for seeing it efficiently through to completion. Philip Saltz prepared the index for which we are likewise grateful.

Finally the publication of this book coincides with the retirement of Owen Harries as founding editor of *The National Interest*. Any periodical necessarily represents an expression of its editor's tastes, temperament, and values. With *The National Interest* during the sixteen years of Owen's tenure this has been acutely the case. Not only bearing the stamp of Owen's own personality—cultured, elegant, intellectually courageous, and sparkling with wit and insight—his journal has also reflected a mind that values integrity, candor, clear thought, and well-crafted prose. Owen is a great editor and remains a great friend and we affectionately dedicate this book to him.

Introduction: Strange Little War

Andrew J. Bacevich and Eliot A. Cohen

Why Kosovo?

The Kosovo war was, for the conventional military historian, small beer. The vast preponderance of forces tilted entirely to one side: The U.S. defense budget was fifteen times the size of Serbia's entire gross national product, and that figure didn't even include the budgets of America's NATO allies. Yet despite Slobodon Milosevic's eventual capitulation and despite the extraordinary absence of combat casualties on the allied side, the unexpectedly protracted two-and-a-half month bombing campaign left a sour aftertaste. Although NATO's air attacks on the whole had been remarkably precise, they had resulted in hundreds of unintended casualties in Serbia and had accidentally turned a wing of China's embassy in downtown Belgrade into rubble, unleashing a furor in Beijing and creating enormous embarrassment for Washington. As initially advertised, Operation Allied Force was supposed to be short and sweet. As those expectations faded, evidence of wrangling, recriminations, and finger pointing within the alliance and between civilian and military leaders became increasingly difficult to conceal. Meanwhile, NATO's abject failure (or inability) to put an end to the displacement and massacre of large (if disputed) numbers of ethnic Albanian Kosovars made a mockery of the campaign's grand moral justification, leaving the United States and its allies fending off accusations of gross miscalculation, callousness, or outright bad faith. Finally, there was the un-savory aftermath of victory itself: Two years after the conflict, Kosovo is nei-ther democratic nor prosperous, its border neither well-defined nor peaceful. That the conclusion of NATO's first significant war found the Supreme Allied Commander Europe, General Wesley Clark, ending his tenure not with a victory parade, but with an unceremonious summons to leave his position early seemed somehow oddly appropriate. Clark's humiliating re-moval (to make room for a loyal lieutenant of the secretary of defense) was just one more reminder that from start to finish, this war—launched by former antiwar activists and draft evaders against a Balkan thug who seemed a throwback to a vintage "B movie"—had been at least slightly bizarre. Why, then, should we care about the war over Kosovo?

In different ways, the authors of this work reply, "because it has important things to tell us about the way developed countries will wage war in years to come." Far more than the Persian Gulf War of 1991, which had showcased much of the technology on display in Kosovo, Operation Allied Force ex-posed the limits of the military capabilities that the United States and its allies had developed to wage the Cold War. Whereas the Gulf War lent itself to neat, if misleading and indeed specious lessons learned, Kosovo stands as an uncomfortable warning about even the lopsidedly successful use of force. No amount of self-congratulation or spin in Brussels or Washington could mask the war's discomforts and anomalies, the bickering and mistakes of its leaders, their lapses and misjudgments.

A New Era of Warfare?

Every century, it seems, has its typical form of large scale war: The eigh-teenth century had its cabinet wars fought with cruel politeness for districts of Europe and swathes of North America; the nineteenth century its mass wars for the creation and exaltation of nation states; the twentieth century its total wars, unlimited in the ambitions that inspired them and the carnage they produced. The twentieth century's last great conflict, the Cold War, had the potential to devastate the planet in one global spasm between two vast blocks of nations armed and prepared for war on the largest scale. Small wars have always existed as a kind of counterpoint to the main event—colonial skirmishing, imperial policing, and eventually revolutionary war as well. These wars shaped, and were in turn shaped by, the larger conflicts for which they were often precursors, interludes, or sequels. For a brief moment of time after the fall of the Berlin Wall and the collapse of the Soviet Union—the events of 1989–91 that marked the real end of the twentieth century—it seemed as if both large and small wars might become obsolete.

Unfortunately, however, events soon proved that peace was not, after all, at hand. The Cold War's gratifying denouement yielded not reconciliation but heightened violence and new fears. The Gulf War did not end substantial international conflict. Epidemics of internal conflicts plagued nations in Europe, Africa, Asia, and Latin America. "Ethnic cleansing" became a seemingly commonplace phrase, while at the other end of the spectrum of conflict India and Pakistan engaged in nuclear posturing, and evidence grew that weapons of mass destruction were becoming increasingly available to the developing world. A rising military power, China periodically flexed its muscles, threatening Taiwan and asserting its claim to various small islands in the western Pacific. Exploiting the openness that is the defining characteristic of globalization, other problems commanded attention: narco-trafficking, international organized crime, and a new breed of cyber-anarchists. Incidents of terrorism occurred with sufficient frequency to persuade many observers that it posed the most insidious and perhaps the most dangerous threat of all.

The international community and major powers such as the United States responded to these developments with an odd combination of boldness and hesitation, at times acting with singular determination, as in the Persian Gulf in 1990, at other times doing next to nothing, as in Rwanda in 1994. When the international community did act—usually but not always with the United States in the van—the results were mixed.

The new century began, in any event, as an era of intense military activity. No nation manifested this more clearly than the United States, the world's sole military superpower. In the 1990s, to an extent that was never the case during the Cold War, the use of force by the United States became routine. Throughout his two terms in the White House, Bill Clinton, the first post–Cold War president, employed American military power more often, in more places, and for more varied purposes than any of his predecessors. For the United States, the military history of the 1990s is, first of all, a story of unprecedented—and, given Clinton's personal background, unexpected—activism.

To be sure, in comparison with any of the "real" armed conflicts of the twentieth century—the World Wars, Korea, Vietnam, or even the Persian

Gulf—Kosovo ranks as a puny event, more on a par with an exercise in old-fashioned gunboat diplomacy than an actual war. Western publics, the American chief among them, have seemingly endorsed this view. A year after the last allied bomb fell on Belgrade the war had all but vanished from public consciousness. Operation Allied Force faded into the ranks of myriad other military actions of the 1990s—cruise missile strikes, bombing campaigns, and armed interventions—that briefly qualified as newsworthy and then were quickly forgotten. Yet in many respects, this strange little war, not the much larger and more spectacular conflict with which the 1990s began, holds the key to understanding that decade—and with it, the emerging security challenges of the twenty-first century.

The Persian Gulf War, which sealed the end of twentieth-century warfare, was supposed to have settled things, an expectation vividly captured in President George Bush's exclamation that the United States had at long last "kicked the Vietnam syndrome." But Americans persuaded themselves—and much of the rest of the world—that victory in the Gulf had resolved more than simply a reluctance to use force carried over from Vietnam. The war put to rest nagging doubts about the basic competence of American arms. It seemingly affirmed the effectiveness of an approach to warfare—to include a preference for employing "overwhelming force"—that the Pentagon had developed and refined over the previous fifteen years. Operation Desert Storm demonstrated the capacity of U.S. forces to integrate and employ cutting edge technology. It set an ostensibly powerful precedent for how the United States would put its vast military power to service on behalf of American diplomacy in the aftermath of the Cold War. It demonstrated beyond the shadow of a doubt that the experiment with an All Volunteer Force had succeeded: The nation embraced "the troops" as the finest that America had to offer. The U.S. military emerged from the war as the embodiment of American greatness. By no means least of all, the war healed the cleavage that since Vietnam had existed between soldiers and civilians and had bred an especially acute antagonism between the officer corps and civilian elites.

In fact, as events would soon make clear, Operation Desert Storm left unsettled more than it had resolved. By the end of 1992, evidence that the Persian Gulf War was less than advertised had already become irrefutable. The victorious commander in chief George Bush had been dismissed from office; the putative loser, Saddam Hussein, remained in power in Baghdad, as he does even today, unbowed and defiant. To replace Bush, Americans had elected a president who brought with him all of the Vietnam-induced divisiveness that Desert Storm had supposedly laid to rest. Even before Bill Clinton became commander in chief, the services were already embroiled in the first of a never-ending series of embarrassing scandals—the Navy's Tailhook fiasco. Meanwhile, a variety of arduous new commitments—large-scale humanitarian interventions into northern Iraq and Somalia, for example—were making short work of expectations that the chief raison d'être of the post–Cold War military would be to fight and quickly win the occasional conventional war.

Reflections on a One-Sided War

The inspiration for this small collection of essays stems from our conviction that Kosovo provides a made-to-order opportunity to assess the implications of the changing international security environment, especially for the United States and its military, in the decade since Operation Desert Storm. This seemingly trivial Balkan war offers an invaluable window through which to gain perspective on the evolving military history of the new century, and with it the Age of Globalization, particularly as it pertains to the United States.

What follows is not a comprehensive narrative of the war as such: This is a task that others will undertake, and in some measure already have.[1] Rather, our intent is to place the war for Kosovo into a broader context. Contributors offer commentary from a variety of perspectives. William Arkin provides a concise account and critical analysis of the air campaign itself. He describes an operation in which the technology worked remarkably well, but in which the high command was internally divided, blundering, and in many ways unprepared for fighting a war in an age of instantaneous sharing of information around the world. Eliot Cohen sees Operation Allied Force as an event bringing into focus a new American approach to war, one that marks a radical break from past practice that originated in the nineteenth century. The difficulty, in his view, lies in the lag between American doctrine and institutions, on the one hand, and the new realities on the other. James Kurth assesses the conflict as an expression of a U.S. grand strategy that since the end of the Cold War has become ever grander. He sees in it, however, recklessly bad strategy, which ignores the interests of potential rivals such as China and Russia and therefore invites future complications. His pessimism finds an echo in Anatol Lieven, who situates NATO's neo-imperial disciplining of the Serbs within the larger tradition of Western military imperialism. At the tactical and operational levels, Lieven argues, Western military superiority is more apparent than real, and he turns to the Russian experience in Chechnya to illuminate his point. Alberto R. Coll explores the troubling moral questions raised by NATO's bombing campaign, both in terms of what the use of force accomplished and what it failed to do. Andrew Bacevich uses the war as a point of departure for reflecting on the evolving and increasingly problematic relationship between soldiers and American society. Finally, Michael Vickers uses Operation Allied Force to assess the American response to the ongoing "Revolution in Military Affairs." Contrary to those who saw in Kosovo a demonstration of new technological capabilities, Vickers is struck by the increasing age of the American arsenal and the unwillingness of those who design and employ that arsenal to break out of a Cold War mold.

Although as editors we confess to feeling at best ambivalent and at worst discouraged about most of the trends that Kosovo has revealed, we do not pretend that the essays that follow present a unified view of the war. When it comes to particulars, our contributors differ among themselves. They may not agree with one another that the war should have been fought at all; they may bring to their analyses different degrees of pessimism about the long-term prospects of conventional military power in a world of low-intensity war. What we all share in common, however, is a conviction that NATO's strange little war against Yugoslavia merits something more than self-congratulation or instant oblivion. As they enter a decade that will prove no less unpredictable than that just passed, the United States and its allies would do well to heed the cautionary tale that emerges from the war over Kosovo.

Note

1. See Ivo H. Daalder and Michael E. O'Hanlon, *Winning Ugly: NATO's War to Save Kosovo* (Washington, D.C.: Brookings Institution, 2000) for a straightforward narrative account of the war.

Contributors

William M. Arkin is a defense expert, independent writer, and consultant. He is a columnist for the Web edition of the *Washington Post* and for the *Bulletin of the Atomic Scientists* and serves as a military analyst for MSNBC. Mr. Arkin consults for Human Rights Watch, the largest human rights organization in the United States, and the Natural Resources Defense Council.

Andrew J. Bacevich is professor of international relations at Boston University, where he also serves as director of the university's Center for International Relations. His most recent book, written with Eliot A. Cohen and Michael Eisenstadt, is *Knives, Tanks, and Missiles: Israel's Security Revolution* (1998).

Eliot A. Cohen is professor of strategic studies at the Paul H. Nitze School of Advanced International Studies of the Johns Hopkins University and is the founding director of the Center for Strategic Education there. In addition to publishing several books related to strategy and military affairs, he serves as military book review editor of *Foreign Affairs* and is a contributing editor with *The New Republic*.

Alberto R. Coll is dean of the Center for Naval Warfare Studies at the United States Naval War College. He is the author of two books and numerous articles on the relationship of morality to statecraft and grand strategy, has served on the advisory board of *Ethics and International Affairs*, and was a principal deputy assistant secretary of defense in the first Bush Administration.

James Kurth is Claude Smith Professor of Political Science at Swarthmore College. Professor Kurth is the author of more than sixty essays and the editor of two volumes relating to international politics and defense and foreign policy, including a series of articles in *The National Interest* examining the interactions between the global economy, postmodern society, culture, and American grand strategy.

Anatol Lieven is senior associate for foreign and security policy in the Russia and Eurasia Center of the Carnegie Endowment for International Peace in Washington. He served previously as correspondent for *The Times* (London) and covered the conflicts in Afghanistan, the southern Caucasus, and Chechnya. His latest book, *Ukraine and Russia: A Fraternal Rivalry*, was published in 1999 by the United States Institute of Peace.

Michael G. Vickers is director of strategic studies for the Center for Strategic and Budgetary Assessments, a Washington-based think tank specializing in military strategy, the defense budget, and the emerging revolution in military affairs (RMA). A former U.S. Army Special Forces officer and CIA operations officer with extensive operational experience, he has published extensively on matters relating to military technology and the RMA.

War Over Kosovo

1   Operation Allied Force: "The Most Precise Application of Air Power in History"

William M. Arkin

At two in the afternoon Washington time, 8:00 P.M. local time on March 24, 1999, the North Atlantic Treaty Organization (NATO) initiated offensive military operations against Yugoslavia. Thirteen (of 19) NATO members committed aircraft, and eight put their planes in action to bomb a sovereign nation that had attacked neither any alliance members nor its neighbors.[1]

Operation Allied Force came after more than a year's effort by the six-nation Contact Group (including Russia) to find a negotiated solution to stop Serbian human-rights violations in Kosovo, one of four jurisdictions of the Federal Republic of Yugoslavia (FRY).[2] In 1998, systematic violence against ethnic Kosovar Albanians erupted, and by the fall an estimated 250,000 Albanians had been driven from their homes by Yugoslav military and paramilitary forces. Intelligence agencies predicted that tens of thousands were threatened by approaching winter weather. The situation prompted the United Nations Security Council to adopt resolution 1199 (UNSCR 1199) on September 23, calling for a cease-fire and the return home of refugees and the internally displaced.[3]

Throughout the crisis, NATO had prepared and refined military options to amplify the diplomatic process. "Activation warnings" for two different air operations were issued the day after the Security Council passed UNSCR 1199. One operation was known as the Flexible Anvil "Limited Air Response" and the other as the Allied Force "Phased Air Campaign."[4] Flexible Anvil, relying predominantly on cruise missiles, "was designed as a quick-strike, limited-duration operation, primarily to be used in response to a specific event."[5]

Richard Holbrooke, the Clinton administration's chief Balkan trouble-shooter, departed for Belgrade on October 5 to meet with Yugoslav President Slobodan Milosevic. To demonstrate allied resolve, NATO on October 13 issued a higher activation "order," threatening air action. In the face of this threat, Milosevic seemingly gave way. He agreed to reduce Serbian security forces in Kosovo and to permit international verification missions in and over the province. The North Atlantic Council (NAC) agreed to a "pause" in its threats, and in late October it suspended execution permission for air operations.[6]

After a brief period when conditions in Kosovo seemingly stabilized, attacks against ethnic Albanians resumed. On January 15, 1999, a massacre of 45 civilians allegedly occurred in the village of Racak. The Contact Group called on both sides to end the cycle of violence, summoning representatives of the Belgrade government and Kosovar Albanians to Rambouillet, France, for direct discussions on how to end the violence in Kosovo. On January 30, the NAC authorized NATO Secretary General Javier Solana to commence air strikes against Yugoslav targets if an agreement was not reached.

But the Rambouillet talks ended unsuccessfully on March 19, and NATO began preparations to initiate bombing. Days before the talks broke down, Belgrade launched "Operation Horseshoe," its methodical campaign of ethnic cleansing—Yugoslav troops and 300 tanks were massing in and around Kosovo.[7] Holbrooke once again flew to Belgrade on March 22 in a last-ditch effort to bring Milosevic to terms. That same day, the NAC authorized Solana, subject to further consultations, to ready a broader range of air options.[8] NATO planned initially to conduct a two-day demonstration strike hitting targets throughout Yugoslavia "in an attempt to convince Milosevic to withdraw his forces and cease hostilities." Two escalating response options would back up the 48-hour plan: the first, a response to continued Yugoslav acts in Kosovo, and the second, a response to aggression against NATO.[9]

Many in the NATO leadership and member governments remained hopeful that a show of force would compel Milosevic to yield. "There was that abiding belief . . . that the campaign will last two nights and that after two nights, Mr. Milosevic would be compelled to come to the table," said one senior U.S. general.[10] After the fact, U.S. officials claimed that they had cautioned allied leaders not to initiate strikes unless they were willing to escalate and go all the way. But there is no evidence that the principal players—Solana, Holbrooke, and General Wesley Clark, the Supreme Allied Commander Europe (SACEUR), in particular—questioned expectations that limited strikes would succeed in coercing Milosevic.[11]

This chapter describes the 78-day air war that ensued—from its diffident beginning on March 24 until its abrupt conclusion on June 10. The focus is on the military dimensions of Operation Allied Force: the conduct and the evolution of the bombing campaign that became in the eyes of its proponents "the most precise application of air power in history."

The Plan

Every military operation begins with a plan, and Operation Allied Force began life as NATO OPLAN 10601. The official history says that preparation of 10601 began in response to a NATO directive in June 1998. In reality General Wesley Clark, who was both SACEUR and commander in chief (CINC) of United States European Command, directed General John Jumper, commanding U.S. Air Forces in Europe, to begin developing options for an air war a month before, in May. In other words, U.S. planning for what would become Operation Allied Force began prior to and proceeded separately from the planning effort within NATO. This penchant for "U.S. only" planning reflected Washington's greater propensity to use force, an assertion of American prerogatives as the dominant partner in the North Atlantic community, and the complicated relationship of Clark, as the theater CINC, with his air-warfare subordinates. As part of the American effort to portray the U.S. role as "supporting [and] not leading" the NATO effort, attempts were made to portray the separate track as existing only to the very limited extent that operational security demanded it.[12] But even as the conflict began, separate NATO and "U.S. only" tracks continued, with alliance members denied the details of U.S. cruise-missile strikes and operations by B-2 and F-117 stealth aircraft.

Between the summer of 1998 and March 1999, NATO and U.S. planners examined an assortment of alternatives, from the limited air response to a robust "U.S. only" option called Nimble Lion, and even to "forced entry" ground campaigns. Planners found themselves responding to General Clark's ever changing "commander's intent," which provided guidance on what targets would or would not be hit in Yugoslavia. First Clark asked for a plan that would focus on five key radio-relay nodes, then for an unlimited campaign, then for strikes limited to below the 44 degree north longitude, then for a campaign employing cruise missiles only, then for one executed exclusively by U.S. and British forces. Throughout, however, certain key requirements remained fixed: Minimize collateral damage, avoid any friendly losses, and preserve the Yugoslav civil infrastructure.[13]

According to General Clark, shifting military priorities reflected an absence of political consensus. "There simply was no consensus on the part of the nations to lay in place the full array of military options," he would later testify.[14] In some ways, then, from the very beginning the prospect of escalation was implicit in any "plan." Alliance members who were determined to use force were willing to sacrifice military realism to secure political unity, believing that, once military action had begun, NATO would have no choice but to expand operations as conditions required. Should a mere show of force be unsuccessful, doubting parties would be lobbied to agree to do more.

By the time Allied Force commenced, NATO had gone through more than 40 iterations of the air-campaign plan. The version actually initiated on March 24 included three combat phases. Phase 1 would establish air superiority over Kosovo and degrade command and control throughout Yugoslavia. Phase 2 would attack military targets in Kosovo and those Yugoslav forces providing reinforcement into Kosovo south of 44 degrees north latitude. Phase 3 would expand air operations against a wide range of military and security-force targets throughout Yugoslavia, including the capital city Belgrade. If Phase 1 did not force the Serbian leadership to accede, Phase 2 and 3 would up the ante.[15]

Within each phase, significant disagreements existed inside both the U.S. and NATO militaries with regard to strategy and priorities. Those engaged in Nimble Lion planning wrestled with a host of constraints: targets within Montenegro were restricted, and critical command and control nodes— particularly telephone exchanges—remained off limits due to concerns about collateral damage, as did electrical-power generating plants and television transmitters. One effect of the restrictions was to preclude a concentrated effort in the initial 48 hours to neutralize Yugoslav air defenses. The ostensible priority at the outset of hostilities would be to establish air supremacy, but the constraints actually worked against that goal.

Looking beyond the 48-hour bombing "demonstration," General Clark and his air-warfare commander, U.S. Air Force Lieutenant General Michael Short, disagreed fundamentally about the proper design of an extended campaign. Should it concentrate on "strategic" targets in Yugoslavia or on "tactical" targets throughout Kosovo? Short believed that "Body bags coming home from Kosovo didn't bother Milosevic, and it didn't bother the leadership elite."[16] Taking Desert Storm's 1991 strikes on Iraq as his model, he argued for delivering a powerful strategic blow against the Serb leadership in Belgrade. "I believe[d] the way to stop ethnic cleansing was to go at the leadership . . . and put a dagger in that heart as rapidly and as decisively as possible," he told Congress after the war.[17]

Clark, applying what Vice Admiral Daniel J. Murphy, commander of NATO naval forces, called "a ground commander's perspective," had other ideas.[18] He wanted Yugoslav forces to bear the brunt of NATO's attacks. His focus was not only the perpetrators of ethnic cleansing on the ground in Kosovo, but also special police and paramilitary forces throughout Yugoslavia.

Among army officers, a belief that wars are ultimately decided on the ground is an article of faith. But if Clark was affected by service bias, other matters also weighed heavily on his thinking. He, and not General Short, was directly responsible for translating political guidance into operational plans. He, not his air commander, appreciated how fragile and tentative was the consensus within the alliance in support of any military action. If commanders became too insistent in demanding a more aggressive approach to using force, they would undermine that consensus and—without a shot having been fired—hand Slobodan Milosevic a victory.

Thus, from his vantage point in Belgium, Clark concluded that his political masters would never agree to opening the war with a Desert Storm–style all-out air assault on Belgrade. Advocating only the most modest bombing campaign enabled Clark to reassure those alliance members hoping that Milosevic might yet have a rapid change of mind. Doing so also seemed to signal that NATO's military chiefs saw no need even to consider mounting a ground invasion, a prospect that several members of the alliance were unwilling to countenance even as a theoretical possibility.

In short, NATO began the war without having achieved any consensus on what the alliance would do if the hostilities extended beyond 48 hours. Although the very fact that it was a "phased" campaign implied the possibility of escalation, the alliance had postponed any decision on what that escalation would entail. Clark and his civilian masters would play it by ear: if Milosevic did not quickly cave in during Phase 1, there would be opportunity to escalate and accommodate alternative approaches.

In practice, this was an invitation to do a little of everything. As General Henry Shelton, chairman of the Joint Chiefs of Staff, said three weeks into the war, the idea was to "gain and maintain air superiority, to put pressure on the Serb leadership by attacking those fielded forces in Kosovo, as well as other leadership and high-priority targets throughout the country, and then to degrade the Serb military capabilities to conduct offensive operations."[19] "Demonstrate, deter, damage, degrade," read other articulations of military objectives.[20] The four "Ds" permitted commanders and politicians alike to extend the bombing beyond Phase 1 with some semblance of purposefulness without committing themselves to having an immediate effect on the ground in Kosovo. To publics that had endorsed NATO's military action with the expectation that bombing would stop the Yugoslav military in its tracks—even Clark in a moment of candor said that his mission "was to halt or disrupt a systematic campaign of ethnic cleansing"—the four "Ds" seemed vague to the point of being devoid of meaning.[21] It is no wonder that the Defense Department would say that the objectives of Operation Allied Force had to be "refined" as the war proceeded.[22]

The plan actually executed on March 24, accommodating the differing notions of air power entertained by both Clark and Short, included both a "strategic attack line" and "a tactical line of operation." The former concentrated on Serb air defenses, command and control, forces of the Yugoslav army, and Ministry of Interior, along with the infrastructure, supply routes, and resources that sustained those forces. The tactical line of operation focused on those Serb forces actually deployed in Kosovo and southern Serbia.[23] Altogether there were eight fixed target groups: airfields and air-defense missile sites and facilities comprising the Integrated Air Defense System (IADS); leadership (or "counter-regime" targets as they were officially called); command, control, communications, computers, and intelligence (C4I); ground forces along with ammunition/military storage and border posts; electrical power; petroleum; lines of communications; and military industry. A ninth "crony" target set was unofficially added in early May, encompassing facilities judged to be of personal, financial, or psychological importance to Milosevic and his associates.[24]

Once the haggling among allies—across civil-military lines, and between services—reached a conclusion, preparations took on the assembly-line atmosphere now standard in any high-intensity air war. As planners moved from the general to the specific, they produced a list of more than 600 prospective targets, with a subset of "approved" targets. Gaining actual approval to strike a target entailed a host of considerations:

> Is this a legitimate target [under international law]? How does it relate to our military goals? What role does it play in our opponent's system of operations and how will it affect him if it is destroyed? Can we constrain our intended damage to this target only? What is the likelihood of unintended damage and how can we minimize unintended damage by changing the time of day or the physical direction of the attack?[25]

Actual sorties were then choreographed in a way that would minimize collateral damage, avoid friendly losses, and preserve Yugoslavia's infrastructure. Reflecting these constraints, among the targets excluded from attack at the outset of the war were headquarters and ministries in "downtown" Belgrade, the electrical-power system, the telephone system, civilian television and radio, non-air-defense targets in Montenegro, dual-purpose industry, and anything that posed the risk of substantial civilian casualties.[26]

Phase 1 would open with strikes mostly against early-warning, air-defense, and military-command and control elements; and ground-force installations, particularly special police and other armed "counter-terrorism" and palace-guard organizations.[27] Follow-on targets, including ground units and supporting installations, were intended to isolate and immobilize Yugoslav forces. The hope, according to General Shelton, was to limit the ability of Yugoslav forces "to move both horizontally [and] laterally on the battlefield" by damaging the road and bridge network and denying units in the field access to the petroleum supplies essential to the operation of mechanized forces.[28]

But most of this was mere window dressing. The *real* plan rested on a single unstated assumption: As soon as Milosevic saw that NATO meant business, he would sue for terms.

Phase 1

Operation Allied Force actually began with U.S. and British air- and sea-launched cruise-missile attacks, followed by a pair of B-2 stealth bombers,

F-117 stealth fighters, and two waves of additional strike aircraft from the United States, Britain, France, Canada, Spain, and Germany. It was the first combat use of the long-range stealth bomber, which flew exhausting missions from the United States to deliver, also for the first time, satellite-guided bombs, released from altitudes of 40,000 feet. In all, during the first night of the war there were four separate waves, with a total of 214 U.S. and 130 allied aircraft. Those attackers dropped just over 100 laser-guided bombs, and launched 27 conventional air-launched cruise missiles (CALCMs), Tomahawk sea-launched cruise missiles, high-speed antiradiation missiles (HARMs), and 8 air-to-air missiles. Compared to the Gulf War, the scope of the effort was modest in the extreme.[29]

By 6:00 A.M. on March 25, NATO reported that it had hit 53 targets.[30] According to the alliance, early-warning radar and air-defense headquarters, command posts, and communications centers had received particular attention, though a couple of industrial and oil targets were also struck. About 20 percent of the targets were Yugoslav army and paramilitary barracks, headquarters, and ammunition depots.

From the very outset, President Bill Clinton made it clear that American ground troops would not be committed to the fight.[31] "What we have indicated to the Congress and to the country is that this is an air operation," Secretary of Defense William Cohen said at his first press conference.[32] Indeed, there would be no need for ground troops because the operation was expected to conclude in short order. Appearing on PBS's *Newshour* the first night, Secretary of State Madeleine Albright breezily announced the administration's expectations. "I don't see this as a long-term operation," she predicted.[33]

Yet the same night, General Shelton gave reporters a different message, indicating that Operation Allied Force would "continue until such time as we achieve our objectives." The campaign, he said, was not "time-phased." As to the precise definition of those objectives, the Pentagon was less clear. "We are determined to discourage and deter [Milosevic] from continuing waging his assault against the Kosovar people," Shelton said. "We are doing that in a way that will send a message." "We would like very much for Mr. Milosevic to stop his slaughter of innocent people," added Secretary Cohen. "In the event he fails to do so, we will continue to damage his capability of waging that in the future."[34]

News reports from Yugoslavia March 25 indicated that, far from stopping the slaughter, Serb forces in Kosovo were actually intensifying their ethnic cleansing.[35] "Operations by the Serbs in Kosovo have continued," acknowledged National Security Adviser Samuel R. ("Sandy") Berger. "I think that pattern has continued and, if anything, has somewhat increased."[36]

President Clinton may have stated that NATO's goal was "to protect thousands of innocent people in Kosovo from a mounting military offensive,"[37] and Secretary-General Solana may have claimed that "we are doing our best to stop the killing which is taking place at this very moment in Kosovo,"[38] but the fact is that Phase 1 was never intended to physically prevent Yugoslav forces from continuing their offensive in Kosovo. To the extent that Phase 1 air operations had anything to do with Yugoslav forces in the field, they were designed simply to deter those forces, not to destroy them. In an interview on CNN on March 26, General Clark said, "It was *always* understood from the outset that there was no way we were going to stop these paramilitary forces who were going in there and murdering civilians in these villages."[39]

Having justified its attack on Yugoslavia as necessary to halt a campaign of ethnic cleansing, NATO found itself conducting air operations largely irrelevant to that purpose. Moreover, Clark and his commanders faced the unwelcome prospect of conducting a military campaign of indeterminate length, with political restrictions on their use of air power, and a seemingly irrevocable prohibition on the use of ground forces. "We are going to systematically and progressively attack, disrupt, degrade, devastate and ultimately destroy these forces and their facilities and support," General Clark asserted on March 25, "unless President Milosevic complies with the demands of the international community. In that respect the operation will be as long and difficult as President Milosevic requires it to be."[40] It was a bold statement indeed, but it contained more than a smidgen of bluff. Unfortunately for Clark, others—not least of all Clinton, Albright, and Cohen—had given Milosevic enough hints to enable him to see through that bluff.

Critics of Allied Force found fault with more than just its operational flaws. Diplomatically, the harshest criticism of NATO came from Russia and China, who demanded an immediate end to bombing. President Boris Yeltsin suspended cooperation with NATO, warning that Moscow reserved the right to take "adequate measures" if the conflict worsened. But within NATO and in the United States, many wondered whether or not the gradualist approach and the preclusion of ground troops had merely emboldened Milosevic's forces. "These bombs are not going to do the job," Senator John McCain told the *New York Times*, reflecting a commonly stated complaint.

"It's almost pathetic. . . . You'd have to drop the bridges and turn off the lights
in Belgrade to have even a remote chance of changing Milosevic's mind.
What you'll get is all the old Vietnam stuff—bombing pauses, escalation,
negotiations, trouble."[41]

Meanwhile, the Yugoslav people reacted to bombing by blaming NATO,
not Milosevic, for their predicament. NATO's restraint may actually have
encouraged a resurgence of Serb nationalism and popular defiance. As one
U.S. Air Force study noted, in the early stages of the war, life in Belgrade
went on virtually as normal: "Buses ran, shops were open, and people went
to cafes and restaurants. . . . The Yugoslav people felt they could carry on
with their lives since they were not being harmed."[42] Serb solidarity and
determination may have encouraged Milosevic to believe that he could wait
NATO out—that the allied consensus would weaken or that international
pressure would force an end to the bombing without obliging him to make
any concessions. "What we saw was a solidification of the [Yugoslav] political
will," says Jumper.[43]

Phase 2

Given Belgrade's refusal to play by the 48-hour script and with the first
of a massive tide of Kosovar Albanian refugees arriving in neighboring countries, the NAC decided on March 27 to escalate the air campaign to Phase
2. At his departure for Camp David on March 28, President Clinton in a
statement at the White House said: "I strongly support Secretary General
Solana's decision yesterday to move to a new phase in our planned air campaign, with a broader range of targets including air defenses, military and
security targets, and forces in the field." The key reference that indicated a
change in emphasis was Clinton's mention of forces in the field. Its hopes
for a prompt resolution of the crisis now dashed, NATO, in the words of
British Defense Minister George Robertson, had "agreed that the range of
targets for our air strikes should be broadened and the attacks intensified to
focus increasingly on the forces involved in the repression."[44]

With the beginning of Phase 2, the disagreements between Generals Clark
and Short over the proper use of air power became more pronounced. Escalation had not removed the restrictions on targets that Short classified as
"strategic," including "downtown" Belgrade, the electrical-power grid, and
civilian communications facilities. Even certain air defenses could not be

attacked to Short's satisfaction due to continuing concerns about collateral damage. On the other hand, the promise to go after the perpetrators of repression turned out to be less than advertised, Short arguing that pursuing mobile forces in the field would put his pilots at risk. Although Clark wanted to intensify the attacks on Serb units in Kosovo, he was hamstrung by his own insistence that there be no allied losses. In effect, he was unable to persuade his own subordinate to carry out his intended purpose. In the end, attacking Serb forces in Kosovo meant bombing fixed facilities such as garrisons and headquarters buildings, most of them probably empty.

With elusive air defenses still surviving in Kosovo, and Yugoslav forces dispersing, Phase 2 had little effect. Strikes against air defenses and infrastructure, Shelton said in an artfully phrased admission of how little was being achieved, continued to "set the conditions for moving on up to the forces in the field."[45] Given the continued refusal even to consider the introduction of NATO ground forces, claims that Serb ground forces had now become the real focus of attention served only to undermine further the campaign's credibility. There was little prospect that air power alone could physically stopping ethnic cleansing, conducted by small, scattered groups in villages throughout the province. From the perspective of allied pilots, attacking forces in Kosovo translated into hunting down and hitting individual vehicles—with negligible effect on the progress of Operation Horseshoe. Secretary Cohen would later claim that the attacks proceeded according to plan, creating the conditions that shifted the "balance of power" toward the Kosovo Liberation Army (KLA). NATO, he said after the war, had been "creating the possibility that the military efforts of the Kosovar Albanians, which were likely to grow in intensity as a result of Milosevic's atrocities in Kosovo, might be a more credible challenge to Serb armed forces."[46] But that is patent nonsense. In claiming that its Phase 2 efforts constituted a serious effort to stop ethnic cleansing by killing its perpetrators, NATO (and by extension the Clinton administration) was being either stupid or disingenuous.

With the shift to Phase 2, disagreement mounted within NATO as to who had the authority to approve additional targets. "There was some . . . confusion in terms of how this is going to operate, in terms of whether or not individual members had to approve or disapprove [targets]," Cohen admitted.[47] "Entire classes of targets were delegated for approval by NATO's military commanders," he said, and were subject to a variety of rules, as well as to an ultimate veto exercised initially by the United States and Great Britain.[48] The widening circle of approved targets did not, however, include "highly sensitive" categories such as the power grid or downtown Belgrade.

Yugoslav civilian casualties also proved an increasing irritant within NATO. Minimizing civilian casualties had always figured prominently in the planning and targeting process. Every target was "looked at in terms of [its] military significance in relation to the collateral damage or the unintended consequences that might be there," General Shelton said. "Then every precaution [was] made [sic] . . . so that collateral damage is avoided."[49] Assessments were performed by feeding prospective targets into several databases to determine whether any facilities off-limits to targeting . . . such as embassies, hospitals or places of worship—were nearby.[50] Using the blast radius of weapons and nearby population density, military planners used a four-tiered grading system to project civilian deaths and injuries likely to result from hitting a particular target. For "sensitive targets" these estimates were distributed directly to President Clinton, French President Jacques Chirac, and Prime Minister Tony Blair, who approved or canceled attacks, restricted the weapons employed, or modified the timing.[51]

Though the impression given by Yugoslav propaganda and a critical press might have suggested otherwise, civilian casualties in the opening days of the war were in fact kept extremely low. One reason was that the bombing effort itself was not all that intense.[52] And 100 percent of NATO weapons expended were precision-guided.[53] Between March 24 and 29, all weapons delivered were guided; only on the fifth day of the war did U.S. forces employ their first "dumb" bomb; only on the sixth day was the first cluster bomb employed. Severe restrictions requiring pilots to positively identify intended targets and to avoid possible civilian damage led to many mission terminations. Poor weather canceled entire waves.[54]

Bad weather or not, tension among key alliance members increased even more when Solana decided on his own volition on March 31 to further escalate the air campaign to Phase 2a (or 2-plus). As a result, on April 3, NATO conducted its first air strike against targets in central Belgrade, attacking the headquarters buildings of the Serbian and Federal Ministries of Interior. The French government protested, and after Presidents Chirac and Clinton consulted with one another they agreed that henceforth France would be informed in advance of any targets that carried a high risk of civilian casualties, as well as of planned attacks against the electrical grid, telephone system, or downtown Belgrade. Chirac specifically asked to review any targets in Montenegro.[55]

As infrastructure attacks expanded during the first week of April, NATO pilots were still wrestling with the daunting and complex problem of figuring out how to get at Yugoslav mobile forces. From experience during exercises and during the Gulf War, pilots and targeters knew that they had a "steep learning curve" to climb. Mountainous terrain, a well-dispersed foe who operated in small contingents and was well-armed with air defense weapons, the Serb tactic of hiding in villages or of using Kosovar Albanian refugees as human shields—all of these complicated the task. "It took all the technology we had to be able to track these guys, learn who they are, learn their habits, be able to predict what they're going to do next," said Jumper.[56]

Operation Allied Force had now lasted well beyond the 48 hours that many speculated would suffice to coerce Milosevic. As the war came increasingly to look like a protracted enterprise, the best that NATO spokesmen and leaders could say was that Milosevic was paying the price for his brutality. They vowed that the alliance would persist.

When Milosevic met with Russian Prime Minister Yevgeni Primakov in Belgrade on March 30, the Yugoslav leader offered a partial withdrawal of his forces from Kosovo if NATO would stop its air strikes, an offer NATO firmly rejected. Was air power indeed having an effect? Or was this just Milosevic's effort to create fissures within the alliance? Regardless, barely a week of bombing had occurred, and the alliance found itself increasingly on the defensive. "I think right now it is difficult to say that we have prevented one act of brutality," acknowledged Pentagon spokesman Kenneth Bacon, stating the obvious on the same day Milosevic met with Primakov. In an interview for CBS-TV, President Clinton pleaded with the American people to "have a little resolve here, to stay with your leaders, to give us a chance to really see this thing through. This air campaign is not a 30-second ad."[57]

Milosevic's War

Milosevic could not defeat NATO militarily. Though Russia was perceived as being in Yugoslavia's corner diplomatically, neither Russia nor China were willing to intervene to save Yugoslavia on the battlefield or in the Security Council. Milosevic's best bet was to erode NATO's political consensus. A combination of resolve, shooting down aircraft, taking prisoners, destabilizing Macedonia and Albania with refugees, and playing on civilian casualties and the image of Yugoslavia as unjust victim just might undermine the fragile public support for Allied Force within NATO. If Milosevic could frustrate NATO's expectations that it could win through air power alone, he might be able to force the alliance to consider the use of ground troops, which almost assuredly would divide the alliance.

In Kosovo, Yugoslav military planners calculated that they could defeat the KLA and expel (or kill) the Kosovar Albanian population in some five to seven days from the onset of hostilities. Some 40,000 Serbian troops were already in Kosovo, manning 859 tanks and 672 armored vehicles, supported by 1,163 artillery pieces.[58] Based on what they had observed in Operation Deliberate Force, NATO's two-week air campaign in Bosnia in 1995, Yugoslav commanders anticipated a demonstration attack and felt confident that they could sufficiently disperse and hide forces to neutralize NATO's air advantage. When bombing began, Yugoslavia did not aggressively challenge NATO aircraft. Fire control radars were not extensively used, negating NATO's electronic dominance. Mobile SA-6 SAM's and shorter-range anti-aircraft artillery and man-portable air defense systems, of which there were many, moved frequently.[59]

Though Yugoslavia initially husbanded its high-altitude missiles and kept its radars "quiet" to thwart NATO's antiradiation missiles, General Short minimized the risk that these SAMs posed to his aircraft by requiring pilots to remain above 15,000 feet in altitude and by flying larger "packages" of strike aircraft accompanied by dedicated jammers and air-defense-suppression fighters. In this way, Short largely frustrated Milosevic's desire to shoot down NATO planes. But this came at a price: flying at high altitude made it even more difficult for NATO to positively identify and attack mobile ground forces.[60]

Even without radar, Yugoslavia fired 845 SAMs, mostly mobile SA-6s, during the course of the war.[61] Although Yugoslav air defenses managed to shoot down only two manned aircraft, by their very survival they contributed to another purpose useful to Milosevic, namely to increase the likelihood of NATO pilots making mistakes. In a sense, civilians paid twice for NATO's determination to avoid its own casualties: First, NATO's reluctance not to "get down in the weeds" and attack the perpetrators of ethnic cleansing facilitated the success of Operation Horseshoe; and second, bombing conducted from higher altitude (at least in the first month of so) reduced the accuracy of NATO pilots, increasing the likelihood of civilian casualties.

"We are taking all possible measures to minimize collateral damage or damage to innocent civilians or nearby property that is not associated with the target," General Clark stressed in his first press conference.[62] Yugoslavia was ready from the outset, using the Internet, state-run media, and an energetic and supportive Serb expatriate community to challenge this claim, charging that NATO was intentionally targeting civilians and civilian facilities. When it came to waging "information war," Belgrade seized the initiative, issuing a barrage of reports, dominating the news media, and sowing dissension within NATO.[63] As soon as the first day's air strikes occurred, Yugoslav Foreign Minister Zivadin Jovanovic was complaining that many civilians had already been killed.[64]

In fact there were no civilian casualties on the first night. Indeed, a week into the war, only a single civilian had been killed in all of NATO's attacks.[65] Yet Clark had to devote a good part of his day to reassuring allied militaries and governments on issues of civilian collateral damage. Despite what was happening on the ground, NATO was always on the defensive and never did succeed in putting Yugoslav's claims into perspective. By April 14, when as many as 73 civilians were killed on the road between Djakovica and Decane when pilots confused tractors pulling farm wagons with military vehicles, Belgrade had succeeded in conveying the impression that this was a regular occurrence.

To protect their own forces on the ground and confound targeting, Serb units intentionally operated among civilian refugees, in villages, and near prohibited targets such as churches.[66] When aircraft did start to go after ground elements in Kosovo, Yugoslavia also made use of a variety of camouflage, concealment, and deception efforts to fool NATO, employing a mix of low- and high-tech decoys.[67] The NATO rule, according to Short, was that "we had to put eyes on target every time we were going to strike a tank or an artillery piece."[68] Before the 15,000-feet restriction was lifted for certain attacks in Kosovo, that requirement, combined with poor weather, meant that far fewer attacks were actually undertaken than were attempted. Still, once attacks on mobile forces in Kosovo got underway around day thirteen, Yugoslav forces were forced to modify their operations.[69] According to Admiral Murphy, "We took away the roads, we took away the day time, . . . we forced them to hide under trees and inside barns."[70] But making life difficult for the Serb forces was not the same as rendering them ineffective.

In late April, just prior to the upcoming Washington NATO summit, General Clark received permission from Solana to begin quietly assessing possible ground options.[71] Within NATO there was still no political consensus to go forward with serious planning for a ground war. Yet the senior military staff at SHAPE headquarters was reportedly telling Clark, "If you want to induce the Serbs to leave Kosovo, you are going to have to use ground forces to do it." Clark also had two ulterior motives for wanting to initiate ground war planning. First, he wanted to shore up his support among American generals, particularly among skeptics in the Joint Chiefs of Staff and in the U.S. Army who were critical of his handling of the war thus far.[72] Second, he wanted to acquire leverage that he could use to expand the air campaign well beyond the parameters permitted by Phase 2. "One of the reasons we were successful in getting the go-ahead to go downtown," he would later testify, "was because it was an alternative to ground troops."[73]

Two weeks into what would become an eleven-week campaign, NATO leaders were insisting that they had always said that the campaign would be "difficult and time consuming."[74] The forces made available to Clark were increasing several fold. By week two, the number of aircraft had reached almost 600, an increase of almost one-third from March 24. Fourteen NATO members committed themselves to providing an additional 500 aircraft.[75] NATO also launched wide-ranging diplomatic efforts to convince Milosevic to pull back his military before bombing destroyed his country. This included, most centrally, enlisting Russia as a partner in the search for a diplomatic agreement. On the day of the Djakovica-Decane incident, the worst case of civilian deaths so far in the war, Yeltsin named former Prime Minister Vladimir Chernomyrdin as his presidential envoy on Kosovo. A week later, Yeltsin stated that Moscow "cannot break with leading world powers" over Kosovo, signaling the narrow limits of Russian support for Belgrade.

The Beginning of the End

The NATO Washington Summit starting on April 23 gave Milosevic his last chance to shatter the political consensus. Leaders and parliamentarians in Italy, Germany, and Greece had all at different times called for bombing pauses. Although the summit suggested the prospect of high drama, alliance leaders merely reconfirmed their commitment to the war and agreed to escalate the air campaign even further. Two decisions in particular were key: electricity and industrial infrastructure were added to the list of authorized targets, and attacks would henceforth occur on a round-the-clock basis.[76] Significantly, Phase 3 would not formally be requested, a move that would have required the NAC to certify a formal "consensus." Instead NATO leaders took the shortcut of authorizing Solana to decide on behalf of the NAC. Clark still had to "request specific additions to target categories," particularly those with "high political connotations."[77] The "U.S. only" targeting circle expanded slightly to include British planners and intelligence experts who would help identify likely targets amongst the personal property and businesses of Milosevic and his cronies.

NATO had already employed economic and political means—sanctions, tightened travel restrictions, frozen financial holdings—to foster "anxiety and discontent within Belgrade's power circles."[78] The United States had also undertaken "Operation Matrix," a covert operation that included harassing and pressuring Milosevic insiders by faxing and calling them on their cell phones.[79] Attacks on factories associated with Milosevic and his associates were used as threats to foment discontent in the inner circle and amongst the Serbian elite. Knocking out electrical power would begin to put pressure on the civilian population as a whole. "We were trying to find additional targets," said Deputy Secretary of Defense John Hamre. "We had hoped that the air campaign would have brought the Milosevic government to a realization that this was a losing cause earlier. . . . it went longer than we thought."[80] Explaining his rationale for attacking targets that just a month before had been considered illegitimate, Clark suggested that "Economic dislocations that are bound to affect the electricity and heating are going to charge up the opposition and bring greater pressure against [Milosevic]."[81]

As the air war proceeded into May, the tempo of attacks increased markedly, as did the resulting damage to the military and civilian infrastructure of Yugoslavia. At the same time, the KLA, which earlier had suffered a string of defeats at the hands of Yugoslav forces, began to regroup. There were signs that military defections and dissent amongst Yugoslav conscripts and reservists were mounting. For the first time since the war had begun, a number of mayors in Serbia were now speaking out against Milosevic. And families of service members were beginning to protest openly—not against NATO but against the regime.[82] NATO also announced on April 24 that, as a result of attacks on fixed SA-2 and SA-3 sites, it had formally achieved air superiority in the mid to high altitudes. General Short revised the applicable rules of engagement to allow certain aircraft to drop to lower altitudes. Attacks on Serb mobile forces in Kosovo finally started to show results.

By the beginning of May, NATO had conducted around 12,000 sorties, 3,500 of which were strikes on some 230 individual fixed targets. Yugoslavia's two oil refineries in Novi Sad and Pancevo were put out of action and sixteen oil storage depots were bombed. NATO aircraft hit a total of 31 fixed communication sites, including nineteen relays between Belgrade and the south. More than twenty road and rail bridges were damaged or destroyed (five over the Danube river in the north). About 20 percent of Yugoslavia's ammunition storage depots was assessed as significantly damaged, and 20 percent of army and paramilitary barracks had also been attacked.

Despite the declaration of air superiority, attacks on Yugoslav air defenses and airfields continued to absorb some 30 to 35 percent of the daily sorties in May. Although Yugoslav aircraft were shot down every time they challenged NATO in the skies, General Short insisted on the time-consuming (and smart-weapons-intensive) effort to destroy planes on the ground by attacking hardened aircraft shelters on Yugoslav air bases. Some 71 shelters were struck by early May with 40 listed as destroyed.

Even during Phase 3 continuing political constraints meant that outside of Kosovo itself Short did not have enough targets to attack. NATO's main effort continued to be against supporting infrastructure and supply lines, more bridges and transmitters, barracks and far-afield storage depots. Although NATO did hit some targets in downtown Belgrade, attacks there continued to be controversial, and targeters managed to get political approval to hit only three Yugoslav telephone exchanges, one in Pristina, Kosovo's largest city. Beginning on May 2, the post-summit emphasis on industry and the psychological targets added electrical distribution to the target list, a change that the alliance trumpeted as a sign that the campaign was coming into its own. "The fact that the lights went out across 70 percent of the country, I think, shows that NATO has its finger on the light switch in Yugoslavia now, and we can turn the power off whenever we need to and whenever we want to," NATO spokesman Jamie Shea said on May 3. By mid-May, 85 percent of Serbia was without power.

Each day in May set a new record in terms of the number of NATO's strikes, with some attacks now originating from NATO air bases in Hungary and Turkey. The number of attacks on Yugoslav forces in and around Kosovo steadily increased, with AC-130U gunships and B-52 bombers loaded with "dumb" bombs entering the fray for the first time. Yugoslav forces in Kosovo remained dispersed, able to operate only in small groups. But if that tactic enabled Serb units to evade the full brunt of NATO's air effort, it also inhibited their efforts to eliminate the KLA. Indeed, from its sanctuaries in Albania, Montenegro, and Macedonia, the KLA was finding a second wind.

Yugoslavia Withdraws

Yet as the air offensive entered Phase 3, the spectacle of public events and controversies eclipsed the campaign itself. The Reverend Jesse Jackson traveled to Belgrade to free three U.S. Army prisoners captured on the Macedonian border. The media reported that NATO was running short of cruise missiles and other guided weapons. The glacial deployment of U.S. Army attack helicopters to Albania and General Clark's inability to bring them into the war provoked both wonderment and sharp criticism. Mounting evidence of civilian collateral damage provoked continuing calls for bombing pauses from various NATO countries, suggesting that allied unity was becoming increasingly precarious. Criticism of the conduct of the war from prominent military historians and commentators, among them retired Army Colonel Harry Summers and John Keegan, mounted. Perhaps worst of all, a targeting error resulted in NATO's bombing of the Chinese embassy. All the while, the action that really counted progressed behind the scenes. Deputy Secretary of State Strobe Talbott, Russian special envoy Chernomyrdin, and Finnish President Martti Ahtisaari, representing the European Union, were engaged in intense negotiations with the Yugoslavs that looked for a way to end the war.

From inside Yugoslavia, independent press reports of civilian protest and speculation regarding growing dissatisfaction with Milosevic's leadership increased. Although NATO admitted that despite its best efforts fresh reserve troops and units were still entering Kosovo to augment the Yugoslav 3rd Army, it also claimed that the reinforcements were a sign of its own success—the additions were needed to replace combat casualties and exhausted troops. On May 20, President Clinton himself reported that "Each day, we hear reports of desertions in the Serbian army, dissension in Belgrade, unrest in Serbian communities."

Toward the end of May, with the support of American intelligence and Albanian artillery, the KLA mounted a counteroffensive. "This is the beginning of a new phase of aggression, the so-called land operation," Major General Vladimir Lazarevic, commander of the Yugoslav Pristina Corps, said.[83] Regardless of the ferocious debate inside NATO about the need for a ground war, Belgrade saw threatening signs that suggested NATO preparations for just that contingency.

When the International Criminal Tribunal for the Former Yugoslavia on May 27 indicted Milosevic for war crimes, time for the Serb dictator was running out. Despite an early shoot-down of a coveted F-117 stealth fighter, Yugoslavia had never been able to inflict any notable damage or any casualties on NATO. Despite collateral damage and the enormous discord over the mistaken bombing of the Chinese embassy, NATO remained united. Opposition to Belgrade within the international community as a whole, now including Russia, actually solidified as the war dragged on. Russia had actively joined NATO in pressing Milosevic to submit. And finally, the street parties in Belgrade had ended: After weeks of isolation and bombing, Serbs were exhausted. There were indeed increasing signs of popular unrest and dissatisfaction—Milosevic himself was potentially threatened by his own people.

As the air war peaked in intensity the last week of May, Yugoslavia began hinting that it would accept the set of principles proposed by the so-called Group of Eight. By implication, Belgrade was signaling a new willingness to withdraw all of its forces from Kosovo and to accept the deployment of an international peacekeeping contingent "with NATO at its core." On June 3, Belgrade formally accepted proposals drawn up and presented by Chernomyrdin and Ahtisaari, paving the way for NATO peacekeepers to occupy the province.

No one could say with certainty why Milosevic had capitulated when he did. U.S. officials were convinced that once NATO and Russia spoke with one voice the Serb dictator Milosevic concluded he had no other options.[84] "It's very difficult to say why tyrants give way because they have their own particular way of behaving," President Chirac said in an interview at the end of the war:

> But I think there were at least two things: the total isolation in which he found himself; he had, without any doubt, banked on Russia's direct or indirect support . . . and also on a split between the democracies, reputed to be weak, particularly the European democracies. . . . Secondly, his power . . . rested on a military and police system which has been considerably weakened by the air strikes to which he's been subjected. . . . So the very foundation of his power has, in a way, been degraded at both the technical and psychological levels, to the point when, as has been said, it was difficult for him to hold out any more.[85]

One very big question was the extent to which the bombing itself had contributed to Milosevic's decision. Was this indeed the first war won by air power alone?

The Score

On June 9, Operation Allied Force came to a close, 78 days after it had begun. In all, the alliance had flown a total of 38,004 sorties, of which 10,484 involved strikes on "strategic" and "tactical" targets while another 3,100 were suppression of air-defense missions.[86] By the end of the war, 829 aircraft from fourteen countries were available for tasking. Strike, electronic-warfare, reconnaissance, refueling, and support aircraft flew from some 47 locations in Europe and the United States.[87]

NATO had expended 28,236 weapons.[88] U.S. and British surface ships and submarines had fired some 218 Tomahawk sea-launched cruise missiles while B-52 bombers launched another 90 conventional air-launched cruise missiles (CALCMs).[89] A total of some 12,000 tons of munitions were expended.[90] Though the raw numbers suggest that an average of 362 weapons were dropped per day, 70 percent or more of the bombs were dropped in the war's final three weeks, meaning that, for the first eight weeks of the war, bombs delivered per day were closer to 150 in number. If the air war was having limited effect in the early days, more than weather and collateral damage constraints were to blame.

The United States was far and away the dominant player. The U.S. Air Force delivered 21,120 weapons (or 75 percent of the total). Including U.S. Navy and Marine Corps aircraft and missiles, weapons delivered by the United States numbered 23,506 (or 83 percent of the total).[91] A mere 22 heavy bombers—five B-1s, six B-2s, and eleven B-52s—delivered close to 12,000 weapons (constituting some 2,400 tons).[92] U.S. and allied planes were flying roughly equal numbers of strike missions at the end of the war,[93] but the vast majority of weapons were being dropped by U.S. aircraft. Notably, two-thirds of the U.S. strikes occurred at night.

By war's end, about 35 percent of all the weapons employed were precision-guided munitions (PGMs), more than three times the percentage expended in the 1991 Desert Storm campaign. In the early weeks of Operation Allied Force, "smart" weapons constituted more than 90 percent of the ordnance employed. By mid- to late-May, only 10 to 20 percent of the weapons dropped were guided. The United States delivered 6,728 PGMs, including the first combat use of the satellite-guided Joint Direct Attack Munition (JDAM) delivered by the B-2. The Joint Standoff Weapon, a long-range cluster bomb, was also used for the first time, being expended in small numbers by the U.S. Navy. JDAM, CALCM, and selected Tomahawk missiles were satellite-guided and therefore impervious to weather. Poor weather adversely affected the operation of all other guided weapons (with the exception of antiradiation missiles).

In all, according to the Defense Department, NATO attacked more than 900 targets, 421 of them fixed installations.[94] Of these, half were military facilities. Of the 421 fixed targets attacked, 232 were "destroyed" or sustained severe damage. Another 135 targets sustained "moderate" or "light" damage, and 51 sustained no damage (see Table 1.1). A total of some 9,815 "aim points" were designated at targets of all types, and 58 percent of these aim points were successfully struck with PGMs.[95] The extensive targeting of ground-force installations focused on paramilitary units and on paramilitary and army barracks, depots, and headquarters. NATO assessed that it had destroyed approximately 111,500 metric tons of Serb ammunition and military equipment. Although installations were bombed throughout the country, the majority of the targets were in Kosovo and in the southern portion of Serbia.

In total, some five hundred Yugoslav civilians were killed in incidents of collateral damage, and some nine hundred were injured.[96] Clark professed that NATO had "no estimate . . . whatsoever" of Yugoslav military deaths,[97] though some NATO sources were claiming 5,000 to 10,000 Yugoslav military casualties at the end of the war.[98] After the fact, Belgrade would report that 240 soldiers and 147 "policemen" were killed by NATO bombs.[99]

NATO attacked Yugoslavia's air defenses throughout the country, but never with sufficient intensity (or design) to neutralize the entire air-defense system. Key nodes in the command and control of the system remained intact at the end of the war. Although the Pentagon stated that two-thirds of the long-range SA-2/3 missile force and a "significant" quantity of mobile SA-6's were destroyed,[100] postwar studies found only three of eighty SA-6 launchers destroyed.[101] In all, Yugoslavia fired 845 SAMs, downing two NATO aircraft and 25 unmanned aerial vehicles.[102] A total of 1,200 Navy and Marine Corps EA-6B sorties were flown in support of air defense suppression, and U.S. and NATO aircraft fired 743 HARM missiles and expended 1,479 towed decoys. Air Force Chief of Staff General Michael Ryan boasted that Yugoslavia's eight airfields "were closed and much of their air defense infrastructure was destroyed."[103] Yugoslavia's air force sustained considerable damage, with shoot-downs or bombing destroying 121 aircraft and helicopters.[104]

TABLE 1.1 Operation Allied Force Targets and Assessed Damage

Category	Total	Level of Damage					
		Destroyed	Severe	Moderate	Light	None	
Infrastructure							
Counter-regime	7	1	1	3	2	0	
Electrical Power	19	6	0	0	9	4	
POL	30	13	10	7	0	0	
C4I	88	31	6	18	9	23	
Bridges and railroads	68	39	8	2	6	12	
Military industry	17	4	5	4	1	3	
Military Forces							
Ground forces facilities	106	23	35	31	16	0	
Border posts	18	5	3	5	3	2	
Airfields	8	0	5	3	0	0	
Air Defenses							
Integrated air defense system	28	12	4	6	4	2	
SAM sites and facilities	32	15	6	5	1	5	
Total	421	149	83	84	51	51	

C4I: Command, control, communications, computers, and intelligence; POL: Petroleum, oil, and lubricants; SAM: Surface-to-air missiles.

Note: C4I counter-regime (leadership) categories include numerous strictly military headquarters, command posts, and communications facilities.

SOURCE: U.S. Air Force, Air War Over Serbia (AWOS) Study Group; data obtained by author.

Attacks on leadership and command and control included two of Milosevic's residences, a number of ministries and army headquarters, and a
half-dozen underground command centers serving the government, military, and air-defense system. More than 30 percent of military and civilian
relay networks were damaged, and the Pentagon rated national command,
control, and communications (C3) capabilities in a "degraded status" by
war's end. Though long-range transmitters were extensively hit, the telephone and cell-phone systems otherwise remained largely intact. Telephone communications had been a major target in the Gulf War, but
remained largely off-limits due to collateral-damage concerns and allied
investments.[105] Forty-five percent of TV broadcast capability was declared
"non-functional," and by the end of the war radio broadcasts were limited
to urban areas only.[106] Two major state broadcast houses were bombed, one
in Belgrade and the other in Novi Sad, the attack in Belgrade killing 16
civilians.[107]

NATO reduced Yugoslavia's capacity to manufacture ammunition by two-
thirds, eliminated its oil refining capacity at Pancevo and Novi Sad, and
destroyed more than 40 percent of its military fuel supplies. Seventy percent
of road bridges and 50 percent of rail bridges attacked throughout Serbia
and Kosovo were damaged or destroyed.

Contrary to Yugoslav propaganda, NATO did not bomb water installations, dams, or pharmaceutical plants, and there were no attacks on food
storage or other targets immediately affecting the survival of the civilian
population. Electrical-transformer stations and power lines were attacked,
first with new so-called "soft bombs" to short-circuit electrical distribution,
and then later with laser-guided bombs. But electrical generation remained
off-limits in an attempt to minimize the long-term effect of bombing on the
civilian population.[108] Although by Phase 3 NATO was eager to pressure the
civilian population, NATO legal officers intervened to keep many prospective targets off-limits. In some instances, legal review was compromised by
inadequate intelligence, resulting in a number of steam-powered central-
heating plants in urban areas being destroyed.

Although a "crony" targeting plan was developed in late April, only two
targets associated specifically with this objective ended up being attacked.
Nor is there any evidence that covert action associated with the crony
strategy influenced Milosevic in his final decisions to agree to the Group
of Eight principles.[109] As the war entered June, new targets had been ap-

proved for attack in the event that Milosevic rejected the Chernomyrdin and Ahtisaari proposal. These included the Yugoslav telephone system.[110]

While 3,000 to 5,000 weapons fell on "strategic" targets in Serbia and Montenegro, the great majority of NATO weapons were dropped in Kosovo, the majority of those against mobile forces. The effectiveness of NATO attacks on Yugoslavia's military and paramilitary in and around Kosovo has proven to be the most controversial aspect of Allied Force. Shortly after the cease-fire, NATO announced that about 47,000 Yugoslav troops and nearly 800 tanks, armored personnel carriers, and artillery guns had left Kosovo. That such a robust force should have survived to retire in good order immediately ignited controversy as to whether NATO during the war had been inflating its claims of what it had destroyed. General Clark told Congress in July that 110 tanks, 210 armored vehicles, and 449 artillery and mortar tubes had been hit.[111] For its part, Yugoslav propaganda was claiming that NATO had hit nearly 500 decoys but only 50 tanks.[112] Numerous articles in the Western media speculated that as little as one-tenth of NATO's damage claims against Yugoslav forces were actually true.

After a three-month assessment of missions flown against Yugoslav forces, Clark in September 1999 released slightly revised figures. A thorough survey by the Kosovo Strike Assessment evaluated some three thousand strike missions flown against mobile targets. In 1,955 of these strikes, pilots dropped weapons, and reported that they had hit 181 tanks, 317 armored vehicles, 600 other military vehicles, and 857 artillery guns and mortars. In the end, this study concluded that NATO aircraft had hit 93 tanks, 153 armored vehicles, 339 military vehicles, and 389 artillery pieces and mortars.[113]

After the war, yet another study group, the Allied Force Munitions Effectiveness Assessment Team (MEAT), visited Kosovo, inspecting 234 locations where mission reports stated that something had been hit. The team found evidence of bombing in 191 locations, but very little evidence of damaged or destroyed equipment. Although Clark claimed in September that the strike assessment had validated more than half of the reports as "successful strikes," the MEAT team could neither verify the mission reports filed by the pilots themselves nor find much evidence of equipment having been removed. On the other hand, the MEAT team did find a significant amount of damaged and destroyed equipment at locations *unrelated* to pilot mission reports.[114] Although the possibility that the Yugoslav army had removed the hundreds of missing vehicles during the war and their withdrawal could not be completely discounted, NATO failed to produce hard intelligence or evidence to substantiate its claim to have dealt the Serb forces in Kosovo a serious physical blow.

Who Shot John?

"NATO accomplished its mission and achieved all of its strategic, operational, and tactical goals in the face of an extremely complex set of challenges." So the Defense Department reported to Congress in October 1999.[115] The dust had hardly settled before competing postwar arguments were being made about which NATO actions "won" the war: Was it strikes in Kosovo and the looming "threat" of a ground war, as General Clark asserted, or was it infrastructure attacks on civilian morale targets such as electricity, media, and leadership, a thesis preferred by air-power advocates?

In truth, we may never know what drove Slobodan Milosevic to finally accede to NATO's demands. But given that Belgrade's strategy hinged on the belief that it could out-wait NATO, the very fact that the bombing continued and that the alliance hung together was probably more important than whether a particular target or group of targets had received a knockout blow. In the end, the phased air campaign that few actually expected to go beyond a couple of days had escalated and accelerated "according to plan." The target list had expanded as more aircraft became available and as NATO's political leaders shed their squeamishness. And the commanders organizing the missions and the pilots flying them proved sufficiently flexible and discriminative to accommodate themselves to the changing political climate in which they labored. But to see in Operation Allied Force the validation of any theory about warfare or doctrine would be sheer nonsense.

Speaking at the International Institute for Strategic Studies in London on the war's first anniversary, Lord Robertson, British Minister of Defense during Allied Force and Solana's successor as NATO Secretary-General, insisted that the alliance had been "absolutely right" to go to war, to act when and how it did. "It may not surprise you that I am saying this," he said, "but frankly, it surprises me that I have to keep repeating it."[116] Yet if NATO and U.S. officials sounded defensive about their victory, one reason was that criticism of Operation Allied Force, both during and after the war, was by no means limited to the usual quarters. Even people usually identified as air-warfare partisans disassociated themselves from NATO's war, complaining about the political and military constraints and about their inability to pursue some optimal air warfare strategy.

Among those complaining the loudest was Clark's own air commander. General Short believed that the conduct of Allied Force had been flawed from the outset. "I'd have gone for the head of the snake on the first night," he told Congress in October. "I'd have turned the lights out . . . dropped the bridges across the Danube . . . hit five or six political-military headquarters in downtown Belgrade." If Short had had his way, "Milosevic and his cronies would have woken up the first morning asking what the hell was going on."[117]

The conventional retort to General Short is that such an idealized air strategy was politically unacceptable. Still, even though Allied Force did not produce the instant gratification promised by Short's scenario, as the campaign progressed the weight of effort did slowly shift to broader "strategic" and infrastructure targets, allowing the Air Force to claim ultimate vindication. To General Ryan, the Air Force Chief of Staff, it was abundantly clear that Milosevic had capitulated because air power brought the war home to Serbia. "The lights went out, the water went off, the petroleum production ceased, the bridges were down, communications were down, the economics of the country were slowly falling apart, and I think he came to the realization that in a strategic sense, he wasn't prepared to continue this."[118] The "strategic center of gravity," Ryan said, "was in and around Belgrade[, the focus of] . . . support for Milosevic and his repressive regime."[119]

Ryan insists that no Air Force officer ever "believed that air power could stop directly the door-to-door infantry thuggery that was driving the Kosovars from their homes. Nor could air power directly stop the slaughter and war crimes that were taking place in isolated villages."[120] Similarly, Air Force General Joseph Ralston, vice chairman of the Joint Chiefs of Staff during the war (and Clark's replacement after the war), rejected the notion that airmen should be held accountable for NATO's failure to knock out Serb ground forces in Kosovo. Those forces were beside the point. "The tank, which was an irrelevant item in the context of ethnic cleansing, became the symbol of Serbian ground forces. How many tanks did you kill today? All of a sudden, this became the measure of merit although it had nothing to do with reality."[121]

In fact, once the 48-hour demonstration attack failed, NATO's assigned task became one of stopping in their tracks the Yugoslav forces perpetrating ethnic cleansing. That is what NATO publics expected, what NATO political leaders promised, and what Clark as the senior military commander vowed to accomplish. Short and other Air Force officers may have believed that the best way to stop ethnic cleansing was indirectly, by mounting a strategic bombing offensive. But both prior to and during the war, they failed to convince Clark or political authorities in Washington and Europe that such an approach was the optimum way to achieve NATO's objectives.

Throughout Operation Allied Force, NATO demonstrated an almost obsessive concern for civilian casualties and damage. It employed a greater percentage of smart weapons than in any other conflict in history. Civilian "micro-management" approached levels not seen since the Vietnam War. Enormous efforts were made, largely successful, to minimize short- and long-term civilian effects. When mistakes did occur in the 78 days of bombing, changes in operational procedures, weapons selection, and limits on targeting were implemented almost immediately. In this sense, the NATO war does merit Secretary of Defense Cohen's description of it as "the most precise application of air power in history," but it was superb technical display concealing a legion of political, military, intelligence, and leadership miscues.

On the political level, leaders failed to take the measure of Slobodan Milosevic despite years of wrangling and negotiations with the Serb dictator. War with Yugoslavia was not Desert Storm, where the coalition was largely in the dark with regard to Iraqi society and Saddam Hussein's intentions. Holbrooke, Albright, Solana, Clark, and others knew the Yugoslav leader intimately. Clark in particular took pride in being a student of Milosevic. Yet at the top, a bizarre confidence in the prospects of a mere demonstration attack prevailed. NATO and the United States had misread their adversary.

On the strategic level, political leaders failed to articulate clear objectives, greatly complicating the efforts of military planners to relate means to ends in a realistic manner. Despite ex post facto claims that alliance leaders had never placed their confidence in the demonstration attack, there was in fact no serious planning for alternative contingencies. No consensus on a proper strategy existed—this despite the luxury of having a "U.S. only" channel where contingency planning could have proceeded without the need to take allied sensitivities into account.

Within the high command, General Clark, the misnamed Supreme Commander, was unable to get his subordinate, General Short, to follow orders, and then he failed to relieve Short when he refused to do so. The Defense Department and Air Force leadership, despite their knowledge of the debilitating tensions between Generals Short and Clark, failed to intervene and resolve them.

The Air Force (and air power advocates generally) clearly failed to educate political leaders, the media, or the public with regard to air power's actual potential and limitations in a setting like Yugoslavia. The end result, regardless of one's devotion to a "tactical" or "strategic" solution in Kosovo, was that the Air Force propagated an exaggerated sense of the ease with which attacks would occur, of the effects of even accurate weapons, of damage potential, and of the ability to properly "read" the opponent.

Most crucially, the Air Force also failed to understand and convey the reality of how long it would take (and what it would take) to coerce Milosevic. There may indeed have been an optimal air-power-only plan for winning in 1999, but the Air Force as an institution failed to produce that plan, and certainly failed to make a convincing case to NATO and Washington decision makers that hitting Yugoslavia hard from the outset might actually shorten the war without entailing unreasonable risk of civilian casualties and friendly losses.

Notes

1. The participating nations were Belgium, Canada, Denmark, France, Germany, Italy, the Netherlands, Norway, Portugal, Spain, Turkey, the United Kingdom, and the United States. Aircraft from the United States, the United Kingdom, France, Canada, and Spain conducted bombing on the first night. Long-range cruise missiles were fired by the United States and Britain.

2. The FRY consists of Montenegro and Serbia, which is made up of Serbia itself, the autonomous province of Vojvodina, and Kosovo.

3. The earlier UNSCR 1160 adopted in March 1998 condemned the excessive use of force by Yugoslav forces in Kosovo and established an embargo against the FRY.

4. DOD, Kosovo/Operation Allied Force After-Action Report, 30 January 2000, pp. A2, 21; discussions with USAFE planners.

5. DOD/JCS, Joint Statement on the Kosovo After Action Review, 14 October 1999.

6. DOD, Kosovo/Operation Allied Force After-Action Report, 30 January 2000, p. A4.

7. James B. Steinberg, "A Perfect Polemic: Blind to Reality on Kosovo," *Foreign Affairs* (November–December 1999): 128.

8.   DOD, Kosovo/Operation Allied Force After-Action Report, 30 January 2000, pp. 2, A7.

9.   Ibid., p. 23.

10. Gen. John P. Jumper, U.S. Air Forces in Europe, presentation at The Eaker Institute for Aerospace Concepts, Operation Allied Force: Strategy, Execution, Implications Colloquy, 16 August 1999.

11. The U.S. Department of Defense contends that it "made clear to our allied counterparts that Operation Allied Force could well take weeks or months to succeed"; DOD/JCS, Joint Statement on the Kosovo After Action Review, 14 October 1999.

12. USAFE Briefing, "Integration of Aerospace Power in Operational Planning, or Doctrinal Implications of our Kosovo Planning Exercise," December 1999.

13. Testimony of General Wesley Clark before Senate Armed Services Committee Hearing on Lessons Learned from Military Operations and Relief Efforts in Kosovo (21 October 1999); Dana Priest, "Bombing By Committee: France Balked at NATO Targets," Washington Post, 20 September 1999, p. A1.

14. U.S. Congress, Senate Armed Services Committee, Hearing on the Situation in Kosovo, Testimony of General Wesley Clark, SACEUR, 1 July 1999.

15. Dana Priest, "Tensions Grew with Divide over Strategy," Washington Post, 21 September 1999, p. A1.

16. John A. Tirpak, "Short's View of the Air Campaign," Air Force Magazine, September 1999, pp. 43–47; Dana Priest, "Tensions Grew with Divide over Strategy," Washington Post, 21 September 1999, p. A16.

17. Testimony before Senate Armed Services Committee Hearing on Lessons Learned from Military Operations and Relief Efforts in Kosovo, 21 October 1999.

18. Dana Priest, "Tensions Grew with Divide over Strategy," Washington Post, 21 September 1999, p. A16.

19. Hearing of the Senate Armed Services Committee, Lessons Learned from Military Operations and Relief Efforts in Kosovo, 14 October 1999.

20. The official military objective was later stated as: "Demonstrate the seriousness of NATO's opposition to Belgrade's aggression. . . . deter Milosevic from continuing and escalating his attacks on helpless civilians and create conditions to reverse his ethnic cleansing; and damage Serbia's capacity to wage war . . . or spread the war to neighbors by diminishing or degrading its ability to wage military operations DOD." Kosovo/Operation Allied Force After-Action Report, 30 January 2000, p. 7.

On the first night of Allied Force, Secretary Cohen stated: "The military objective of our action is to deter further action against the Kosovars and to

diminish the ability of the Yugoslav army to continue those attacks if necessary";
DOD News Briefing, Wednesday, January 24, 1999.

NATO listed its political objective in a statement issued at the Extraordinary
Meeting of the North Atlantic Council held on April 12, 1999 (reaffirmed on
April 23 at the Washington Summit). They included:

> a verifiable stop to all military action and the immediate ending of
> violence and repression;
> the withdrawal from Kosovo of Serb military, police and paramilitary
> forces;
> the stationing in Kosovo of an international military presence;
> the unconditional and safe return of all refugees and displaced persons
> and unhindered access to them by humanitarian aid organizations;
> and
> the establishment of a political framework agreement for Kosovo on the
> basis of the Rambouillet Accords, in conformity with international
> law and the Charter of the United Nations.

21. General Wesley Clark, Remarks to the American Enterprise Institute regarding
     military action in Yugoslavia, 31 August 1999. This position is consistent with
     Gen. Clark's attitude before the war as well.
22. DOD, Kosovo/Operation Allied Force After-Action Report, 30 January 2000,
     p. 7.
23. Special Department of Defense Press Briefing with General Wesley Clark,
     Supreme Allied Commander, Europe, Topic: Kosovo Strike Assessment Also
     Participating: Airmen and Analysts from Operation Allied Force and Post-strike
     Assessment Work, Brussels, Belgium, 16 September 1999.
24. William M. Arkin, "Smart War, Dumb Targeting?" *The Bulletin of the Atomic
     Scientists* (May-June 2000): 46–53.
25. Statement of the Honorable John J. Hamre Deputy Secretary of Defense Before
     the House Permanent Select Committee on Intelligence, 22 July 1999.
26. DOD/JCS, Joint Statement on the Kosovo After Action Review, 14 October
     1999; Testimony of Secretary Cohen, Hearing of the Senate Armed Services
     Committee, Lessons Learned from Military Operations and Relief Efforts in
     Kosovo, 14 October 1999; see also testimony of General Shelton to the House
     Armed Services Committee, 14 April 1999.
27. Such attacks emulated Iraqi attacks in December 1998 against Saddam Hus-
     sein's "special" Republican Guard and Presidential security forces; see William
     M. Arkin, "The Difference Was in the Details," *Washington Post*, 17 January
     1999, p. B1.

28. Hearing of the Senate Armed Services Committee, Lessons Learned from Military Operations and Relief Efforts in Kosovo, 14 October 1999.
29. On the first day of Desert Storm, 2,388 coalition sorties were flown, with more than 1,000 strikes, 400 against Iraqi ground forces.
30. Dana Priest, "Tensions Grew with Divide over Strategy," *The Washington Post*, 21 September 1999, p. A1.
31. "I do not intend to put our troops in Kosovo to fight a war," President Clinton declared in his March 24 address to the nation; Statement by the President to the Nation, the Oval Office, 24 March 1999.
32. DOD News Briefing, Wednesday, January 24, 1999. Secretary of Defense William S. Cohen and CJCS Gen. Shelton. "Others in the administration reiterated the no ground force pledge. Secretary of State Madeleine Albright said on March 24: "I think that NATO had some contingency planning for this, but this is not our plan to use ground forces." Transcript, Interview of Secretary of State Madeleine K. Albright on *Newshour with Jim Lehrer*, PBS, 24 March 1999. National Security Advisor Samnuel R. Berger made the same point on March 25: "We do not have, as the President indicated, an intention to put ground forces in Kosovo in a combat situation"; Transcript, Press Briefing by National Security Advisor Sandy Berger, 25 March 1999.
33. Transcript, Interview of Secretary of State Madeleine K. Albright on *Newshour with Jim Lehrer*, PBS, 24 March 1999.
34. DOD News Briefing, Wednesday, March 24, 1999.
35. Transcript, NATO Press Conference, Secretary General Dr. Javier Solana and SACEUR General Wesley Clark, 25 March 1999.
36. Transcript, Press Briefing by National Security Advisor Sandy Berger, 25 March 1999.
37. Statement by the President to the Nation, the Oval Office, 24 March 1999.
38. Transcript, NATO Press Conference, Secretary General Dr. Javier Solana and SACEUR General Wesley Clark, 25 March 1999.
39. Emphasis added.
40. Transcript, NATO Press Conference, Secretary General Dr. Javier Solana and SACEUR General Wesley Clark, 25 March 1999.
41. Quoted in R. W. Apple Jr., "Conflict in the Balkans: News Analysis, A Fresh Set of U.S. Goals," *New York Times*, 25 March 1999, p. A1.
42. Air Force Doctrine Center, "Operation Allied Force: An Initial Doctrinal Assessment," (December 1999).
43. Presentation at The Eaker Institute for Aerospace Concepts, Operation Allied Force: Strategy, Execution, Implications Colloquy, 16 August 1999.
44. Transcript of briefing, Defense Minister George Robertson and the Chief of Staff, General Guthrie, London, 28 March 1999.

45. Testimony of General Henry Shelton to the House Armed Services Committee, 14 April 1999.

46. Hearing of the Senate Armed Services Committee, Lessons Learned from Military Operations and Relief Efforts in Kosovo, 14 October 1999. See also DOD/JCS, Joint Statement on the Kosovo After Action Review, 14 October 1999.

47. Testimony of the Honorable William S. Cohen to the House Armed Services Committee, 14 April 1999.

48. Hearing of the Senate Armed Services Committee, Lessons Learned from Military Operations and Relief Efforts in Kosovo, 14 October 1999.

49. Testimony of General Henry Shelton to the House Armed Services Committee, 14 April 1999.

50. Director of Central Intelligence Statement on the Belgrade Chinese Embassy Bombing, House Permanent Select Committee on Intelligence, Open Hearing, 21 July 1999.

51. Dana Priest, "Bombing By Committee: France Balked at NATO Targets," *Washington Post*, 20 September 1999, p. A1. See also U.S. Congress, House Permanent Select Committee on Intelligence, Hearing on the Bombing of the Chinese Embassy, 21 July 1999.

52. By the end of the first week, reportedly only some 90 attacks against 70 targets had been carried out. The majority of targets — 16 radar and early warning sites, 18 surface-to-air missile sites, 12 other air defense facilities, and eight airfields — were associated with air defenses and the establishment of air superiority.

53. Secretary of Defense William S. Cohen, Remarks as Delivered to the International Institute for Strategic Studies Hotel del Coronado, San Diego, Calif., 9 September 1999.

54. Weather would continue to be a problem throughout the war. Only 21 of 78 days were 50 percent or better cloud-free; in Kosovo, NATO operated under conditions in which there was at least 50 percent cloud cover more than 70 percent of the time. The Air Force says 16 percent of all strike sorties were lost due to weather. DOD/JCS, Joint Statement on the Kosovo After Action Review, 14 October 1999. Also, U.S. Air Force, "Air War Over Serbia," hereinafter cited as AWOS. This Pentagon study has not been declassified or released. The author has had extensive discussions with the AWOS study team and has reviewed AWOS documents and draft materials.

55. Dana Priest, "Bombing By Committee: France Balked at NATO Targets," *Washington Post*, 20 September 1999, p. A1.

56. Hearing of the House Armed Services Committee on Support of Operation Allied Force, 26 October 1999.

57. Transcript, Interview of the President by Dan Rather, CBS, The Cabinet Room, 31 March 1999.

58. AWOS data obtained by the author.

59. Yugoslavia's long-range air defenses, according to the U.S. Air Force AWOS, were made up of three SA-2 systems, 16 SA-3s, and 80 SA-6s. It had 130 SA-9s, and 404 air defense artillery guns (ZSU-57-2 and M53/59). Man-portable SAM systems (SA-7/14/16) numbered 10,000 plus.

60. Testimony before Senate Armed Services Committee Hearing on Lessons Learned from Military Operations and Relief Efforts in Kosovo, 21 October 1999; DOD/JCS, Joint Statement on the Kosovo After Action Review, 14 October 1999.

61. AWOS data obtained by the author. Yugoslavia fired 188 SA-3s, 477 SA-6s, 124 man-portable SAMs, and 56 unknown SAMs.

62. Transcript, NATO Press Conference, Secretary General Dr. Javier Solana and SACEUR General Wesley Clark, 25 March 1999.

63. William M. Arkin, "NATO Info Strategy Bombs," washingtonpost.com, 26 April 1999 (http://www.washingtonpost.com/wp-srv/national/dotmil/arkin 042699.htm).

64. Yugoslavia, Ministry of Foreign Affairs (MFA) Daily Dispatch, 26 March 1999.

65. Human Rights Watch, "Civilian Deaths in the NATO Air Campaign," February 2000.

66. DOD/JCS, Joint Statement on the Kosovo After Action Review, 14 October 1999.

67. Statement of Lieutenant General Marvin R. Esmond, Deputy Chief of Staff Air and Space Operations, United States Air Force, 19 October 1999.

68. Testimony before Senate Armed Services Committee Hearing on Lessons Learned from Military Operations and Relief Efforts in Kosovo, 21 October 1999.

69. The Defense Department says this "limited the Serb ground forces' combat effectiveness" and "and made them ineffective as a tactical maneuver force"; DOD/JCS, Joint Statement on the Kosovo After Action Review, 14 October 1999.

70. Hearing of the House Armed Services Committee on Support of Operation Allied Force, 26 October 1999.

71. U.S. Congress, Senate Armed Services Committee, Hearing on the Situation in Kosovo, General Wesley Clark, SACEUR, testifying, 1 July 1999.

72. Dana Priest, "A Decisive Battle That Never War," *Washington Post*, 19 September 1999, p. A1.

73. Testimony before Senate Armed Services Committee Hearing on Lessons Learned from Military Operations and Relief Efforts in Kosovo, 21 Oct 1999.

74. Statement of Secretary of Defense William S. Cohen, Brussels, 7 April 1999.

75. This included combat aircraft from Belgium, Denmark, France, Germany, Italy, The Netherlands, Norway, Portugal, Spain, Turkey, the United Kingdom, and the United States.

76. Secretary of Defense William S. Cohen, Remarks as Delivered to the International Institute for Strategic Studies, Hotel del Coronado, San Diego, Calif., 9 September 1999.

77. U.S. Congress, Senate Armed Services Committee, Hearing on the Situation in Kosovo, General Wesley Clark, SACEUR, testifying, 1 July 1999; DOD/JCS, Joint Statement on the Kosovo After Action Review, 14 October 1999; Dana Priest, "Bombing By Committee: France Balked at NATO Targets," *Washington Post*, 20 September 1999, p. A1.

78. DOD/JCS, Joint Statement on the Kosovo After Action Review, 14 October 1999. See also speech by National Security Adviser Samuel R. Berger at the Council on Foreign Relations, Washington, D.C., 26 July 1999.

79. William M. Arkin, "Ask Not for Whom the Phone Rings," washingtonpost.com, 11 October 1999 (http://www.washingtonpost.com/wp-srv/national/dotmil/arkin 101199.htm).

80. U.S. Congress, House Permanent Select Committee on Intelligence, Hearing on the Bombing of the Chinese Embassy, 21 July 1999.

81. Testimony before Senate Armed Services Committee Hearing on Lessons Learned from Military Operations and Relief Efforts in Kosovo, 21 October 1999.

82. DOD/JCS, Joint Statement on the Kosovo After Action Review, 14 October 1999.

83. Dana Priest, "A Decisive Battle That Never Was," *Washington Post*, 19 September 1999, p. A1.

84. Speech by National Security Adviser Samuel R. Berger at the Council on Foreign Relations, Washington, D.C., 26 July 1999; U.S. Congress, Senate Armed Services Committee, Hearing on the Situation in Kosovo, General Wesley Clark, SACEUR, testifying, 1 July 1999.

85. Television interview given by M. Jacques Chirac, President of the Republic, to TF1, Paris, 10 June 1999.

86. UK Ministry of Defense, Kosovo: An Account of the Crisis, A Paper by Lord Robertson of Port Ellen, September 1999.

87. Hearing of the House Armed Services Committee on Support of Operation Allied Force, 26 October 1999.

88. AWOS data provided to the author.

89. AWOS data provided to the author; DOD, Kosovo/Operation Allied Force After-Action Report, 31 January 2000, p. 92.

90. This is based on the delivery of some five thousand 2,000-lb.-class weapons, five thousand 1,000-lb. weapons, seventeen thousand 500-lb. weapons, and one thousand sub-500-lb. weapons of all types, including cruise missiles, JDAMs, guided and unguided bombs, cluster bombs, HARMs, etc.

91. AWOS data provided to the author.

92. AWOS data provided to the author. No more than two B-2s were in the theater
     at any one time. See also William M. Arkin, "In Praise of Heavy Bombers,"
     The Bulletin of the Atomic Scientists (July-August 1999): 80.
93. Testimony of William Cohen, Secretary of Defense, to the Senate Armed Ser-
     vices Committee, on Operations in Kosovo, 20 July 1999. The allies were able
     to conduct 47 percent of the strike sorties, but provided only about 29 percent
     of the overall support sorties.
94. Statement of the Honorable John J. Hamre, Deputy Secretary of Defense,
     before the House Permanent Select Committee on Intelligence, 22 July 1999.
95. AWOS data provided to the author (excludes Tomahawk cruise missile).
96. Human Rights Watch, "Civilian Deaths in the NATO Air Campaign," Feb-
     ruary 2000. On 29 August 2000, the Serbian Public Prosecutor brought charges
     against NATO for Yugoslav attacks, stating that 504 civilians had been killed
     and 913 injured, 454 of them seriously.
97. Special Department of Defense Press Briefing with General Wesley Clark,
     Supreme Allied Commander, Europe, Topic: Kosovo Strike Assessment Also
     Participating: Airmen and Analysts from Operation Allied Force and Post-strike
     Assessment Work, Brussels, Belgium, 16 September 1999.
98. Nick Cook, "War of Extremes," *Jane's Defence Weekly*, 7 July 1999.
99. Agence France Press (Belgrade), "Belgrade to Try Clinton, Blair for NATO
     'warcrimes,'" 29 August 2000.
100. Nick Cook, "War of Extremes," *Jane's Defence Weekly*, 7 July 1999.
101. AWOS data provided to the author.
102. AWOS data provided to the author.
103. General Michael E. Ryan, Chief of Staff, United States Air Force, Remarks at
     the AFA National Convention,14 September 1999.
104. This included 14 MiG-29s, 24 MiG-21s, 23 Galebs, 22 Super Galebs, 2 Oraos,
     7 Curls, 15 helicopters, and 14 "other."
105. William M. Arkin, "Ask Not for Whom the Phone Rings," washingtonpost.com,
     11 October 1999 (http://www.washingtonpost.com/wp-srv/national/dotmil/arkin
     101199.htm).
106. Testimony of William Cohen, Secretary of Defense, to the Senate Armed Ser-
     vices Committee, on Operations in Kosovo, 20 July 1999; U.S. Congress, House
     Armed Services Committee, Subcommittee on Military Procurement, Hearing
     on the Performance of the B-2 bomber in Kosovo, testimony of Lieutenant
     General Marvin R. Esmond, Deputy Chief of Staff for Air and Space Opera-
     tions, Department of the Air Force, 30 June 1999.
107. Human Rights Watch, "Civilian Deaths in the NATO Air Campaign," Feb-
     ruary 2000.
108. William M. Arkin, "Yugoslavia Unplugged," washingtonpost.com, 10 May 1999
     (http://www.washingtonpost.com/wp-srv/national/dotmil/arkin051099.htm).

109. William M. Arkin, "Smart War, Dumb Targeting?" *The Bulletin of the Atomic Scientists*, (May-June 2000): 46–53.

110. William M. Arkin, "Ask Not for Whom the Phone Rings," washingtonpost.com, 11 October 1999 (http://www.washingtonpost.com/wp-srv/national/dotmil/arkin 101199.htm).

111. U.S. Congress, Senate Armed Services Committee, Hearing on the Situation in Kosovo, General Wesley Clark, SACEUR, testifying, 1 July 1999.

112. *Aviation Week & Space Technology*, 26 July 1999, p. 68.

113. Special Department of Defense Press Briefing with General Wesley Clark, Supreme Allied Commander, Europe, Topic: Kosovo Strike Assessment Also Participating: Airmen and Analysts from Operation Allied Force and Post-Strike Assessment Work, Brussels, Belgium, 16 September 1999.

114. In all, the MEAT found 26 tanks and self-propelled artillery guns on the ground, 30 armored vehicles and air defense guns, and eight artillery pieces. They also found 136 destroyed or damage military vehicles. The MEAT expected to find tanks at 64 geographic locations, but only physically found 14 tanks.

115. DOD/JCS, Joint Statement on the Kosovo After Action Review, 14 October 1999.

116. Dinner Speech by Lord Robertson, NATO Secretary General, International Institute for Strategic Studies, Arundel House, London, 22 March 2000.

117. Testimony before Senate Armed Services Committee Hearing on Lessons Learned from Military Operations and Relief Efforts in Kosovo, 21 October 1999.

118. "Reconstitution Efforts Won't Impact Readiness," Air Force Policy Letter Digest, August 1999.

119. General Michael E. Ryan, Chief of Staff, United States Air Force, Remarks at the AFA National Convention,14 September 1999.

120. General Michael E. Ryan, Chief of Staff, United States Air Force, Remarks at the AFA National Convention,14 September 1999.

121. Dana Priest, "Tensions Grew With Divide Over Strategy," *Washington Post*, 21 September 1999, p. A16.

2 Kosovo and the New American Way of War

Eliot A. Cohen

The Kosovo war marks a departure from the traditional American way of war. From a style of warfare that has been since the middle of the nineteenth century direct, simple, and overwhelming, the United States has turned to a style of conflict that is quite different, and to which it has not yet completely adapted. The Kosovo war did not by itself force that change; the conflict did, however, crystallize it.

The Old American Way of War

"Facing the Arithmetic"

By the end of 1862, little had gone well for the Union. After dramatic successes in the first half of the year, the Confederacy had launched counteroffensives that first hurled the Army of the Potomac off the peninsular approaches to Richmond, scattered a newly assembled army at the approaches to Washington, and invaded Maryland, scooping up over 12,000 prisoners at Harper's Ferry along the way. In the West, Confederate General Braxton Bragg had nearly succeeded in wresting Kentucky from the Union. Although driven back to Tennessee, Bragg remained a looming menace to Northern gains there. Back in Washington, Union finances were in shambles, the Emancipation Proclamation was a sham, and the November elections had gone against the Republican Party. The gentle, melancholic man in the White House grieved over the death of a favorite son earlier in the year, and many friends who had fallen in combat since.

To cap it all off, the Army of the Potomac, under its fumbling new commander—the third in four months—had just failed spectacularly at Fredericksburg, Virginia. On December 13, General Ambrose Burnside had launched an assault on a naturally strong ridge, fronted by half a mile of open field swept by Confederate rifle and artillery fire. During fighting that lasted from dawn until the early afternoon, some 12,500 men had fallen as casualties, many of the wounded dying of exposure on the open fields. Robert E. Lee's Army of Northern Virginia had suffered perhaps a third as many casualties.

How did the grieving President react? According to a secretary, William Stoddard, Lincoln remarked a few days later that:

> if the same battle were to be fought over again, every day, through a week of days, with the same relative results, the army under Lee would be wiped out to its last man, the Army of the Potomac would still be a mighty host, the war would be over, the Confederacy gone, and peace would be won. . . . No general yet found can face the arithmetic, but the end of the war will be at hand when he shall be discovered.[1]

After Fredericksburg, as he had after so many other defeats and disappointments, Abraham Lincoln would continue his search for the general who "understood the arithmetic." When Lincoln finally found him in the person of Ulysses S. Grant, he placed Grant in charge of all his armies and backed him unflinchingly. "Grant is the first general I've had," he said approvingly. When Grant presided over his own bloody fiascoes such as the battle of Cold Harbor in June 1864—an ill-conceived assault every bit as bungled as Fredericksburg, costing perhaps 7,000 casualties in the space of an hour—Lincoln uttered not a word of protest.

Lincoln is one of the fathers of the modern "American Way of War."[2] If the long and brutal conflict of 1861–1865 provides the most vivid expression of that approach to waging war, subsequent conflicts are replete with reminders that the convictions manifested by the likes of Lincoln and Grant lived on after Appomattox. It echoes, for example, in the speech given by Lieutenant General Leslie McNair on the eve of America's first large European operation during World War II, the TORCH landings in North Africa:

Our soldiers must have the fighting spirit. If you call that hating our
enemies, then we must hate with every fiber of our being. We must
lust for battle; our object in life must be to kill; we must scheme and
plan night and day to kill. There need be no pangs of conscience, for
our enemies have lighted the way to faster, surer, and crueler killing;
they are past masters. . . . Since killing is the object of our efforts, the
sooner we get in the killing mood, the better and more skillful we shall
be when the real test comes.[3]

McNair's call for his fellow citizens to get into a killing mood serves as a
useful reminder: The bloodlust that Americans have come to associate with
George S. Patton was by no means unique to Patton himself. In World War
II, it permeated a generation of officers schooled in the traditions of Grant
and William T. Sherman, many of whose members in 1918 had experienced
killing in close quarters on the Western Front.

A quarter of a century later, the American way of war was alive and well
in Vietnam, finding expression in a thinly fictionalized account of the war
by Josiah Bunting, a Vietnam veteran who was then teaching at West Point:

[Colonel] Manley could build a battle, could 'orchestrate forces' better
than any commander in Vietnam. His casualties were quite heavy—
indeed, a cynical reporter once called him a 'butcher'—but his body-
count for two months running had been the highest for a unit its size
in the whole combat theater. It was gratifying to the General to have
such a commander working for him.[4]

Even in the Persian Gulf War of 1990–1991, viewed as the antithesis of
Vietnam and the incubator of so much that was novel or even revolutionary,
the classic American way of war found expression. Surely, when Chairman
of the Joint Chiefs of Staff General Colin Powell declared that the American
objective in Kuwait was "to cut off the [Iraqi] army and kill it," Lincoln
would have approved. Here—seemingly—was another general who did not
flinch when confronting the arithmetic of battle.

Aggressiveness, Decision, Maximum Effort, Bright Lines

Four qualities distinguish the old American way of war. The first is extreme aggressiveness, at all levels of conflict, from the tactical (the conduct

of individual fights) to the operational (the orchestration of battles in time and space) to the strategic (the planning out of campaigns to achieve the objectives of war). Whether fighting Indians on the Western frontier, Spaniards in Cuba, Germans in the Argonne or Normandy, a compulsion to seize the first available opportunity to close with and destroy the enemy characterizes the preferred American approach to warfare. (One of the very first moves in the American Revolution—fought nominally to defend against George III's repression—was a lunge to grab Quebec.)

American military heroes are the bold, the dashing, the audacious— whether they are Stonewall Jackson evading and then striking multiple Union armies attempting to trap him in the Shenandoah Valley in 1862, or Jimmy Doolittle attacking Tokyo with a handful of bombers in 1942. The quintessential American military leaders are those eager to attack: Ulysses S. Grant, pushing into the Wilderness in 1864 and declaring himself determined to "fight it out on this line if it takes all summer," or John J. Pershing who insisted that a vast American army would end World War I by undertaking offensives that European powers had given up as suicidal. Admiral Ernest King's insistence upon a quick riposte at Guadalcanal in response to Japan's devastating offensives in 1942, or General Marshall's desire to invade France in 1943, or the aspirations of General Hap Arnold to win the war through strategic bombing—all manifest the urgent determination to take the fight to the enemy that is the essence of the traditional American way of war.

Nor did this aggressiveness manifest itself only in the realm of strategy. The American armed forces have, in the twentieth century at least, favored offensive tactics. In between the world wars the Marine Corps sedulously cultivated the art of amphibious assault written off as impossibly bloody by the British veterans of Gallipoli. "Search and destroy," not pacification, dominated the American military style in Vietnam, and more than a few Air Force generals still believe that a less restrained use of air power might have brought that war to a different conclusion. The residual desire to carry the war to the enemy in the old way—to "go downtown" as fighter pilots like to put it, appeared in Kosovo as well, as frustrated Air Force generals made clear repeatedly. But such yearnings had by then become vestigial and, more importantly, operationally irrelevant.

Closely coupled to American aggressiveness at the outset of war has been the quest for decisive battle, the clash of arms that could clinch a decision. This search for the engagement that would finish the war has obsessed American generals from Robert E. Lee hoping to bring the Union to its knees at Gettysburg to Douglas MacArthur attempting to conclude the Korean conflict with a decisive lunge to the Yalu River.

Colonel Harry Summers began a short study of the Vietnam war with a telling anecdote that captured the American military's discomfort with the Indochina war. "You never beat us in a single battle," he recalled telling a North Vietnamese counterpart during the final armistice negotiations. "That's true," the Vietnamese colonel replied, after a moment's thought. "That's also irrelevant." That brief exchange captures the frustration and outrage that American officers felt when fighting a war in which undoubted, and hard-won tactical victories, measured by ground taken and casualties inflicted, did not translate into strategic success. Virtuosity in grand tactics— the big battle, rather than the campaign, much less strategy—has obsessed generations of American officers who pore over Lee's brilliant flanking ma- neuver at Chancellorsville, convinced that it will yield profound insights into the art of generalship despite the fact that Lee's victory came at an unaffordable cost in casualties and produced no lasting gains. Similarly, in the decades before World War II, the quest for the decisive engagement obsessed U.S. Navy war planners who could not imagine that a war with Japan might be decided not by a super-Jutland of the massed fleets in the Philippine Sea, but by attrition.

The third characteristic of the American way of war, again tied to the previous two, is discomfort with ambiguous objectives, constricted resources, and political constraints. The revulsion of the American military from the Vietnam experience represented not only its reaction to that war, but a sense that somehow the rules for successful warfighting had been violated at their core. In November 1984, Secretary of Defense Caspar Weinberger—ex- pressing that revulsion on behalf of the officers who had fought the Vietnam war—articulated preconditions for the use of force, henceforth to become canonical within the defense establishment. The "Weinberger doctrine" consisted of six principles:

1) The United States should not commit forces to combat overseas unless the particular engagement or occasion is deemed vital to our national interest or that of our allies. That emphatically does not mean that we should declare beforehand, as we did with Korea in 1950, that a particular area is outside our strategic perimeter.
2) If we decide it is necessary to put combat troops into a given situ- ation, we should do so wholeheartedly and with the clear intention of winning. If we are unwilling to commit the forces or resources

necessary to achieve our objectives, we should not commit them at all. Of course, if the particular situation requires only limited force to win our objectives, then we should not hesitate to commit forces sized accordingly. When Hitler broke treaties and remilitarized the Rhineland, small combat forces then could perhaps have prevented the holocaust of World War II.

3) If we do decide to commit forces to combat overseas, we should have clearly defined political and military objectives. And we should know precisely how our forces can accomplish those clearly defined objectives. And we should have and send the forces needed to do just that. As Clausewitz wrote, "No one starts a war—or rather, no one in his senses ought to do so—without first being clear in his mind what he intends to achieve by that war, and how he intends to conduct it." War may be different today than in Clausewitz's time, but the need for well-defined objectives and a consistent strategy is still essential. If we determine that a combat mission has become necessary for our vital national interests, then we must send forces capable to do the job and not assign a combat mission to a force configured for peacekeeping.

4) The relationship between our objectives and the forces we have committed—their size, composition, and disposition—must be continually reassessed and adjusted if necessary. Conditions and objectives invariably change during the course of a conflict. When they do change, then our combat requirements must also change. We must continuously keep as a beacon light before us the following basic questions: Is this conflict in our national interest? Does our national interest require us to fight, to use force of arms? If the answers are "yes," then we must win. If the answers are "no," then we should not be in combat.

5) Before the United States commits combat forces abroad, there must be some reasonable assurance that we will have the support of the American people and their elected representatives in Congress. This support cannot be achieved unless we are candid in making clear the threats we face; the support cannot be sustained without continuing and close consultation. We cannot fight a battle with Congress at home while asking our troops to win a war overseas or, as in the case of Vietnam, in effect asking our troops not to win, but just to be there.

6) The commitment of U.S. forces to combat should be a last resort.[5]

Setting an impossible standard of purity and simplicity, the Weinberger rules did not survive long in practice. But they did represent an ideal to which succeeding political and military leaders pledged allegiance. Officers imbibed them at war colleges, and though criticized sharply by some—including Secretary of State George Shultz—they continued to exercise an influence well after Weinberger had departed office. Even in the late 1990s a retired four star general would recall: "As a young officer, I literally carried a copy of that for 10 years with me in my briefcase because I thought it was so important, and it had such a dramatic effect on me when I read it, to think, 'Holy mackerel, it's really as simple as this.' I said, 'Finally, there's a realization about what a military can and cannot do for a democracy.'"[6]

The Bush administration during the Persian Gulf crisis of 1990–91 prided itself on having conducted the war in a way that adhered to the Weinberger doctrine. The administration insisted that in going to war with Iraq it did so in pursuit of four well-defined objectives. In reality, they were anything but well-defined. Only one of the avowed American objectives during the Gulf War (driving the Iraqi army out of Kuwait) could be fairly described as straightforward. The others were far more ambiguous than advertised. The first, ensuring the security of American citizens, had been rendered nugatory by Saddam Hussein's release of American hostages. The restoration of the legitimate government of Kuwait depended on one's definition of legitimacy, and the last, "ensuring the security and stability of the Persian Gulf," offered ample room for confusion and misinterpretation. What mattered, however, was to convey the *impression* that ambiguity had been banished from the planning and conduct of war. At about this same time, the term "exit strategy"—having in hand a plan to extricate oneself from a messy military commitment even prior to launching that commitment—became a popular term of art in the defense establishment.[7]

Finally, the traditional American way of war has rested on a similarly clear-cut understanding of civil-military relations, in which the tasks of soldiers and politicians are discrete and well understood. Two overarching principles define a proper civil-military relationship. The first is a prohibition on civilian "interference" in military operations. The second is the obligation of apolitical officers to dutifully execute the policies laid down by the political leadership. In short, the tradition of civil-military relations draws a bright line to separate the realm of the soldier from that of the politician. This tradition goes back to the Civil War, or rather to the reaction of regular officers to that war, evidenced most notably by Major General Emory Upton's posthumously published study *The Military Policy of the United States*.[8] A brilliant (and definitely offense-minded) tactician, Upton scorned the incompetence of civilian notables turned generals, the indiscipline of hastily raised volunteer units, and the meddling of politicians, as he understood it. His book crystallized an orthodox disdain for citizen-soldiers and interfering statesmen that has lasted for well over a century.

Here too, the American way of war has been framed by an understanding of the Vietnam and Gulf wars as morality tales of how wars should not, and should be conducted. The former, in the telling that retains wide credibility with most military and many civilian leaders, is a sorry tale of President Lyndon Johnson personally selecting bombing targets. The latter, in contrast, is portrayed as an exemplary case study in civil-military effectiveness, with primary credit given to President George Bush as a commander in chief who provided broad overall guidance and ample resources, and then allowed his field commanders to fight the war as they saw fit.

As described here, the old American way of war is, of course, something of a caricature. In practice, it has never commanded universal support among American political and military leaders. Rarely in actual practice has the United States been able fully to live up to it. (This was true even of the Persian Gulf War, the claims of Bush administration veterans notwithstanding). The traditional American way of war stands more as a statement of ideal conditions than real circumstances—what war ought to be more than what it has actually been.

The Kosovo war did not represent a conscious abandonment of this tradition, which in the Pentagon and within policy circles remains even today the conventional wisdom. But the war did illustrate the extent to which modern conditions had rendered that tradition inadequate and, indeed, obsolete. Furthermore, Kosovo demonstrates the extent to which the circumstances of the post–Cold War era have obliged American military and civilian leaders to extemporize an approach to war that differs radically from past practice—even as they trumpet their fealty to the approved lessons of Vietnam and the Persian Gulf. Indeed, the continuing influence of those two conflicts on American thinking about war, the former seeming to violate all the precepts of the old way of war, the latter affirming them, constitutes a barrier that conceals from view the emergence of this new way of war. Among civilians and soldiers alike, the old doctrines—now hardened into prejudices—remain intact. Unable or unwilling to grasp the extent to which actual practice—not just in Kosovo—has already superseded the traditional

American way of war, they cannot even begin to assess the implications, military and otherwise, of the tradition that is emerging to replace it.

The New American Way of War: From Weinberger's Rules to the "Beauty of Coalitions"

During the Cold War Americans told themselves that their country should wage war for concrete, vital interests—a conviction codified as Weinberger's first principle. Such too seemed to be the lesson of Vietnam, when America's leaders threw away lives, apparently, in pursuit of intangibles. The result ever since has been a tendency on the part of political leaders to define the purposes of American military action as being overwhelmingly large, to inflate the significance of the object pursued and the clarity with which that object has been defined.

Yet in Kosovo, as in other 1990s U.S. military interventions such as in Somalia or in Haiti, vital American interests were never at stake. To be sure, President Bill Clinton, in his first address to the nation on the Kosovo conflict, said the opposite. He insisted that the United States and its allies were obliged to "act to prevent a wider war; to diffuse a powder keg at the heart of Europe that has exploded twice before in this century with catastrophic results."[9] Despite President Clinton's references to World War I originating in the Balkans—a prime example of the inflation of strategic purposes—the likelihood that Serb repression in Kosovo would somehow trigger a great power confrontation between Russia and the West was minimal. If anything, the reverse was true: NATO's intervention in the war was likely to precipitate friction with the shrunken remnants of the Soviet empire.

Administration rhetoric also emphasized a moral imperative for U.S. and NATO action, finding in Serb actions parallels with the crimes perpetrated by Nazi Germany. But the suffering of the Kosovar Albanians, if awful enough, did not match the agony of Rwanda during the spring of 1994, which the Clinton administration had largely ignored. Serb forces in Kosovo sought to expel the province's ethnic Albanian inhabitants, not to exterminate them, and the atrocities, although substantial, did not rise to the level of genocide. Just as the remnant of Yugoslavia in 1999 was not the Balkan powder keg of 1914, so too Slobodan Milosevic was not Adolf Hitler.

Why then did the U.S. and its allies intervene? The administration's actual motivation for war in Kosovo seems to have stemmed from a number of lesser concerns, all of them legitimate, but none of them qualifying even remotely as "vital interests." One objective was the desire to forestall the second- and third-order consequences of another Yugoslav war, for example, the destabilization of Macedonia and its absorption by Greece, possibly triggering a conflict with Turkey. A second objective was to maintain the cohesiveness of NATO, a self-referential objective (taking an alliance to war in order to preserve the alliance with which one might at some point wish to go to war). Finally, humanitarian concerns no doubt played a role in motivating the United States to intervene. Ending the suffering of Kosovar Albanians would testify to the unacceptability of such behavior, particularly in other parts of Europe but also beyond.

None of these purposes could be considered objectionable; by the same token, however, none qualify as self-evidently vital, much less meriting President Clinton's assertion that the objectives envisaged included "A future in which leaders cannot keep, gain or increase their power by teaching their young people to hate or kill others simply because of their faith or heritage. A future in which young Americans who set out . . . to serve our country will not have to fight in yet another major European conflict."[10] Yet in their ambitious reach these lofty goals mirror the equally hazy or remote interests that motivated the United States to use force in a variety of contexts since the Cold War. The Bush and Clinton administrations alike lavished these operations—the invasions of Panama and Haiti, for example, or the deployments to Somalia as well as the periodic (now all but continuous) military operations against Iraq—with a rhetorical justification well beyond the limited and prudent calculations that brought them about. The December 1989 intervention in Panama, for example, became a crusade to "defend democracy in Panama" and combat drug trafficking;[11] the standoff with Iraq became a decisive test of world order.

Conceivably, the politicians who compared the Balkan crisis of 1999 to the Balkan crisis of 1914 were deceiving not only their publics, but to some extent themselves, about the actual stakes for which they had gone to war. To most members of the public since the Vietnam War, the notion of using force to overawe opponents, to demonstrate commitment, to send signals, and in general to create an international climate of deference to American wishes (or at least fear of American displeasure) has been anathema. The political leader willing to confess publicly that he or she was putting American soldiers at risk merely to defend such discredited concepts as "credibility" or "reputation" would be brave to the point of foolhardiness. Yet in virtually every instance in which the United States employed military power in the 1990s such considerations in all likelihood provided the deeper rationale leading to the use of force. "The reputation of power is power," wrote Thomas Hobbes in *Leviathan*. For no state is this more true than an imperial state—a state like the United States since the end of the Cold War.

Long unwilling to admit the implications of their position of global dominance, Americans have tended to think of power as something like a checking account—draw it down with trivial expenditures and the balance will be inadequate for the larger emergencies of national security. It would be no less plausible, however, to think of power as a muscle, its strength maintained and enhanced through exercise. Such, at least, appears to have become the implicit, and perhaps the unconscious doctrine of U.S. foreign policy.

In this the United States does not differ from any other great imperial power, seeking to sustain its position by periodically employing military power to remind friend and foe alike of its capacity and willingness to exert its power. Like the imperial powers of bygone years, the United States throughout the first decade of the post–Cold War era has used force for purposes that are not merely less than vital, but indirect. The hazard posed by an ethnically cleansed Kosovo on Balkan stability is a good example of not a secondary but a *tertiary* interest: The United States went to war over Kosovo—a place of almost no intrinsic value—less to correct Serb misbehavior there, than to preclude adverse consequences elsewhere, for example, a general deterioration in the relations of the Balkan states that could ultimately pit Greece against Turkey and, hence, undermine NATO. In a similar vein, British nineteenth-century statesmen embroiled their soldiers in the Sudan—a place of little intrinsic value—to protect Egypt, which was essential to protect the Suez Canal, which was crucial to defending the sea lanes to South Asia, which enabled Great Britain to secure the real prize, India.

Both logics—that of reputation, and that of second-order interest—smack of the sort of calculus that led to Vietnam, and hence cannot be introduced into public discourse about strategy. Ambiguity and nuanced political objectives have acquired an equally ill repute. Of all the supposed lessons of Vietnam, none has received wider endorsement than an insistence on defining "precise and achievable objectives." Fuzzy purposes and open-ended commitments helped doom the U.S. effort in Vietnam, and hence the language of American strategy now pointedly employs terms like "end states" and "exit strategies," which are viewed as essential to the conduct of war.

In truth, during the various U.S. military interventions of the past decade, an absence of clarity and precision has been the rule, not the exception. Nearing the end of his term in office, George Bush dispatched U.S.
forces to Somalia on a limited humanitarian aid mission scheduled to conclude by Bush's last day in office on January 20, 1993. In fact, Operation
Restore Hope was nowhere near completion on that date and soon thereafter
metamorphosed into a bloody—and ultimately unsuccessful—vendetta
against a local warlord. Efforts to impose precision, to include pre-an-
nounced exit dates, on the U.S.–led intervention in Bosnia met similar failure. Secretary of Defense William Perry vowed, on November 30, 1995 that
American forces would be out of Bosnia within a year of their arrival.[12]
Speaking for the uniformed military, General John Shalikashvili, chairman
of the Joint Chiefs of Staff, offered public assurances that the U.S. could
and would adhere to such a deadline. Both would eat crow a year later,
when the U.S. military commitment to Bosnia was extended and eventually
became all but permanent.

These lapses from the sort of clarity mandated by the Weinberger doctrine
may reflect muddiness of thought on the part of political and military leaders.
They reflect as well, however, the intrinsic uncertainties of strategy itself. To
the extent that the old American way of war accepted Clausewitz's iron
dictum that war is an extension of politics by other means, it did so by
limiting politics to the setting of larger objectives that victory in battle would
secure. Once those objectives were defined, Americans preferred to keep
politics as far apart from war as possible.

Yet in defining the relationship between war and politics so narrowly,
Americans misconstrued Clausewitz, whose actual intent was to argue that
politics suffuses war. Viewing war in this light, the objectives for which any
conflict is fought must of necessity be adjusted in accordance with political
exigency, changing moods and preoccupations, shifting constellations of domestic and international political forces, and the consequences of success
or failure on the battlefield.

American leaders insist otherwise. During the Kosovo war, for example,
the scramble for an unambiguous statement of political purpose led to an
absurd formulation of allied objectives. Thus, when President Clinton explained to the nation the purpose of American-led air strikes he declared:

Our strikes have three objectives: First, to demonstrate the seriousness
of NATO's opposition to aggression and its support for peace. Second,

to deter President Milosevic from continuing and escalating his attacks on helpless civilians by imposing a price for those attacks. And, third, if necessary, to damage Serbia's capacity to wage war against Kosovo in the future by seriously diminishing its military capabilities.[13]

At almost the same time, the Secretary General of NATO (who claimed that it was he who had actually ordered the bombing) indicated that the purpose of Operation Allied Force was to "prevent more human suffering and more repression and violence against the civilian population of Kosovo."[14] Both leaders indicated—as did their subordinates—that Serb acceptance of the proposed Rambouillet accord would cause the war to cease.[15]

Thus, the ostensible purpose for which the American-led alliance fought was the deal proposed at Rambouillet: the creation of an autonomous (not independent) Kosovo, composed of an Albanian majority and a Serb minority living together, under continued Yugoslav sovereignty. Yet the solvent of violence—both Serb repression and NATO's bombing—made the erection of such intricate structures all but impossible. A vengeful Albanian population would accept neither long-term affiliation with Yugoslavia, nor the presence of Serb neighbors who had, in many cases, cooperated in their expulsion from their homes. In Kosovo, the quest for simplicity, clarity, and finality in war objectives led, by the beginning of a new century, not to a genuine settlement imposed by arms but only to a precarious and violent truce.

America's allies often think of the United States as a lone gunslinger; American statesmen sometimes think of themselves the same way—as Henry Kissinger, to his later regret, once confessed to Italian journalist Oriana Fallaci. American defense planning assumes that the United States will wage its wars on its own—at least such are the assumptions embedded in the doctrine of "two major theater wars," which shapes American force structure. American politicians and soldiers prepare for wars in which the United States confronts its opponents alone. Critics, both domestic and overseas, deride the United States for its lack of understanding of foreign cultures and its blithe assumption that the psychology of other peoples differs in no material way from that of the American heartland. There is some justice in all this, but the purely unilateral way of war died in the United States a long time ago. The change did not occur all at once. Since 1917 the United States had always fought as a member of a coalition, but until Kosovo in most cases it did so while insisting upon maximum freedom of action. In World War I the United States was careful to identify itself as an Associated, not an Allied Power, and it strove to keep its forces independent from those of France and Great Britain. In World War II, it attempted, insofar as possible, to exclude its allies from participation in the Pacific save in a completely subordinate role. (Europe, where the U.S. was a latecomer to the war, was admittedly a different situation). In Korea, Vietnam, and the Gulf, the United States thoroughly dominated its allies, who had very little say in the broader direction of the war. The United States today goes to war leading coalitions into battle, and over the space of a century it has made itself a remarkably adroit leader of multinational military enterprises.

Kosovo marked a departure, though, in that here, to an even greater extent than in the Gulf War, the maintenance of a coalition became something of an object in itself. In Operation Allied Force, for the first time, coalitional concerns intruded upon the strategy and operational concepts of the war. Thus, in a Pentagon briefing Major General Charles Wald responded to a question about NATO's 18 other members:

> They all have a vote on everything. They can vote on whether we start this or not. They can vote on whether we continue. They can vote on everything. That's the strength and probably the weakness a little bit of what we have going on here. But the beauty of the fact is we're a coalition. This is not one nation against Serbia. Therefore, as 19 nations we all have an equal vote, so I won't talk on specific targeting, but the fact of the matter is this is 19 nations going against Serbia together. We're not the only ones that vote. Everybody votes.[16]

In fact, one might say that American strategy now has a coalitional habit. When General Wald continued—"I will tell you that as we go down this campaign, the mission that's been given to General Clark has been given by 19 nations to execute. That's who we answer to."—he spoke with an air of irritated but unquestioning acceptance.[17] Politicians and military planners alike are uncomfortable with the prospect of going to war without allies. On occasion they provide some military support that the United States requires—basing, peacekeeping, a few military specialties like minesweeping, or a greater tolerance for risk and loss (particularly true of the British, and to some extent the French). By and large, however, the quest for coalition partners stems primarily from a desire for political legitimacy abroad and at home. This yearning stems as well from years of institutionalized coalition building and operations—NATO may have outlived its original purpose of sheltering Europe from a Soviet onslaught, but for half a century now it has taught American officers to work with foreign militaries. What is customary has become desirable; to this extent, the decades of mobilization during the Cold War had the effect on the American military mind that a hot war would. It created an instinct to work with allies, whether or not doing so was strictly necessary or even beneficial. The coalitional impulse received further reinforcement from the desire to legitimize the use of force. A multinational operation allows Americans and others to pretend that, say, keeping Iraq down is not a constabulary act of American imperial will, but a mere discharge of the mandate of the United Nations. Hypocrisy, perhaps, but humbug has its place in the conduct of foreign policy.

The coalitional habit extends well beyond a mere wish to have troops of other nations side by side with Americans. It includes a fine web of procedures and protocols that allows military organizations to work harmoniously with one another; a prime example of this is the air tasking order that specifies not only which targets aircraft will attack but such mundane matters as radio frequencies, tanker rendezvous points, and the like. American units have developed experience in sharing intelligence with not entirely trustworthy friends, in attaching liaison units to unfamiliar armies, in conducting maritime operations with multinational flotillas. The spread of English as the world's *lingua franca*, and the enormous number of foreign officers who have studied in the United States (and American officers who have served for extended periods abroad) facilitates America's coalitional habit.

Coalition leadership comes, of course, with a price. Some times this is no more than the dollar cost of providing logistical support and equipment; at others, as in Kosovo, it is the wearing irritation of coping with allies who usually wish to hold the United States back from waging war in its preferred style. (Kosovo was unusual in this one respect, however: One ally, Great Britain, actually preferred a more aggressive course, to include the early use of ground forces if air power did not drive the Serbs out.) But the benefits, to this point at any rate, far outweigh the costs, so much so that the United States may lose the willingness to consider (although not, in all likelihood, the physical ability to conduct) operations in the face of universal disapproval. On the other hand, the Kosovo war, in which allies as reluctant as Greece nonetheless took part, suggests that the United States will never lack for partners. After all, states join alliances out of mutual interest, but among lesser partners that interest may well include a desire to constrain a leader as much as to assist in achieving a common purpose.

Operational Style: Air Power and the Long March to 73 Easting

Since the early days of World War II, air power has commanded a central place in the American way of war. Still, until the Persian Gulf War, a deep and abiding skepticism about the utility of air power as an independent instrument permeated the United States Army, and through it the defense establishment. The Air Force, of course, disagreed. But the Navy was divided, seeing air power as a powerful but far from decisive tool of military action, and the Marine Corps, self-sufficient unto itself, played little role in national debates over the proper role of air power. The Army, however, which provided many of the chairmen of the Joint Chiefs of Staff and theater commanders in Europe, the Persian Gulf, and Latin America, had the last word—and the last word was to be wary of the extravagant claims of air advocates. Moreover, such Army prejudices exercised a more subtle influence on strategic thought through civilian leaders such as Weinberger whose own military service had been with the Army.

After Operation Desert Storm, however, and despite the continuing skepticism of General Colin Powell, the extraordinarily influential chairman of the Joint Chiefs of Staff, civilian elites came to see air power as the ideal vehicle for deriving political utility from U.S. military dominance in a unipolar world. The apparent contribution of air power to the triumph over Iraq, and its subsequent application—however inelegant—in Bosnia, Serbia, and Kosovo persuaded many that air weapons employed independently offered the ideal tool for the sorts of military problems facing the United States in the 1990s, and the new century beyond. As a result, in the first decade of the post–Cold War era, air power became the weapon of choice for American statecraft.

Two technological developments (reinforced by formidable tactical expertise) account for this development. The first is the routinization of precision. American warplanes can now deliver ordnance with something approaching pinpoint accuracy as a matter of course. "Dumb" (i.e. unguided) munitions still remain in the U.S. military inventory, but the norm in all four services is to employ bombs or missiles guided by any of a number of means—homing on laser reflections or infra-red signatures, electro-optical guidance, or through use of Global Positioning System navigation. To be sure, bombs still go awry, and the friction and fog inherent in war means that—as in the bombing of the Chinese embassy in Belgrade—the wrong target will occasionally get hit. But by any historical standard the technological advance in weapons accuracy has been immense: after centuries of warfare in which the vast majority of ordnance expended hit nothing except unoccupied land or sea, today most weapons actually hit their intended targets.

The second advance is no less critical, but more subtle. It is the ability to employ weapons against an adversary without suffering losses, except very rarely and indeed almost by accident. Hardware, organization, and skill enable American forces first to locate, identify, and accurately characterize enemy defenses and then to avoid, neutralize, or destroy them. This means that in many cases, and certainly against fixed targets, American air power can operate with near impunity. By and large, American politicians and commanders can realistically plan for the punishment of smaller opponents without anticipating the loss of pilots or expensive aircraft.

The combination of precision and virtual invulnerability makes air power overwhelmingly attractive for medium scale applications of force (as in the Balkans) and for more routine forms of policing (as in Iraq). In practice, the American high command can titrate the amount of violence it wishes to apply to a potential opponent. As it demonstrated in Kosovo (and continues to demonstrate in the no-fly zones over Iraq), the United States can conduct combat operations over a period of months, even with some civilian casualties on the other side, without arousing a furor of opposition at home.

Air power offers precision and impunity—and, one might add, the appearance of control. Unlike ground forces committed to combat, air forces can cease operations within hours or minutes. Unlike ground forces, air forces can decrease, increase, or redirect the amount of violence they deliver on comparatively short notice. Air operations against third-rate opponents such as Yugoslavia or Iraq offer the peculiar prospect of war without real combat interaction. Opponents may counterpunch in some asymmetric fashion—by speeding up ethnic cleansing as the Serbs did in Kosovo or by firing off a few missiles as Saddam Hussein did in 1991. But "surprises" of this type are still very different from the shock of close combat. The inability of NATO warplanes to stop Slobodan Milosevic's Operation Horseshoe in Kosovo may have been an embarrassment; but the bloody punishment that Mohammed Farah Aidid's militiamen administered to American Rangers in Mogadishu in 1993 was a military defeat that led directly to policy failure. The preference for aerial warfare seems a way to bypass the hazards of ground combat: in Kosovo, in fact, the American government went out of its way to deny itself that option. Thus, the attractiveness of the scalpel seems to rule out the military equivalent of bone saws; but scalpels are not a solution to every surgical problem.

As has often been noted, precision air warfare is not without its drawbacks. Formidable though it appears, it actually exercises a relatively narrow range of military effects. Fielded forces can reduce their vulnerability by "hugging" the civilian population or by taking cover in forests and urban areas. More importantly, as precision becomes technically possible, it quickly becomes politically imperative; accidents as an inevitable byproduct of war become less acceptable. Public opinion abroad and at home, diplomatic reactions by foreign governments (allied, neutral, and hostile alike) are all less forgiving.

Reliance on air power (albeit a radically different kind of air power than the bludgeon of World War II strategic bombing) represents some elements of continuity with the old American way of war. The same cannot be said of changed American attitude toward ground combat. Here too, a combination of training and technology have produced what is, from one point of view, tremendous increases in military effectiveness. The demoralized, ill-disciplined semiconscript force of the late Vietnam era has given way to an all-volunteer, and highly professionalized Army and Marine Corps.[18] The long march from Hamburger Hill to 73 Easting—the former the scene of a notorious battle in the A Shau valley that cost 450 Americans killed or wounded, the latter a notable victory over Iraqi forces in 1991, won without friendly casualties—has provided the United States with exceptionally effective ground combat forces.

Assuming, that is, that Americans are willing to use them. Kosovo suggests just how hesitant the U.S. officials have become in that regard. The agonizing deliberations over the deployment of Task Force Hawk—fewer than two dozen Army helicopters, guarded and muffled by nearly 5,000 men and women—showed that politicians and generals alike found it increasingly difficult even to conceive of ground forces participating in a limited ground war. In contrast to modern air war, ground combat is more likely to mean casualties, except in some extraordinary circumstances—the Kuwait theater of operations in 1990–91, for example, offered a uniquely favorable situation for the heavily armored forces the United States deployed there. But casualties, even in numbers that are minute by any historical standard, have seemingly become unacceptable. When, as occurred earlier in the Yugoslavia intervention, U.S. commanders tell their troops that the first mission is force protection, this represents a fundamental change in American attitudes to ground warfare.

Why this shift in attitudes has occurred is uncertain.[19] Military leaders attribute casualty sensitivity to a public that is unwilling to face up to the realities of war. But survey data among military and civilian elites suggest otherwise. It appears, in fact, that the American military has become more sensitive to casualties than civilians. This stands to reason: in the absence of conscription, the public seems to regard America's servicemen and women much as they view police and firefighters—as people who deserve honor for the risks they run, but who have volunteered to put themselves in a position to do so. The roots of the present-day aversion to casualties are probably several. They may include a deep-seated reaction to the trauma of Vietnam, in two ways: a mistrust of military adventures launched for murky or merely limited political purposes, and a professional disgust at the squandering of human life. Casualty sensitivity may go deeper yet, being the military manifestation of broader trends in civil society. In a world that no longer accepts, with a fatalistic shrug, the notion of accidents and bad luck, in which, for example, corporations find themselves held accountable for the lung cancer that afflicts smokers who have chosen their habit, tolerance for combat losses has declined precipitously. It is not only that the stakes of war appear to be (and are) low; it is that the hazards of war—once a common phrase—no longer evoke the philosophical resignation they once did.

It is no coincidence that one slang for getting killed in Vietnam was "getting wasted." War is nothing if not waste on a hideous scale. But a society, including its military, which is fundamentally unwilling to accept the idea of waste has accepted a peculiar notion of war. And, for the moment, that is exactly what the United States has done.

The New Proconsuls

In 1986 the United States overhauled its system of defense organization. The Goldwater-Nichols Department of Defense reorganization act of that year continued trends evident in defense legislation going back to 1947. Since the end of World War II, the influence of the services on the conduct of military operations has diminished, with power moving to the Chairman of the Joint Chiefs of Staff (and the Joint Staff which now reports to him alone) and to the theater Commanders in Chief, or CINCs. Although it would only become apparent years after the fact, the Goldwater-Nichols Act had the further unanticipated consequence of draining power from the Office of the Secretary of Defense as well, increasing military authority at the expense of civilian control.

General Wesley Clark, Supreme Allied Commander Europe (SACEUR) and commander in chief of European Command (CINCEUCOM), dominated decision-making during the Kosovo conflict. Precisely, he served as the focal point for strategic decision-making, even if, in retrospect, cross-cutting pressures from NATO members limited his autonomy. Clark's was the dominating personality, even if he endured more than his share of frustration in gaining the decisions he wished. In some ways he represented a throwback to an eighteenth-century style of warfare. Clark carried much of the burden of negotiating with the multiple governments that contributed forces to the coalition battle. Indeed, one of the peculiarities of the Kosovo conflict lay in the deference that the United States showed to allied leaders. Despite providing more than three-quarters of the effective force—that is, those elements that delivered precision guided weapons, coordinated and controlled air operations, and assessed their effects—the United States yielded to a style of collective decision-making that soldiers found agonizingly slow. What seems *not* to have occurred was shaping of alliance strategy and action by political and military authorities in Washington—the kind of central control exercised during World War II by Roosevelt and his chiefs of staff. Not only did the President and the Secretary of Defense seem remarkably detached from the conduct of operations; their statutory advisers, the Joint Chiefs of Staff, contributed little to the planning and conduct of the war. Indeed, their first meeting with the President occurred the day the Milosevic regime announced its intention to withdraw from Kosovo.

The rise of the CINC reflected, no doubt, the effect of personality. Clark, a brilliant, politically sophisticated, and assertive soldier, exercised perhaps disproportionate, or at least unusual control over a foreign policy establishment at home that had sent American forces off to limited engagements before, but evinced little stomach for war leadership. But Clark's dominant role reflected as well the bureaucratic consequences of Goldwater-Nichols, which, in reducing the role of the service chiefs had left political leaders with but two channels of military advice—the CINC overseas, and the Joint Chiefs of Staff chairman at home. The latter, General Henry Shelton, seems to have been a cautious and not terribly forceful bureaucratic player, thus reversing the pattern of the Gulf War, when a dominant chairman, General Colin Powell, controlled all communications between the CINC, General Norman Schwarzkopf, and civil authority.

What seems, in all events, to have dropped out of the civilian-military dialogue was a presentation of different options and a debate among military authorities about the best course of action, conducted in the presence, and for the ultimate benefit of, civilian leadership. Indeed, implicit in the Goldwater-Nichols legislation was the view that such debates produced confusion or tawdry bargaining, a questionable interpretation of the historical record.

Beyond this military centralization, however, lay a further more pervasive and subtle development, the rise of the CINC as imperial proconsul. Gone are the days when senior generals and admirals think of themselves as the mere executors of policy rather than its formulators. Clark's record in pushing for operations against Milosevic, and his dominance of the intra-Allied debate is mirrored in other theaters of the world. America's Asian security policy bears the clear imprint of the views of the commander in chief of the Pacific Command (CINCPAC). American drugs and security policy in Latin America likewise reflects the influence of the commander in chief of Southern Command (CINCSOUTH)—and (during the Clinton Administration) of the retired four-star general who is the "czar" of White House counter-narcotics policies. American generals and admirals, having experienced a half-century of the Cold War, have become more than comfortable with a strong role in setting policy, negotiating deals, and even setting the objectives for which force should be used. Admiral Leighton ("Snuffy") Smith, the NATO commander during operation DELIBERATE FORCE in 1995 summarized his view of civil-military relations this way:

> I said this publicly a number of times. In Western militaries, the military follow the guidance of their political leaders, their authorized and rightful political leaders, okay? 'If you want me to go after the war criminals—and I do not think that's a good idea right now—if you want me to go after them, give me the order, get the hell out of my way, and stand by for the consequences.'[20]

Within ten days of the beginning of the war in Kosovo, a senior officer told the *Washington Post* that "I don't think anybody felt like there had been a compelling argument made that all of this was in our national interest"—as if that were for the military itself to decide.[21]

The development of a military that no longer sees sharp lines between the making of policy and its execution, between a necessary literacy in political matters and the arts of manipulating government to do what it believes desirable, is a troubling development. It has occurred, in part, because civilian leaders have in large measure abdicated responsibility for shaping the course and conclusion of military operations. When General Norman Schwarzkopf went to negotiate an end to the Gulf War he did so without the benefit of instructions or guidance from his civilian superiors, who seem to have delegated to him and to Chairman of the Joint Chiefs of Staff, General Colin Powell, the final decision on how to end the Gulf War. In this, as in other cases, the differences between the first Bush and the Clinton administrations, often proclaimed by members of both administrations, are more apparent than real.

Beyond Kosovo

To be sure, no way of war is a fixed thing. Under the right set of circumstances leaders and their society may accept very different styles of conflict. But barring some cataclysmic event—a twenty-first-century Pearl Harbor—it seems likely that the American way of war will prevail for some time to come. Given that prospect, three large consequences follow.

First, the United States now operates with a kind of cognitive dissonance with respect to force structure and doctrine. Its soldiers, sailors, airmen and marines live the new American way of war. Their arms, their training, their doctrine, and their fundamental beliefs about war bear the imprint of the old one. Adapting the legacy of the old way of war to meet the imperative of the new one has proven a daunting challenge. The new American way of war demanded by the new responsibilities undertaken by U.S. soldiers requires something other than an old Cold War–era force—fewer armored brigades and more B-2 bombers; the abandonment of military jargon about "end states" and "exit strategies;" the development of organizations dedicated to peacemaking and other "Operations Other Than War"; and the recruitment of personnel whose primary interest lies in such activities rather than becoming "warriors." None of these changes will come easily.

Secondly, the United States must face up to the vulnerabilities inherent in its new way of war. First and foremost among them is casualty sensitivity, but those potential vulnerabilities also include increasing deference to allied opinion and an unwillingness even to contemplate serious land operations. These problems are societal and political in nature, but they may respond, at least to some degree, to technological and organizational solutions. The more advances in military technology allow the United States to wield effective, and above all sustained military power without exposing itself to losses, the better. One piece of good news in the Kosovo war was America's ability to conduct relatively modest operations over a prolonged period. From a traditional point of view such an operational style has little to recommend it; but if political circumstances require chronic, incremental, and highly constrained military operations, better to execute them well than badly.

Finally, the American leaders, civilian and military alike, must consider whether the current balance in civil-military relations is the right one. The narrowing of channels of military advice may have had the effect of undermining real civilian control. To regain freedom of maneuver civilians may find it useful to pit their chief military adviser—the Chairman of the Joint Chiefs of Staff—against the theater CINC. Another alternative would be an effort to reinvigorate the Joint Chiefs of Staff as a collective body offering advice. In any event, civilian leaders must re-establish the clear lines between making policy and executing it, strongly advocating courses of action and attempting to influence them. Conceivably, such an effort to re-assert civilian supremacy may produce uncomfortable confrontations, and perhaps a few dismissals or resignations—if so, however, the price is worth it.

These challenges for the American way of supreme command are compounded by the peculiar difficulty Americans now have in speaking frankly about war. The old way of war may have been brutal, but at least it was honest. It is symbolic, perhaps, of a larger change in how the countries of the West now think about conflict that Secretary General Javier Solana could declare, while announcing the bombing of Serbia: "Let me be clear: NATO is not waging war against Yugoslavia."[22] Some amount of disingenuousness characterizes most war. But there is something more than usually disheartening in the quibbles, evasions, and semantic contortions that pervaded the Kosovo operation—in which war was not war, in which an absence of results signified progress, and in which an utterly implausible objective was declared a precise and achievable "end state." Perhaps Western leaders, including Americans, have concluded that waging war is a subject that no longer merits serious consideration. If so, they are making a grave mistake.

The end of the Cold War transformed America's role in the world. Prior to World War II the United States was but one of several Great Powers. By the end of that conflict it had become the undisputed leader of a grand coalition. Today, it views itself, in the possibly unfortunate phrase of Secretary of State Madeleine Albright, as "the indispensable nation," or, as others might term it, "the global hegemon." American power pervades the international system. Civil war in Rwanda, border disputes in the Levant, jousting over coastal waters in the South China Sea—all engage American interests, and ultimately, American power. These inescapable interests and commitments occur in a radically changed international environment, in which the bipolar conflict of the Cold War has irretrievably collapsed, and in which the United States, because of the strength of its economy and culture, bestrides the world. The strangely successful Kosovo war—the bloodless victory that left the winners disconcerted and discontented—marked another milestone in an era that has evoked a new way of war. Like all others, that approach to war will last for a duration of time—years or decades—that its practitioners cannot hope to know.

Any way of war has its strengths and its weaknesses; all ultimately succumb to altered political circumstances and changing techniques and technology. For the moment, devising an open formulation of the new American way of war, perfecting its methods, clarifying its assumptions, and recognizing its limits—while accepting the likelihood that it too, will, at some point, prove inadequate—will be challenge enough.

Notes

1. Don E. Fehrenbacher and Virginia Fehrenbacher, eds., *Recollected Works of Abraham Lincoln* (Stanford, Calif.: Stanford University Press, 1996), p. 426.
2. For the classic description of the "American Way of War," see Russell Weigley's book of that name (Bloomington: Indiana University Press, 1973).
3. E. J. Kahn, *McNair, Educator of an Army, by Chief Warrant Officer E. J. Kahn, Jr.* (Washington, D.C.: The Infantry Journal, 1945), p. 8.
4. Josiah Bunting, *The Lionheads: A Novel* (New York: Braziller, 1972), p. 56.
5. Caspar Weinberger, National Press Club, 28 November 1984, reprinted in *Defense* (January 1985): 1–11. Also at: http://www.amsc.belvoir.army.mil/ecampus/gpc/prework/strategy/use.htm
6. General Howell Estes Jr., in "Give War a Chance," Program 1715 of *Frontline*, PBS, 11 May 1999. Transcript at http://www.pbs.org/wgbh/pages/frontline/shows/military/etc/script.html
7. See Gideon Rose, "The Exit Strategy Delusion," *Foreign Affairs* 78, no. 1 (January-February 1998).
8. Emory Upton, *The Military Policy of the United States* (1904; reprint, New York: Greenwood, 1968). See also a commentary by this author, "Making Do

With Less, or Coping with Upton's Ghost," Strategic Studies Institute mono-graph (Carlisle Barracks, Pa.: U.S. Army War College, 1995).

9.   Statement by the President to the Nation, 24 March 1999. http://www.pub. whitehouse.gov/uri-res/I2R?urn:pdi://oma.eop.gov.us/1999/3/25/1.text.1

10. Remarks by the President at the Commencement of the United States Air Force Academy, 2 June 1999. http://www.pub.whitehouse.gov/uri-res/I2R?urn:pdi:// oma.eop.gov.us/1999/6/4/7.text

11. President George W. Bush, Address to the Nation Announcing United States Military Action in Panama, 20 December 1989. http://bushlibrary.tamu.edu/ papers/1989/89122000.html.

12. David E. Johnson, "Wielding the Terrible Swift Sword: The American Military Paradigm and Civil-Military Relations," (Cambridge, Mass.: Harvard University Olin Insitute for Strategic Studies, 1996); http://data.fas.harvard.edu/cfia/olin/ pubs/no7.htm

13. Statement by the President on Kosovo, 24 March 1999. http://www.pub. whitehouse.gov/uri-res/I2R?urn:pdi://oma.eop.gov.us/1999/3/24/5.text.1

14. Press Statement, Dr. Javier Solana, Secretary General of NATO, 23 March 1999. http://www.nato.int/docu/pr/1999/p99-040e.htm

15. See, for example, Secretary of State Madeleine K. Albright's interview on *Face the Nation*, CBS, 28 March 1999; http://secretary.state.gov/www/statements/ 1999/990328.html

16. DOD News Briefing, 19 April 1999. http://www.defenselink.mil/news/Apr 1999/t04191999_t0419asd.html

17. Ibid.

18. There is an important distinction. When, as in the case of the Marine Corps, the bulk of infantry consists of troops serving only one term of enlistment, the term "professional" must be qualified. But that is an extreme case, and as re-cruitment becomes more difficult the armed services have turned their atten-tion to the need to retain personnel in lieu of bringing more in.

19. For a good overview of this issue, see Eric V. Larson, *Casualties and Consensus: The Historical Role of Casualties in Domestic Support for U.S. Military Opera-tions* (Santa Monica, Calif.: RAND, 1996).

20. "Give War a Chance," Program 1715 of *Frontline*, PBS, 11 May 1999.

21. Bradley Graham, "Joint Chiefs Doubted Air Strategy," *Washington Post*, 5 April 1999, p. A1.

22. Secretary General Solana, press statement, 23 March 1999.

3 First War of the Global Era: Kosovo and U.S. Grand Strategy

James Kurth

NATO's war for Kosovo has been widely seen as the first example of a new kind of armed conflict, the prototype for a twenty-first century way of war. Indeed, observers have touted the war as first of its kind in at least four different ways. To begin with, Kosovo was ostensibly the first truly humanitarian war, fought not for national interests as traditionally defined but for the furtherance of human rights alone. Second, Kosovo was the first real war undertaken by the NATO alliance, fought with the full authorization and participation of NATO members acting as an organization. Third, in the estimation of many well-informed analysts, the war for Kosovo provides the first real example of victory achieved through air power alone, a war won without having to engage in ground combat operations. And finally, the war was the first case of a completely bloodless victory, a war in which NATO prevailed without suffering a single combat casualty. Any one of these unique features would assure the Kosovo War a distinctive place in the annals of military history. The conjunction of the four should make that place truly extraordinary.

As we will see, all of these claims about the Kosovo War are true, but they are also incomplete. They could therefore be misleading both about the causes of the war and about its implications for future conflicts. To understand these causes and consequences, we will need to examine the war in the context of the grand, or national, strategy of the United States. For the Kosovo War was, inter alia, an outgrowth of a new grand strategy that the United States has developed in the aftermath of the Cold War.

Among the Kosovo War's distinctions, it was the first American war of the global era.

The United States and Grand Strategy

It is often thought that grand strategy—a concept that historically was most articulated by the centralized nation-states of Europe—cannot really apply to the United States, with its free-wheeling democracy, fragmented political system, and disorderly decision-making process. Alexis de Tocqueville, writing in the 1830s, was the first of a long line of distinguished analysts to argue that democracies, particularly pluralistic ones like the United States, are incapable of adhering to coherent and consistent foreign policies.[1] They are, in short, incapable of adhering to anything remotely resembling a genuine grand strategy.

In practice, however, diplomatic historians (as well as foreign adversaries) have discerned a good deal of coherence and consistency in U.S. policy, sustained over long periods of time. These periods include much of the nineteenth century (when the grand strategy was defined by continental expansion and the Monroe Doctrine); the first three decades of the twentieth century (when it emphasized commercial expansion and U.S. leadership in the world balance-of-power system); and the Cold War (when it comprised containment, nuclear deterrence, and the promotion of an open international economy). The "new" grand strategy of each successive period builds on the strategy it supercedes, revising and expanding it to fit the altered realities and opportunities created by American victories in successive wars. In a sense, there has been a single U.S. grand strategy, continuing, developing, and evolving for over two centuries.[2]

U.S. grand strategy has always included both security objectives and economic objectives, as well as particular approaches to achieving these ends at particular times. During the Cold War, for example, the United States emphasized military containment and free trade.[3] During the same period, the U.S. also supported the development of rather sophisticated international institutions with which to achieve its security and its economic objectives. These included international security organizations, such as the North Atlantic Treaty Organization (NATO) and the Organization of American States (OAS), and international economic organizations, such as the International Monetary Fund (IMF), the World Bank, and the General Agreement on Tariffs and Trade (GATT). The U.S. also developed a rather sophisticated ideology, one that gained wide international appeal and comprised both political and economic ideals. This was liberal internationalism, whose political ideal was liberal democracy and whose economic ideal was free markets. All of these features were elements of U.S. grand strategy during the Cold War.[4]

After the collapse of the Soviet Union and the end of the Cold War, the United States modified and expanded elements from its earlier grand strategies and used them as the basis for a revised grand strategy. The result reflected not only new realities and opportunities created by the American victory in the Cold War; it also reflected particular transformations that had developed during the last decade or so of the Cold War. Indeed, U.S. grand strategy at the beginning of the twenty-first century is the product of six new realities that characterize the contemporary United States and its role in the world. Two of these new realities pertain primarily to the international security system, two to the global economic system, and two to the American social system. Several of these converged to bring about the Kosovo War.

The New Realities and the Global Era

With regard to the international security system, the most obvious new reality is that the United States now finds itself the sole superpower. But although it is the greatest power, the U.S. is not the only power. Since its power, although formidable, is not great enough that it can act alone in world affairs, the United States must lead and cooperate with other states to achieve its own purposes.

This points directly to the second new reality about the international security system, namely, the enhanced American reliance on selected international organizations as vehicles to legitimize U.S. grand strategy. As we have seen, the United States has a long tradition of using international organizations through which to exercise leadership and gain cooperation. Now that the United States is the sole superpower, one whose leadership can readily be interpreted by other states as domination, the imperative of working through international organizations—even if only as a cloak for de facto unilateral action—has become even more pronounced. Among security or-

ganizations, NATO clearly is seen by U.S. policymakers as the most useful
for these purposes.

The new security realities are the result most obviously of the American
victory over the Soviet Union in the Cold War. The new economic and
social realities result from particular developments that began even before
the Cold War ended and that developed within the United States itself,
coming to maturity in the 1990s.

Any nation's grand strategy must take into account that nation's economic
and social conditions. U.S. grand strategy during the Cold War era—a strategy whose core elements consisted of containment, nuclear deterrence, and
the promotion of an open international economy—reflected particular economic and social realities that existed during most of that time. The economic realities were American industrial power and American leadership in
the international economy. The social realities were the ordering of Americans into large, hierarchical organizations—a distinctive feature of what has
been termed "modern society"—and the existence of a basic national consensus around an ideology of liberal internationalism.

Today, more than ten years after the end of the Cold War, economic and
social conditions are radically different. The American economic reality no
longer centers on industrial power, and the American social reality no longer
adheres to classic liberalism. Four great economic and social transformations
have displaced the old reality. These transformations have been most pronounced in the United States, but their impact has been global in scope.
Indeed, they have brought about a whole new era that can best be identified
as "the global era." These transformations have had a corresponding effect
on American grand strategy, which U.S. policymakers have redesigned to fit
their conception of the global era. The Kosovo War was among the first
fruits of that revised strategy.[5]

The Four Great Transformations and Liberal Globalism

The four transformations giving birth to the global era are the following:
the emergence of a global economy, replacing what had been merely an
international economy; the development of an information economy, replacing what had been the industrial economy; the development of the
postmodern society, replacing what had been modernity; and the decline of
the nation-state, superseded in some countries (particularly the United

States, Canada, and Western Europe) by a multicultural society along with a new form of liberalism.[6]

The current era has been given different names. Three of the more common ones—the "global era," the "information era," and the "postmodern era"—testify to the prominence and defining power of the first three of the transformations. The fierce debates about multiculturalism in American society testify to the prominence of the fourth.

Although the consequences of these four transformations are truly global, they have developed more in some countries than in others. Among the major powers, they have advanced most within the United States and Britain, somewhat less so in Germany and Japan, and still less in Russia, China, and India. Indeed, the *uneven* advance of these global transformations, combined with the U.S. leadership in promoting them, probably will produce even greater international misunderstandings and conflicts in the future than will the simple transformations themselves. Within the United States itself, these transformations have made America a very different country from what it was as recently as the Cold War. These transformations have also accentuated the ways that the United States differs from the other major powers.

The four transformations have had major consequences for American ideas, ideology, and even identity. For example, the development of *the global economy* has increased the freedom and mobility of business enterprises and weakened the constraints of governments. The global economy has thus reinforced the traditional American idea of free markets. But it also has promoted a newer and broader idea, that of the open society.

Similarly, the emergence of an *information economy* that has displaced the industrial economy has increased individual choice and devalued conventional hierarchies. The information economy has thus reinforced the traditional American idea of liberal democracy—but it too has promoted the newer and broader idea of the open society.

The global economy and the information economy are therefore two powerful forces whose ideological bias favors openness. But the ideology of the open society implies, indeed advocates, the limitation of state sovereignty and the weakening of the nation-state. This is particularly the case in regard to state-imposed barriers or regulations concerning the free movement of goods, capital, migrants, and information across national borders. This ideology of the open society, which most American political, economic, and intellectual elites now endorse, represents a fundamental challenge to traditional conceptions of international relations, still held by policymakers in many states, including Russia and China.

The development of *the postmodern society* has eroded the great pillars of modern society—government bureaucracies, military services, and business corporations—and the attitudes of deference, duty, and loyalty that often went with them. In their place, the postmodern society has promoted the two interrelated ideas of expressive individualism and universal human rights. Together, they form a new ideology in which individual rights are universal, universal rights are individual, and such rights are fundamental, even absolute. Conversely, the nation-state does not bestow rights, and the nation-state has no rights.

The development of a multiracial or *multicultural society* celebrates the idea of cultural diversity. Like the postmodern society, the multicultural society also promotes the idea of human rights. Although it might seem that a multiplicity of cultural groups would lead logically to an emphasis on the rights of the community, in practice it has led instead to an emphasis on the rights of the individual. Like the ideology of the open society, the ideology of human rights also points toward the limitation of state sovereignty and the decline of the nation-state. This is particularly the case in regard to international institutions overruling national governments in order to enforce human rights.

Traditional American ideology advocated liberal democracy and free markets. In foreign affairs, this ideology translated into liberal internationalism, and its most prominent proponents were Presidents Woodrow Wilson and Franklin Roosevelt. Because of the four great transformations, the 1990s saw a revival of this traditional ideology and, indeed, its expansion with a more explicit emphasis on promoting human rights and the open society. This modified version of liberal internationalism is more accurately termed "liberal globalism"; its most prominent proponents have been President Bill Clinton and Secretary of State Madeleine Albright.

The new American ideology of human rights and the open society—liberal globalism—in turn has provided the justification, and sometimes a compulsion, for a new kind of U.S. military interventionism. This has been humanitarian intervention, as in Somalia, Haiti, and then Bosnia. The U.S.-led war against Serbia over Kosovo represented the culmination of this trend toward humanitarian intervention. Vaclav Havel and others have described the Kosovo War as an altogether new kind of conflict, one in which the objectives are not traditional national interests but instead universal human rights.[7] These observers saw the Kosovo War as the first purely humanitarian war and, on that score, gave it their approval. But, as we shall see, this is not the whole story; Kosovo was also the first war fought in response to the new U.S. grand strategy of the global era.

The Grand Strategy of the Global Era

The new U.S. grand strategy of the global era reflects the changing realities that we have described. The elements of Cold War–era grand strategy have undergone their own transformation to become the elements of the new grand strategy. In most cases, this transformation has involved expansion, in regard to both the scope of objectives and the particular means employed to achieve these objectives.

The American interest in promoting an open international economy has expanded into support for an open global economy, even an open global society. U.S. grand strategy aims ultimately to eliminate all economic or social borders everywhere in the world. Borders separating nation-states would become about as significant as the borders separating the fifty states of the Union. The preferred means of achieving this open international order have expanded correspondingly. Support for free trade has given way to all-out advocacy of globalization.

The policy of containing the communist great powers, particularly the Soviet Union and China, has also expanded, this despite the Soviet Union itself having disappeared. The United States still pursues a de facto policy of containing (or more subtly of managing) Russia and China. To this has been added a policy of containing or managing several lesser powers that no longer have strong alliance ties with Russia or China. These are the usual suspects: Iran, Iraq, Libya, North Korea, Cuba, and occasionally Syria. These states are nationalist in their identities, authoritarian in their regimes, statist in their economies, and anti-American in their public rhetoric. They represent the antithesis of the American ideology of liberal globalism. The United States has often classified such states as rogues.[8] The military strategy employed to implement the policy of containment has likewise expanded. Whereas during the Cold War that strategy centered on nuclear deterrence, of late it has shifted to one that, while not abandoning nuclear deterrence, emphasizes conventional capabilities to deter, but also to retaliate against and punish by employing precision weapons.

The enlarged ambitions and objectives of liberal globalism have also encouraged the United States to expand its use of international organizations to achieve American security and economic objectives. In regard to security organizations, the United States has expanded the functions of the United Nations, the Organization for Security and Cooperation in Europe (OSCE), and NATO, particularly concerning peace-enforcement (no longer just peacekeeping) operations undertaken in the name of human rights and humanitarian intervention. In regard to economic organizations, the U.S. has broadened the functions of the IMF and the World Bank. It has led the campaign to transform the GATT into a fully-parallel economic institution, the World Trade Organization (WTO). Consistent with the so-called "Washington Consensus," this troika of economic institutions presses relentlessly to break-down national borders and supplant state enterprises, all in the name of the global economy and the open society.

Opposition to the U.S. Grand Strategy: Losers and Winners

Within a few years after the end of the Cold War, all the elements of the new U.S. grand strategy for the global era were in place. But by the mid-1990s, that strategy was already beginning to produce a backlash.

American promotion of the new realities of the global era, the American ideology of liberal globalism, and the consequent new U.S. grand strategy together are revolutionizing human affairs. This revolution is one of the most profound in human history, and it is certainly the most wide-ranging. Indeed, it is the first truly *world* revolution, its reach extending well beyond even the grandest claims of Marxism in its day.

Great revolutions can be expected to generate great opposition. The American-led global revolution has already generated significant opposition among important states. The major sources of opposition are found in three large nuclear powers (Russia, China, and India) and one large religious realm (the Islamic world). Some of this opposition comes from losers in the new global economy, but some, perhaps even most, comes from winners.

The first and most obvious sources of opposition to the American-led global revolution are the *losers* in the new global economy. These include

Russia and, more generally, most countries with an Eastern Orthodox religious tradition. They also include most of the Islamic world.

For a variety of reasons that are related to cultural traditions, Orthodox countries (Russia, Belarus, Ukraine, Moldova, Romania, Bulgaria, and Serbia) have been unsuccessful in making the transition from communism to liberal-democratic and free-market structures adaptable to an open society and a global economy. In contrast, most countries with a Roman Catholic tradition (Poland, Lithuania, the Czech Republic, Slovakia, Hungary, Slovenia, and even Croatia) have made this transition successfully. Largely Protestant nations (Estonia and Latvia) also have been successful. This dichotomy among ex-communist countries—between the more Western and the more Eastern, between the Roman Catholic or Protestant and the Eastern Orthodox—means that the political and economic developments of the 1990s revived and reinforced an ancient historic divide, corresponding to the great schism between Western and Eastern Christianity, even to the ancient division between the Latin and Greek halves of the Roman Empire. This particular cultural divide provided a major illustration of Samuel Huntington's famous argument about "the clash of civilizations."[9]

In their current condition of political and economic weakness, the governments of Russia and the other Orthodox countries cannot mount an effective and sustained opposition to the United States and its promotion of the global economy, the open society, and humanitarian intervention. But among the populations of these countries, there is now substantial resentment of and resistance toward the United States. The Kosovo War against Orthodox Serbia sharpened this resentment and resistance.

In Islamic countries as well, efforts to establish viable and resilient liberal democracies and market economies have failed. Most today are alienated from the American global project. As in the Orthodox world, governments in the Islamic world are neither willing nor able to mount a sustained and effective opposition to that project. But again, within their populations exists widespread resentment and resistance, manifested most obviously in militant organizations based upon Islamic revivalism.[10]

Even among the *winners* in the new global economy, opposition to the American-led global revolution is growing. These winners include China (and more generally many countries with a Confucian cultural tradition) and India.

Most Chinese, both in China itself and overseas, attribute their economic success to their own culture—to "Asian values" and a distinctive approach to the global economy in their own way. The Asian interpretation of the region's economic crisis of 1997–1999 has reinforced this conception. The countries with the most open currency-markets (South Korea, Thailand, and Indonesia) suffered the greatest disruption and decline; those whose currency-markets were most regulated (China and, ironically, Taiwan) experienced little disruption and continued their economic growth.

India's entry into the global economy has been recent, and its benefits for that country have been unevenly distributed. For now, however, India (or at least its vibrant information sector) qualifies as an emerging winner in the global economy. This success has occurred, however, in tandem with growing Hindu nationalism and India's development of a nuclear arsenal.

Thus the opposition to the United States and its global project is quite disparate. Some opponents are politically and economically weak and divided (the Orthodox and Islamic countries). Some are economically strong but still divided among themselves (the Confucian countries). But together, these sources of opposition constitute a vast region, really all of Eurasia and more; resistance to the American global project stretches from Russia and Eastern Europe, through the Middle East, through South Asia, to China and East Asia. This vast region contains four of the great civilizations that Huntington has identified as most likely to clash with the West: "Slavic-Orthodox," Islamic, Hindu, and "Sinic-Confucian." In this region too are four nuclear powers—Russia, Pakistan, India, and China—each seeing itself as the center of its particular civilization.[11]

U.S. leadership in humanitarian intervention, especially in Kosovo, has sharpened the opposition to the American global project. Humanitarian intervention presents a serious and specific threat to the norm of national sovereignty, and most of the opposition states saw the Kosovo War as a prime example of a U.S. grand strategy that aims to impose and enforce globalization. Furthermore, when the circumstances leading to humanitarian intervention in one state seem analogous to circumstances existing elsewhere, that intervention can also suggest a serious and specific threat to states worried that they may be next. This was the case with the Kosovo War, where Russia saw analogies between Kosovo and Chechnya, China saw analogies between Kosovo and Tibet, and India saw analogies between Kosovo and Kashmir.

The Balkans and Grand Strategy

By the late 1990s, the Balkans had become the central theater for implementing the new U.S. grand strategy of the global era. That such a marginalized place should serve such a grand purpose might seem strange, but of course it was not the first time that this poor and violent region has served as the arena for the grand strategies of the great powers.

The Balkans had been the crucible of bloody conflicts on four major occasions in the twentieth century. In the 1910s, the decay of the Ottoman Empire led to the Balkan Wars, and the recently-independent and expansionist Serbia conquered Kosovo at that time. A characteristic tactic in these Balkan Wars, one used by the Serbs against the Albanians in Kosovo, was state-organized massacre of ethnic groups, with the objective of ethnic cleansing. Serbia was an ally of Russia, which protected and promoted it in the international arena. As is well-known, Serb ambitions to acquire Bosnia led to the assassination of Archduke Franz Ferdinand, heir to the throne of Austria-Hungary, and to the outbreak of the First World War.

In the 1930s, tensions within the Kingdom of Yugoslavia (cobbled together by the victorious Allies after the First World War) led to conflict between Serbs and Croats, to German invasion and occupation, and to a sort of civil war between the different ethnic groups of Yugoslavia, within the larger conflict of the Second World War. Once again, a characteristic tactic in this Yugoslav civil war was ethnic massacre, combined with the new tactic of guerrilla warfare. The most successful guerrillas were the Communists, many of them Serbs who were supported by the Soviet Union. A new Yugoslav federation ruled by the Communist Josef Broz Tito was the result.

In the late 1940s, the decay of the British Empire led to a civil war in Greece, pitting conservatives against Communists. Communist Yugoslavia supported the guerrilla insurrection of Greek Communists until 1948, when Marshal Tito broke with Stalin. However, the United States thought that the Soviet Union itself was providing the principal support for the guerrillas, and this perception formed the basis for the Truman Doctrine in 1947 and for a sharper definition of the emerging Cold War.

Finally, the decay of Communist Yugoslavia in the 1980s after Tito's death led to a new civil war in the 1990s between the different ethnic groups of that country. As at the time of the Balkan Wars of the 1910s, the Serbs once again conquered the territories of other groups, employed state-organized massacres with the objective of ethnic cleansing, and enjoyed broad Russian support. This latest round of ethnic conflict in Yugoslavia, involving Orthodox Serbs, Catholic Croats, and Muslim Bosnians and Albanians, seemed a prototype of a new kind of larger world conflict, the "clash of civilizations."

This periodic centrality of the Balkans in great power conflicts in part results from the region's ambiguous geographical position between Europe and the Middle East. Indeed, observers have differed over whether the Balkans are in or out of Europe or in or out of the Middle East.

The Balkan people themselves have commonly perceived themselves as being part of Europe, as have many Americans. In the last decade, the U.S. State Department has often referred to the region as South-Eastern Europe, a term which implies that the Balkans are important to the security of Europe and (since Europe is manifestly important to the United States) also important to that of the United States. Conversely, the Balkans have also been seen as lying beyond Europe, part of a vaguely-defined East. This view is common among many Europeans. During the first half of the twentieth century, the Balkans were often referred to as part of "the Near East."

In any event, whether the Balkans are in Europe or merely near it, the region also exists in proximity to the Middle East, and thus to the vast U.S. economic interests in the oil of that region and to the important U.S. political interests in the security of Israel. For more than two decades, the United States has believed that Iraq and Iran posed a threat to these important interests. In the 1990s, these two nations numbered among those rogue states accused of developing weapons of mass destruction that would pose a serious threat to U.S. national security. This threat from the Middle East exercised an important influence on the way that the Clinton administration came to conceive of new purposes for NATO and to perceive the conflicts in the former Yugoslavia.

Reinventing NATO's Strategic Concept

Prior to the 1990s, when the Soviet Union posed the most serious threat to U.S. national interests, NATO offered the primary instrument to contain that threat. With the collapse of the Soviet Union, NATO became a very strange institution, magnificent in its capabilities, deluged with applicants for membership, but without any obvious purpose. Throughout the 1990s, U.S. policymakers wrestled with the problem of reinventing NATO, particularly the redefinition of both its purpose and its membership.

The first step in the redefinition of NATO was "enlargement," the admission to membership of the three Central European states of Poland, Hungary, and the Czech Republic. But this kind of redefinition did not fundamentally change NATO's purpose. Although the Russian threat was greatly diminished, to NATO's three new members—its Eastern flank—that threat still seemed very real. So the enlarged, post–Cold-War NATO, like the smaller Cold War NATO, was still focused on Russia.

At the same time, however, the Clinton administration was developing the conception that U.S. national interests in the Middle East, threatened by rogue states such as Iraq and Iran, could be better protected if NATO's responsibilities included not only new territories within but also beyond Europe. A NATO willing to go "out-of-area" could make itself most useful in the region of the Middle East, important both in regard to "the flow of vital resources" and "the proliferation of NBC weapons and their means of delivery."[12]

Since the formation of NATO in 1949 its purpose and strategy had been elaborated in a formal and authoritative document known as "The Strategic Concept." NATO had adopted the previous version of the Strategic Concept in 1991, just after the end of the Cold War. The Clinton administration sought to redefine and expand the purpose of NATO in an easterly direction by promoting a new Strategic Concept that would focus on new threats and tasks. The goal was to have the alliance formally adopt this new document at the most important and symbolic NATO meeting of all, the 50th Anniversary Summit to be held in Washington in April 1999. The new Strategic Concept would articulate an expanded and expansive redefinition of "security challenges and risks":

> The security of the Alliance remains subject to a wide variety of military and nonmilitary risks which are multidirectional and often difficult to predict. These risks include uncertainty and instability in and around the Euro-Atlantic area and the possibility of regional crises at the periphery of the Alliance, which could evolve rapidly. . . . Some states, including on NATO's periphery and in other regions, sell or acquire or try to acquire NBC weapons and delivery means.

Any armed attack on the territory of the Allies, from whatever direction, would be covered by Articles 5 and 6 of the Washington Treaty
[the central articles in the original NATO treaty of 1949, which spec-
ified a direct attack upon members of the Alliance]. However, Alliance
security interests can be affected by other risks of a wider nature, including acts of terrorism, sabotage and organized crime, and by the
disruption of the flow of vital resources.[13]

Other members of NATO were not as convinced as the United States
that the alliance should shoulder out-of-area responsibilities, and particularly
in the Middle East. They were also not as convinced that NATO had the
military wherewithal to enforce this new purpose. However, the Clinton
administration was determined to press forward with its own new strategic
concept (and with NATO's new Strategic Concept). For the administration
to make its case, it became important to demonstrate the necessity of NATO's
out-of-area expansion and to affirm NATO's military capabilities to undertake such operations effectively.

Kosovo as Strategic Testbed

The Balkans—which are both in Europe and out of it and which are
the bridge between Europe and the Middle East—were the obvious place
to begin the great march of NATO out-of-area and into vital resources.
Increasing violence and repression in Kosovo in 1998 provided occasion
and opportunity. A NATO war against Serbia would provide the defining
or rather redefining moment, one that would redefine NATO's central
purpose from the containment and management of Russia to the containment and management of rogue states and that would shift NATO's central
theater from Central Europe first to South-Eastern Europe or the Balkans
and then to the Middle East. Such a war would demonstrate NATO's new
purpose and its new capabilities. Of course, the war would have to be both
successful and short (something like the "splendid little war" of a hundred
years before, the Spanish-American War of 1898). Indeed, it would have
to be so successful and short that it would come to a triumphal end in
time for the opening ceremony of the Washington Summit on April 23,
1999.

The Clinton administration had convinced itself that an air war against

Serbia would indeed be both successful and short, that Serbia would yield to NATO demands after only a few days and a few sorties of bombing. This confidence stemmed from the administration's reading of NATO's role in the climactic chapter of the Bosnian civil war in 1995, when limited bombing had seemingly caused the Bosnian Serbs to yield to the demands of the international community. By crediting its own action with ending the Bosnian War, the administration engaged in analysis that was incomplete and self-serving. In truth, the main force that paved the way for a negotiated settlement over Bosnia in 1995 was not the bombing by NATO but an offensive by Croat and Bosnian Muslim armies that threatened to overrun most of the territory held by the Bosnian Serbs.[14] The Bosnian War, like all previous wars, was decided not with an air war alone, but with a land war. But in its enthusiasm to go to war with Serbia over Kosovo, the Clinton administration overlooked all of that.

Reinventing NATO was not the sole purpose that U.S. policymakers had in mind when they decided to go to war with Serbia over Kosovo. More traditional security and economic interests, however, were not among those purposes. By any conventional definition of such interests, the United States had virtually none at stake in Kosovo. Serbia did not obviously threaten aggression against any other state, even Albania. Granted, some observers worried that violence in Kosovo might spill over into neighboring states such as Albania and Macedonia, leading somehow to a wider conflict pitting Greece against Turkey, but this security argument was so indirect (not to say far-fetched) that, by itself, it could hardly provide a rationale for NATO intervention. As for U.S. economic interests in Kosovo, these were nonexistent. It seems clear that the United States did not undertake the Kosovo War in order to achieve any of the traditional security and economic objectives of its grand strategy.

There were, however, ideological and political objectives that a war for Kosovo might serve. As noted above, the new realities of the global economy and the multicultural society have brought into being the new ideology of liberal globalism, with its emphasis on human rights and openness. Liberal globalism has also brought into being a political constituency on behalf of these ideas, located principally within the American media and universities. Some U.S. officials eager for war in Kosovo were responding to this ideology and constituency. But as we shall argue in a later section, humanitarian objectives may be necessary for the United States to go to war in the global era, but they are not sufficient.

Rambouillet and the Pretext for War

The actions of the U.S. diplomats in the Rambouillet negotiations in February and March 1999 strongly indicate that the United States wanted Serbia to reject a political solution to the problem posed by Kosovo. This rejection would then be used to justify a NATO war against Serbia.[15]

The main text of the proposed "Interim Agreement for Peace and Self-Government in Kosovo" consisted of thirty pages of small print and dealt with Kosovo itself.[16] Although it included stipulations that were disputed by the Serbs, the document contained nothing that was particularly unusual or unacceptable by normal diplomatic practice. However, the agreement also included two appendices. Appendix A was a boring list of weapons cantonment sites in Kosovo. Appendix B, entitled "Status of Multi-National Military Implementation Force," was altogether different from what had gone before.

Appendix B authorized NATO forces to have free movement and to conduct military operations anywhere within the Federal Republic of Yugoslavia (FRY) and therefore within Serbia itself. Clause 8 reads:

> NATO personnel shall enjoy, together with their vehicles, vessels, aircraft, and equipment, free and unrestricted passage and unimpeded access throughout the FRY including associated airspace and territorial waters. This shall include, but not be limited to, the right of bivouac, maneuver, billet, and utilization of any areas or facilities as required for support, training, and operations.

Other clauses further amplified the rights of NATO military forces within Serbia.

Appendix B obviously posed a direct threat to the sovereign independence of Serbia, as well as to the practical security of the Milosevic regime. It was predictable that the Serbs would reject it and therefore would have to reject the agreement.[17]

That the Serbs would reject Appendix B was more predictable still, given a particular event in their history. In the Serb understanding of their past, the ultimatum which Austria-Hungary presented to Serbia on July 23, 1914 in the aftermath of the assassination of Franz Ferdinand stands out as a particularly infamous document. Much of that ultimatum contained nothing that was very unusual or unacceptable in normal diplomatic practice, and indeed, the Serbs agreed to accept several burdensome stipulations. However, one clause gave the Austro-Hungarian security officers unimpeded access throughout Serbia for purposes of investigating the assassination.[18] Serbia saw this as a direct threat to its sovereign independence. It also saw it as a deliberate move by Austria-Hungary to provoke Serbia to reject that clause and therefore the ultimatum. That rejection would then be used to justify a declaration of war against Serbia. Despite this understanding of the consequences, Serbia did reject the clause. Thus began the long and terrible chain of events consisting of the Austro-Hungarian declaration of war upon Serbia; Russia's declaration of war upon Austria-Hungary; the invasion and destruction of Serbia; the explosion of the Balkan war into the First World War; and, ultimately, Serbia's resurrection within the new and greater Yugoslavia. The Serbs view their rejection of the Austro-Hungarian ultimatum as being tragic but heroic and ultimately vindicated by history.

In any event, Serbia did reject the Rambouillet Agreement, and NATO led by the United States did go to war over Kosovo on March 24, 1999. Eleven weeks later, when Serbia accepted a new agreement with NATO on Kosovo in order to end the war, that agreement contained no clauses authorizing the movement of NATO forces within Serbia itself. In explaining to the Serbian people why it went to war rather than sign the first agreement and why it had agreed to sign the second, the government of Slobodan Milosevic gave a prominent place to this difference.

The Kosovo War came about as a consequence of the new U.S. grand strategy, and the war itself has had consequences for that strategy. But these consequences are not quite as momentous as has often been argued. To understand what the consequences actually are, we will examine the war as it relates to five strategic issues: humanitarian war, NATO enlargement, victory through air power, U.S. relations with Russia, and U.S. relations with China.

The Kosovo War and Humanitarian War

The Kosovo War has been seen by many as the first humanitarian war, a war fought for the furtherance of human rights alone, rather than for the traditional objectives of national interests. This writer has argued above that the main U.S. purpose in the war was in fact the furtherance of NATO. However, the Kosovo War did achieve clear humanitarian results, such as the end of the Serbian atrocities and the return of the Albanian refugees. In that sense, the war was indeed a humanitarian war.

What are the future prospects for more humanitarian wars, such as the Kosovo War appeared to be? Alas, countries where the potential exists for the state to undertake large-scale massacres of ethnic groups, comparable to the Serb-organized massacre of Albanians in Kosovo in 1999 (as well as of Croats in Croatia in 1991 and of Muslims in Bosnia in 1992–1995) are plentiful. The most obvious current candidates to become victims of state-sponsored massacres in the future are the Kurds in Iraq, Christians in Sudan, and Hutus in Burundi (the obverse of the Tutsis slaughtered in Rwanda in 1994). Indeed, these peoples have been the victims of such massacres in the recent past or are even suffering them at present. There are also the well-known, but disputed, cases of the Chechens in Russia and the Tibetans in China.

Massacres organized by a state and directed against an ethnic group approach the definition of genocide given in the *United Nations Convention on the Prevention and Punishment of the Crime of Genocide*; preventing and punishing them would clearly qualify as humanitarian.[19] And since such massacres are implemented by the organized force of a state, stopping them would normally require a comparable organized force, i.e., one or more other states undertaking a war against the perpetrators. State-organized massacres would thus be the most suitable, and perhaps the only suitable, targets for humanitarian war, following the prototype of the Kosovo War.

The doleful history of state-organized massacre suggests, however, that other states, even when representing "the international community," are not inclined to undertake a purely humanitarian war to stop them. This was true not only of the state-organized massacres that occurred during the Cold War era, but also those occurring after the Cold War ended but before Kosovo.

It is, of course, easy enough to understand why humanitarian war was not a practical option for the international community (such as it was) or for the United States (as its purported leader) during the Cold War. In the bipolar conflict between the United States and the Soviet Union, almost every U.S. military intervention had to be grounded and justified in terms of concrete U.S. national interests related to that great struggle. The United States could not afford to expend military resources on matters totally unrelated to its own interests. During the Cold War, there were many cases of large-scale, state-organized massacres of ethnic groups in response to which the United States did nothing. These cases include the Baltic states in 1949,

Tibet in 1959, Indonesia in 1965, Burundi in 1972, Syria in 1982, and Iraq in 1988.

The removal of constraints that had been imposed by Soviet-American bipolarity, along with the advent of U.S. global hegemony, gave rise to the notion that humanitarian war against state-organized massacres had at last become feasible. The actual experience of the 1990s, however, revealed other reasons why, in most cases, the United States could not be relied upon to wage humanitarian war against massacring states. Sadly, in the 1990s, the actions of the Serb government against the Albanians in Kosovo and earlier against the Croats and the Bosnian Muslims were not especially unique. The decade saw at least four comparable examples where a state representing one ethnic group undertook systematic violence against another ethnic group living within the boundaries of the state. This was the case in Rwanda in 1994 (the Hutu regime against the Tutsis), Burundi from 1993 to the present (the Tutsi regime against the Hutus), Sudan throughout the 1990s (the Islamic regime against the Christians), and Iraq through much of the 1990s (the Iraqi Ba'ath regime against the Kurds).

Each of these four cases had similarities to the conflict between the Serb state and the Kosovar Albanian population and Kosovo Liberation Army (KLA). But with the exception of Iraq, U.S. military intervention in these cases was never seriously considered. And in Iraq the United States's use of military force to protect the Kurds was largely fitful and ineffective. As in Kosovo, in each case no traditional, obvious U.S. national interest was at stake. Unlike Kosovo, though, where a less obvious but significant U.S. national interest was involved (the promotion of NATO, an international institution that was central to U.S. grand strategy), in these other four cases no other U.S. national interest was at stake. For all its rhetoric about human rights and humanitarian intervention, the Clinton administration was actually quite unwilling to undertake any war on *purely* humanitarian grounds, no matter how compelling the situation.

In this regard, the administration was merely responding to political realities within the United States. In truth, the political base for humanitarian intervention is quite narrow. The idea that the United States should undertake military operations—and sustain military casualties—to support human rights or even prevent genocide is one that most segments of the American public and of the American military reject. Only among the professional liberals and liberal professionals who inhabit the worlds of the media and academe does the idea of purely humanitarian intervention find favor. Few members of this liberal elite have actually ever served in the U.S. military; nor are their children likely to do so.

Humanitarian intervention is the consequence of liberal globalism carried to its logical conclusion, in which the United States as the sole superpower, without any "peer competitor" and without apparent constraints, is obliged to "do something" in the face of evil. Humanitarian intervention represents a rejection of that other great tradition of thinking about international relations, realist internationalism, prominent in U.S. foreign policy under the constraining conditions of the Cold War.

Humanitarian intervention also represents a rejection of the "Weinberger-Powell doctrine" governing the use of force. For the U.S. military, the Weinberger-Powell doctrine summed up the "lessons learned" from the failures of the Vietnam War. In the eyes of the doctrine's adherents—especially soldiers themselves, but also their supporters in Congress and the public— the successful Persian Gulf War of 1990–1991 seemingly confirmed the validity of those lessons.

But the Weinberger-Powell doctrine constitutes a huge obstacle to military operations conceived for humanitarian purposes. During the 1990s, this would have important consequences for the politics of military interventionism. First, the narrow political base for humanitarian intervention causes supporters of liberal globalism to avoid seeking approval for such operations from the more conservative Congress, and to justify this avoidance by saying that Congress is isolationist and irrational. Since this avoidance of Congress, composed of the elected representatives of the American people, evades a principal element of the Weinberger-Powell doctrine (public and congressional support as a precondition of military operations), the liberal elite is driven to denigrate the doctrine itself. Second, the narrow political base forces that elite to avoid the use of ground forces in combat operations, and therefore to avoid the use of overwhelming force, because unacceptable casualties would likely result. Since this avoidance of overwhelming force is an evasion of another principal element of the Weinberger-Powell doctrine, the liberal elite is again driven to denigrate the doctrine as wrongheaded and obsolete.

The military consequences are not without irony. Proponents of liberal globalism call for military action in response to humanitarian catastrophe, but political realities place off-limits the sort of action most likely to be effective: the massive and aggressive deployment of ground troops. This leaves only air operations, in particular punitive bombing, as in Bosnia in

1995, in Iraq sporadically after the Gulf War and especially in 1999, and in Serbia in 1999. But as Operation Allied Force suggests, these air operations by themselves may only achieve their political objectives when they expand to the point of hurting civilians, either by killing them "collaterally" or by deliberately targeting their economic necessities, such as electric-power grids and water-supply systems.[20] In the air war against the Serbs, when mere symbolic bombing proved insufficient, moves toward strategic bombing proved necessary. These actions against civilians hardly seem to fit the normal definition of "humanitarian."

As for the future, the United States does not seem likely to undertake a humanitarian war in large areas of the world where it has no traditional or obvious national interests, in particular sub-Saharan Africa and South Asia. Elsewhere, where the United States does have obvious national interests, these interests will likely inhibit U.S. intervention to protect the rights of ethnic minorities, especially when regimes friendly to the United States are doing the abusing. While the United States may well wage a war against a state such as Iraq or Iran for conventional security or economic reasons and then justify that war as being a humanitarian enterprise, this is humanitarianism as fig leaf rather than as actual motive. But such may well be the only role that humanitarian war will play in U.S. grand strategy in the near future.[21]

The Kosovo War and NATO Enlargement

The second way in which the Kosovo War has been seen as a new kind of war lies in it being the first real NATO war, with the full authorization and participation of alliance members acting collectively. This feature of the war is both true and important.

This writer has argued that the major U.S. objective in the Kosovo War was to expand NATO's purpose into regions that had hitherto been "out-of-area." Formal NATO enlargement (the admission of new members, such as Poland, the Czech Republic, and Hungary) was to be supplemented by informal NATO enlargement (imposing order on new areas, such as the Balkans and the Middle East). If Serbia had yielded after a few days of bombing, as the Clinton administration had expected, Operation Allied Force would have demonstrated that similar methods of coercion (NATO-authorized bombing) would work again against similar "rogue" adversaries (Libya, Syria, Iraq) in a similar area (the Middle East).

In some sense, NATO won the Kosovo War as the Clinton administration had originally expected. Bombing by itself, without the use of ground forces and without any American combat casualties, did bring about a Serb surrender. NATO did adopt the new Strategic Concept at the 50th Anniversary Summit, despite the fact that at the time the war was still being waged and its outcome appeared uncertain. However, the bombing campaign took eleven weeks rather than one; it required attacks on civilian targets rather than a limitation to military ones; and it produced disputes among NATO decision-makers that often put the alliance's political consensus at risk. Indeed, in a sense, beyond an agreement to begin bombing, there never was a consensus within NATO: no consensus on how to orchestrate the campaign, no consensus on how to escalate, and no consensus on how long to persist. The lesson that most NATO decision-makers took from Operation Allied Force was not how easy it is to bomb even a weak adversary into submission, but how difficult. The subsequent NATO occupation of Kosovo has also been disappointing due to the reverse ethnic cleansing of the Serbs by the Albanians, as well as continuing violence and corruption among the Albanians themselves. The lesson that most NATO decision-makers have taken from the ongoing occupation is that, however easy it may be to send military forces into a country, getting them out may be another matter altogether. As a result, among the European members of NATO, there has been little triumphalism about its Kosovo victory. Indeed, for the purposes of facilitating future out-of-area operations and informal NATO enlargement, that victory now seems to have been a Pyrrhic one.[22]

The Kosovo War and Air Power

A third way in which the Kosovo War has been seen as a first is as the first-ever fulfillment of the long-sought dream of victory through air power alone. Related to this unique and pioneering feature of the war is the fourth way in which it was a first: The war was the first case of a completely bloodless victory—NATO prevailed without suffering a single combat casualty. These two features of the war most obviously involve U.S. military doctrine and operations. However, they are closely connected to U.S. grand strategy as well.

A military doctrine emphasizing air power has been a crucial part of U.S. grand strategy since the Second World War. During the Cold War, a military doctrine of nuclear deterrence was integral to the grand strategy of containing the Soviet Union. Since the end of the Cold War, a military doctrine of punitive bombing has become integral to the grand strategy of managing rogue states.

In the second half of the twentieth century air power played a role in U.S grand strategy similar to that which naval power played in British grand strategy in the nineteenth century. In each case, the leading world power of the day tried to convert its comparative advantage in industry and technology into a way of war that minimized its military casualties. Britain and the United States have shared a number of qualities during the periods when each was the leading great power. Economically, each has been the leading industrial, technological, and financial power of its time. Politically, each has been a leading liberal democracy, with governments responsive to public opinion expressed in regular elections.

In the industrial era of the nineteenth century, Britain had a comparative advantage, really an absolute one, in capital-intensive industrial products and also in capital-intensive weapons systems, above all in warships. In the industrial era of the twentieth century, America had a similar advantage in capital-intensive industrial products and also in capital-intensive weapons systems, above all in bombers, missiles, and aircraft carriers. Now, in the information age, the United States has acquired a new comparative and absolute advantage, this time involving knowledge-intensive or high-technology products and services and knowledge-intensive and high-technology weapons, above all in surveillance systems, stealth aircraft, and precision munitions. Conversely, when it comes to labor-intensive commercial products and labor-intensive weapons systems, Britain and the United States have been at a comparative disadvantage. In military affairs, this has meant a disadvantage in the fielding of traditional land forces, particularly infantry and artillery.

Britain and the United States have also been the leaders in liberal-democratic politics. In liberal democracy, governments must respond to public opinion. This has not prevented British and American governments from expending great numbers of lives in combat, as the two world wars in the British case and the Civil War and the Second World War in the American case attest. But democracies will endure great sacrifices only when the cause itself is manifestly great (as in those great wars). When the stakes are more modest—as with Britain's nineteenth century colonial wars or U.S. interventions in the Caribbean through much of the twentieth century—democracies expect that operations will be conducted with economy, especially when it comes to the sacrifice of their own troops.

These features of the British economy and political system drove Britain to adopt a particular way of engaging in war. The British way of war comprised a particular trinity, which consisted of naval power, financial power, and diplomatic skill.[23] Whenever possible, Britain deployed these assets within a strategy of grand coalitions. In the obvious sense, this meant a grand coalition of several powers who united to defeat the hegemonic ambitions of some overwhelming European land power. In another sense, however, it meant a grand coalition of comparative advantages, in which Britain provided the bulk of the coalition's naval forces, its financial power bought or supported the land forces of the other powers, and its diplomatic skill kept the coalition in place.

Similar economic and political features seem to be driving the United States to an analogous form of waging coalition warfare. The present-day American way of war comprises its own particular trinity, consisting of air power, technological superiority, and international organizations. In deploying these assets against some rogue power, the United States prefers to act through a grand coalition rather than unilaterally. Furthermore, it organizes that coalition with an eye toward comparative advantage, in which the United States provides air power and a technological edge while persuading its coalition partners to provide land forces (and to sustain any casualties entailed by the operation). The Gulf War and the Kosovo War lent apparent plausibility to this strategy. The Gulf War demonstrated that the United States could fight a land campaign and sustain very few casualties. The Kosovo War demonstrated that it could win a war without any land campaign and without any casualties at all.

Whatever advantages a military strategy based on air power and punitive bombing may offer in the abstract, there are major limitations to its application in practice. The range of states susceptible to such a strategy is quite narrow. On the one hand, a target-state has to have reached a certain level of urban and industrial development so that it has something essential to lose through bombing, and its government must be responsive to popular pressure from the people who feel pain caused by that loss. Although Serbia fit these conditions in the Kosovo War, Iraq during the Gulf War did not. (Despite intense bombing of Baghdad, a land campaign was still necessary to defeat Iraq and to achieve the U.S. war aims.) Nor is it clear that North Vietnam fit them in the Vietnam War. (The actual impact of the U.S. bombing of Hanoi and Haiphong in 1972 remains a matter of debate.) The less advanced the level of political and economic development, the less likely it is that punitive bombing will be effective. It did not work against the guerrillas in South Vietnam, and it would not work against the guerrillas in Colombia.

Conversely, of course, the target-state cannot be so developed that it has acquired its own weapons of mass destruction, and therefore the capacity to deter the United States through mutual assured destruction. It is inconceivable that the United States would employ a Kosovo-type strategy against Russia or China, i.e., the bombing of Moscow or Beijing in expectation of extracting political concessions. Indeed, it is not even clear that it would be able to employ such a strategy against North Korea by bombing Pyongyang.

Excluding potential adversaries who are too developed and those who are not developed enough leaves only about a half-dozen rogue states that are plausible target-states for a doctrine of punitive bombing. These are, again, the usual suspects: Iran, Iraq, Libya, and, at the lower end of development, perhaps Sudan and Afghanistan. As it happens, four of these (Iraq, Libya, Sudan, and Afghanistan) have already been the target at some point of some kind of U.S. punitive bombing, and in no case has the bombing yielded decisive results. In short, the new American way of war displayed in Kosovo may well have at best limited applicability for the future.

From War to War: The Mismatch of Military Strategies

More generally, the military strategies used by the United States in winning one war have rarely fit a later war; strategies that have brought victory in some circumstances have failed to do so in different ones. The U.S. military strategies that won the Second World War against Germany and Japan (the offensive use of mobile armored forces by the Army, carrier task forces by the Navy, and large-scale strategic bombing by the Air Force) were based upon the U.S. advantages in both mass and mobility. However, these strategies soon became obsolescent in the Cold War against the Soviet Union. They were replaced with the military strategy of nuclear deterrence, within the context of the generally static grand strategy of containment. A strategy of mass and mobility was succeeded by a strategy of mass destruction and rigid lines.

The United States did try to apply its World War II strategy of mass and mobility in the early stages of the Korean War. (General MacArthur's invasion at Inchon followed by the break-out from the Pusan Perimeter offers the most conspicuous example). This worked against North Korea, but failed once Communist China intervened in the autumn of 1950. The "new war" against China obliged the United States to develop an alternative military strategy in Korea, that of attrition within the context of a limited war. Although this military strategy could not result in a victory in the World War II sense, it could achieve the objective of preserving South Korea, which adequately served the grand strategy of containment.

In turn, the United States initially tried to apply its Korean War strategy of attrition and limited war to Vietnam. (General Westmoreland's search-and-destroy operations during the period 1965–1968 were the most controversial example). Although not without success (the U.S. and its South Vietnamese allies did destroy much of the Viet Cong at the time of the 1968 Tet Offensive), for the most part, this military strategy failed in the different circumstances of Vietnam.

In the 1980s, the venerable strategies of mass and mobility (especially the latter) that had won the Second World War enjoyed a second coming—updated and modernized with high-technology weapons. In the army and air force this expressed itself as the Air-Land Battle Doctrine and in the navy as the Forward Maritime Strategy, both designed to win a conventional war against the Soviet Union. As it happened, the Soviet Union collapsed a few years later, and these strategies were never implemented as planned. However, after Iraq's invasion of Kuwait in 1990s, the Air-Land Battle Doctrine (along with much of the U.S. Army in Europe) was transported from the north German plain to the vast expanse of the Arabian desert, where it won the Gulf War.

In short order, the U.S. military strategy that won the Gulf War against Iraq became obsolescent. It did not fit the new great challenge for U.S. military operations, the ethnic conflicts of the 1990s, particularly those in Yugoslavia. The Air-Land Battle Doctrine and the massive and mobile armored forces that were suitable for the North German plain and for the Iraqi desert were not suitable for the mountainous terrain of the Balkans. As General Colin Powell put it, in contrasting Iraq with Bosnia, "we do deserts, we don't do mountains."

This record of mismatch between the strategies of one war and the necessities of the next one suggests some caution about the applicability of

Kosovo to future conflicts. The particular military strategy that appeared to win the Kosovo War—precision bombing of civilian targets—is unlikely to fit the particular circumstances of the next war that engages the United States. The potential adversary that most resembles Serbia is probably Iraq, but the United States has already tried a version of the precision bombing strategy there in the past few years, and that strategy has not yet achieved its objectives.

The Kosovo War and the Russian Problem

Russia viewed the U.S.-led NATO war against Serbia as a serious threat, not just to its traditional national interests in the Balkans but also to its neo-traditional cultural identity as an Orthodox country. The war confirmed and sharpened Russian suspicions of the real purposes of the United States and NATO in international politics, suspicions which had already become wide-spread in Russia in the previous year or so, due to NATO enlargement and the Russian financial crisis of 1998.[24]

Russia has considered the Balkans to be its natural sphere of influence since at least the 1870s. Its victory in the Russo-Turkish war of 1877–1878 resulted in the independence of Serbia and Bulgaria from Turkey. Both became Russian allies. The original Russian alliances with Serbia and with Bulgaria were based upon ties of mutual national interests, Slavic ethnic identity, and Orthodox religious tradition. The Russian alliance with Bulgaria fell victim to the intricate calculations and maneuvers of Balkan politics in the First and Second World Wars, when Bulgaria sided with Germany. However, the Russian alliance with Serbia continued right up until 1948, when Tito's Yugoslavia (containing Serbia) broke with Stalin's Soviet Union. This break in the traditional alliance was relatively brief, since Stalin's successors restored generally good relations with Yugoslavia. When the Soviet Union and Yugoslavia both dissolved in the same year, 1991, their largest constituent nations, Russia and Serbia respectively, were re-established as independent states, and the old alliance between them was also revived.

Similar ethnic and demographic situations reinforce this renewed Russo-Serb alliance. About 25 percent of Russians reside outside the boundaries of Russia, where they lived as minorities in former Soviet republics, espe-cially in the Baltic states, Ukraine, and Kazakhstan. Similarly, about 25 per-cent of Serbs reside outside the boundaries of Serbia, where they lived as minorities in former Yugoslav republics, especially in Croatia and Bosnia. Conversely, within Russia itself, many non-Russian minorities remain, particularly Caucasian Muslims who comprised a substantial majority of the population in Chechnya. Similarly, within Serbia itself, a substantial number of non-Serbian minorities remain, particularly the Albanian Muslims, who comprise a 90-percent majority in Kosovo. Given these similarities, Russia sees Serbia as a smaller version of itself. In Russian eyes, an attack on Serbia is an attack on Russia, or at least on Russian interests and identity.

These historical and cultural factors help explain Russia's attitudes and behavior during the Kosovo War. The U.S.-led NATO campaign against Serbia directly challenged Russia's conception of its traditional sphere of influence and its neo-traditional Orthodox culture. Not surprisingly, Russia opposed the war throughout its duration, and it voiced this opposition, vociferously if ineffectively, in every international organization where it was a member, most importantly in the UN Security Council. The surprise occupation of the Pristina airport by a small contingent of Russian troops at the war's end—an action seen in the West as reckless, annoying, or just silly—was a desperate Russian attempt to preserve a symbolic presence in its traditional sphere, while NATO's occupation of Kosovo was extinguishing the substance.

During Operation Allied Force itself, it appeared that the war might cause serious and long-term damage to U.S. and NATO relations with Russia. By the time that the war was a year in the past, however, a clearer perspective had emerged. The war largely confirmed and crystallized previous Russian views toward the United States and NATO, ones that already existed even before the bombing of Serbia began; it did not fundamentally alter these views. Russia had already become concerned about the United States dominating international politics as the sole superpower—about "U.S. hegemonism." So too, it had already become concerned about NATO enlargement. Russia saw the Kosovo War as amply demonstrating the validity of these concerns.

Conversely, however, the war did not permanently prevent Russia from re-establishing normal, if wary, relations with the United States and other NATO states on other issues; Vladimir Putin tried to do so soon after he was elected as president. In short, the Kosovo War will become one more difficult chapter in the complex history of relations between Russia and the West since the end of the Cold War, a history composed of both competition and cooperation. Drawing on an analogy from an earlier era, the impact of the

1999 U.S.-led NATO war against Serbia on Russian-American relations will probably be about the same as the impact of the 1968 Soviet-led invasion of Czechoslovakia on Soviet-American relations.

Yet for the United States to think that it could get away with another Kosovo-like war that threatened Russian interests or identity would be a serious error. Russia generally accepted the 1995 U.S.-led military intervention against Serbia in Bosnia. It greatly resented the 1999 U.S.-led war against Serbia in Kosovo. A third such military intervention anytime soon, especially in a country in a traditional Russian sphere of influence (e.g., in the Caucasus or in Central Asia) would very likely produce a fundamental and enduring Russian reaction. Here the historical analogy would be more like the U.S. reaction to the 1979 Soviet invasion of Afghanistan.

The most important consequence of the Kosovo War for Russia involves not its relations with the West but its relations with itself, i.e., its relations with the Russian minorities outside of Russia and with the non-Russian minorities within Russia. Russia can readily interpret the Kosovo War as establishing useful precedents for its own future wars. If the United States and NATO can use military force to protect a repressed minority within another state, then surely Russia could legitimately use military force to protect a repressed minority, particularly a Russian one, within a neighboring state. In the future, Russia could use Kosovo to justify military intervention in such states as Estonia, Latvia, Ukraine, and Kazakhstan, even if the real motive was not the protection of the Russian minority and its safety but the restoration of Russian power. Such a Russian intervention would lack the legitimation bestowed by an international organization, as the U.S. intervention was legitimized by NATO, but it would gain legitimation, at least in Russian eyes, by the fact that Russia was only acting to protect its own people in its own backyard.

Also, if the United States and NATO can bomb cities and civilians, then surely Russia can legitimately do so as well. Indeed, Russia has already done so with the bombing of Grozny during the Chechnya war of 1999–2000, citing NATO's bombing of Belgrade as a precedent. Moreover, the U.S. success in ending Serbian repression of the Albanians in Kosovo obviously did not deter Russia from engaging a few months later in similar repression of the Muslims in Chechnya. Indeed, it may have prompted the Russian action, since Russia was now convinced that a rebellious province eventually could provide the opportunity for a disruptive U.S. involvement of some sort.

The Kosovo War and the Chinese Problem

China also viewed the U.S.-led NATO war against Serbia as a serious threat, even though its stakes in the war were not as obvious as Russia's. China's concerns involved its own version of national interests—Kosovo as possible precedent for U.S. involvement in Taiwan or in Tibet—and its own version of cultural identity—the indignity of having its embassy in Belgrade bombed.

As with Russia, the war confirmed and sharpened Chinese concerns about "U.S. hegemonism." Like Serbia and Russia, China has its own rebellious province (Taiwan) and repressed minority (Tibet), and it was concerned about the precedent that the Kosovo War could set for international and especially U.S. meddling in such cases. This was enough to cause China to join Russia in opposing the war throughout its duration, particularly in the forum of the UN Security Council. However, although the analogy between Kosovo and Taiwan or Tibet may have been potentially relevant in the abstract, it was certainly remote in the concrete details, to say nothing of geographical distance. By itself, this Chinese concern about the precedent of the war would not have had a major impact on Sino-American relations.

The U.S. bombing of the Chinese embassy in Belgrade, however, transformed the war from minor irritant to major issue. From a Chinese perspective, that bombing could only have been deliberate. The Chinese credit the United States (as the United States credits itself) with the highest technology in military intelligence. Since the particular embassy floor that was hit housed a Chinese intelligence unit and since the CIA had selected this particular target, U.S. claims of having bombed the building by accident were simply not plausible. The Chinese were furthered angered by the American refusal to offer a convincing explanation or to punish the responsible officials. The embassy bombing transformed the Kosovo War from being just another chapter in the long history of Balkan wars into being yet another chapter in the long history of Western contempt for China, a dramatic reminder of what the Chinese call "the century of humiliation."

As was the case with Russia, the U.S. success in ending Serbian repression of the Albanians in Kosovo did not deter China, a few months later, from issuing harsher threats against Taiwan and from increasing repression in Tibet. Indeed, it may have prompted these actions, since they served to make a statement that China (unlike the Serbs) could not be intimidated and humiliated.

The Kosovo War and Grand Strategy: The First and the Last

The Kosovo War was the first war that the United States undertook to carry out its grand strategy for the global era. It was fought not for traditional security and economic objectives but for new institutional and ideological ones. It was not fought for the old purpose of defending NATO but for the new purpose of enlarging it. It was not fought for the old ideology of liberal democracy and free markets but for the new ideology of cultural diversity and global society. It was not fought to contain Russia or China but rather as if Russia and China did not even exist. Most importantly, it was not fought with the expectation of it being a serious military ordeal that might entail significant American casualties but as a splendid little war to be won easily by American high technology.

Even in the global era, however, the United States will still have traditional and vital security and economic interests to defend. It will still have to live with other great powers, particularly Russia and China, without driving them into permanent opposition and into being a permanent threat to those vital interests. And it will still need a grand strategy that is based upon these old realities as well as the new ones.

The Kosovo War was the first U.S. war of the global era. But it will not be the last. It should, however, be the last U.S. war fought to enlarge an international organization. It should be the last U.S. war justified as being a purely humanitarian war. It should be the last war fought in disregard of Russia or China. Above all, from the perspective of U.S. grand strategy and the American people that strategy is supposed to serve, the Kosovo War should be the last U.S. war fought with the expectation of victory after a few days of limited bombing and with no American casualties. That is, it should be the last war fought by the United States in the expectation that it won't really be a war at all.

Notes

1. Alexis de Tocqueville, "Conduct of Foreign Affairs by the American Democracy," in *Democracy in America*, vol. 1 (1835; reprint, New York: Vintage Books, 1945), pp. 240–245.

2. James Kurth, "America's Grand Strategy: A Pattern of History," *The National Interest*, no. 43 (Spring 1996): 3–19. Also see Walter A. McDougall, *Promised*

Land, Crusader State: The American Encounter with the World Since 1776 (Boston: Houghton Mifflin, 1997).

3.   In this sense, U.S. grand strategy has always been both realist and liberal. Realist theories of international relations focus on international security, while liberal themes focus on the international economy. In practice, however, successful strategies in the real world have combined both, e.g., the British grand strategy in the nineteenth century and the American grand strategy during the Cold War. At its best, the Anglo-American tradition in grand strategy has been *both* realist and liberal. See my "Inside the Cave: the Banality of I.R. Studies," *The National Interest*, 53 (Fall 1998): 29–40.

4.   James Kurth, "The American Way of Victory: A Twentieth-Century Trilogy," *The National Interest* 60 (Summer 2000): 5–16.

5.   Some analysts might argue that the U.S. bombing of the Bosnian Serbs in 1995 was the first such war. But that bombing was very limited in virtually every respect: the type, number and location of the targets; the number of sorties; and the duration of the bombing. The U.S. bombing helped to end a war, but it did not itself add up to one. On the relationship between globalization and U.S. military operations, see Andrew J. Bacevich, "Policing Utopia: The Military Imperatives of Globalization," *The National Interest*, 56 (Summer 1999): 5–13.

6.   I have discussed the four great transformations at greater length in my "Global Trends and American Strategic Traditions," in Pelham G. Boyer and Robert S. Wood, eds., *Strategic Transformation and Naval Power in the 21st Century* (Newport, R.I.: Naval War College Press, 1998), especially pp. 8–18. The following discussion of the transformations and the opposition to them draws from my "American Strategy in the Global Era," *Naval War College Review* 53, no. 1 (Winter 2000), especially pp. 7–16.

7.   Vaclav Havel, "Kosovo and the End of the Nation-State," *The New York Review of Books* 46, no. 12 (10 June 1999): 4.

8.   The United States has also described Sudan as a rogue state because of its support of terrorism; Sudan is certainly a rogue, even though it is not much of a state. In June 2000, Secretary of State Madeleine Albright announced that the U.S. government was replacing the term "rogue states" with the term "states of concern." The change reflected improvements that were now perceived in the internal politics of Iran and the foreign relations of Libya, North Korea, and Syria. *New York Times*, 20 June 2000, p. A8.

9.   Samuel P. Huntington, *The Clash of Civilizations and the Remaking of World Order* (New York: Simon and Schuster, 1997), especially pp. 158–163.

10.   One might have thought that the Kosovo War, with the United States fighting on behalf of the Bosnian Muslims, might have softened this Islamic resentment and resistance. It appears, however, that many in the Islamic world view the

Kosovo War as simply more evidence that the United States is determined to impose globalization by force, and the fact that particular Muslim peoples (in Kosovo and earlier in Bosnia) were beneficiaries is merely an accident.

11. Paul Bracken, *Fire in the East: The Rise of Asian Military Power and the Second Nuclear Age* (New York: Harper Collins, 1999).

12. Robert E. Hunter, "Maximizing NATO: A Relevant Alliance Knows How to Reach," *Foreign Affairs* 78, no. 3 (May-June 1999), especially pp. 201–202. Hunter was U.S. Ambassador to NATO from 1993 to 1998. The quoted phrases are used in NATO Office of Information and Press, "The Alliance's Strategic Concept," *NATO Review* 47, no. 2 (Summer 1999): D9.

13. Ibid.

14. Adam Roberts, "NATO's 'Humanitarian War' over Kosovo," *Survival* 4, no. 3 (Autumn 1999), especially pp. 109–112. Also see the account by Richard Holbrooke, *To End a War* (New York: Modern Library, 1999), especially 142–162.

15. Christopher Layne and Benjamin Schwarz, "For The Record," *The National Interest* 57 (Fall 1999): 10–11.

16. U.S. Department of State, "Rambouillet Agreement: Interim Agreement for Peace and Self-Government in Kosovo." http://www.state.gov/www/regions/eur/ksvo_rambouillet_text.html

17. Charles Simic, "Anatomy of a Murderer," *The New York Review of Books* 47, no. 1 (20 January 2000): 29. Simic states about the specific clause 8, "The U.S. introduced, at the last minute, an additional demand."

18. A classic and thorough account of the Austro-Hungarian ultimatum and the Serbian rejection is given by Sidney Bradshaw Fay, *The Origins of the World War*, 2nd ed., vol. 2, chapters 5 and 7 (New York: Macmillan, 1930). The text of the ultimatum is given on pp. 269–273; that of the reply is given on pp. 344–347.

19. The text of the UN Genocide Convention is given in George J. Andreopoulos, *Genocide: Conceptual and Historical Dimensions* (Philadelphia: University of Pennsylvania Press, 1994), pp. 229–233.

20. Roberts, "NATO's 'Humanitarian War' over Kosovo," pp. 114–116. A thorough analysis of the air campaign is given by Daniel L. Byman and Matthew C. Waxman, "Kosovo and the Great Air Power Debate," *International Security* 24, no. 4 (Spring 2000): 5–38.

21. Humanitarian war is analyzed and debated by Charles Krauthammer, "The Short Unhappy Life of Humanitarian War," *The National Interest*, 57 (Fall 1999): 5–15; and Elliott Abrams, "To Fight the Good Fight," *The National Interest* 59 (Spring 2000): 70–77.

22. For an overview of NATO after the war, see United States Institute for Peace, "Transatlantic Relations in the Aftermath of Kosovo," *Special Report* (15 May 2000). The prevailing attitude of NATO members one year after was summed

up by a senior NATO official: "Kosovo was such a resounding success that no one in the Alliance wants to repeat it ever again." *The New York Times* (18 June 2000), "The Week in Review," p. 5.

23.   For a comprehensive account of British grand strategy, see Paul Kennedy, *The Rise and Fall of British Naval Mastery* (New York: Scribners, 1976).

24.   See the analysis of Russian decision-making on the Kosovo War in Oleg Levitin, "Inside Moscow's Kosovo Muddle," *Survival* 42, no. 1 (Spring 2000): 130–140.

4 Hubris and Nemesis: Kosovo and the Pattern of Western Military Ascendancy and Defeat

Anatol Lieven

A scrimmage in a border station—
A canter down some dark defile.
Two thousand pounds of education
Drops to a ten-rupee jezail . . .

With home-bred hordes the hillsides teem.
The troopships bring us one by one,
At vast expense of time and steam,
To slay Afridis where they run.
"The captives of our bow and spear"
Are cheap, alas! as we are dear
—Rudyard Kipling, Arithmetic on the Frontier

I

NATO's victory in Kosovo in 1999 confirmed proponents of the "Revolution in Military Affairs" in their belief that technological development is bringing about changes in warfare comparable in its implications to the greatest military transformations of recent centuries. They also believe that for decades to come the advantages stemming from this revolution will accrue overwhelmingly to the West and, primarily, to the United States. Above all, Kosovo is taken to prove that aerial bombardment alone can in fact win wars. In the wake of Kosovo, even distinguished military commentators like John Keegan, who were previously skeptical of such claims, have been won over.[1]

This essay will argue that to see Kosovo as the paradigm for war in the first half of the twenty-first century would be a grave mistake. It would, of course, be pleasant to think that all wars could be decided in the West's favor by the use of high-precision weapons from a safe distance, thereby discouraging potential adversaries from confronting the West in the first place. But the success of NATO's air campaign in Kosovo is unlikely to deter those adversaries. Rather, it will persuade those adversaries to confront the West indirectly, using nonstate actors against Western troops on the ground in circumstances that will render the West's technological edge moot.

Rather than ushering in a new paradigm of warfare, NATO's victory in Kosovo represents the further evolution of that technological superiority that has helped Western powers repeatedly to defeat their non-Western opponents and dominate the world over the past five centuries. Yet this long period of Western military dominance has not been without its share of defeats at the hands of ostensibly inferior opponents. On numerous occasions in every age, Western powers have suffered local setbacks so severe as to jeopardize their claim to political preeminence. The reasons for these defeats derive from multiple sources, prominent among them difficult local conditions and over-confidence on the part of Western nations. But looming largest of all is culture.

The operations undertaken by Western powers in places such as the Balkans display more than a passing resemblance to old-fashioned imperial policing, however much that particular term may have fallen out of fashion. Yet in contrast to the imperial policing of the nineteenth and twentieth centuries—the French in Indochina and North Africa, the Americans in the Philippines and the Caribbean, the British in any number of places—these new operations proceed in a more tangled context. Public tolerance for failure or even minor missteps has shrunk. Meanwhile, the risks accompanying intervention are vastly greater. On the one hand, Western publics expect that their militaries will bring these operations to a quick, tidy, and cheap conclusion. On the other hand, the prospect of these "small wars" escalating into something much larger—to include the potential use of weapons of mass destruction by nonstate actors—means that the consequences of miscalculation are potentially disastrous.

In 1879, the British could lose more than 1,500 men in a single hour at

Isandhlwana, shrug it off, and go on to conquer Zululand. In 1993, the loss of 18 American Rangers sufficed to force the United States out of Somalia. But the issue goes beyond the willingness to sustain casualties. Mogadishu—along with Beirut, Grozny and other battlefields—suggests that the locus of political and military struggle is shifting from the mountains and jungles of the past, into the "urban terrain" of Third World cities—conditions unfavorable to the style of warfare preferred by American or Western European forces. Within those cities, the most dangerous enemy is not the general schooled in the conventions of traditional warfare, but the cunning, charismatic irregular who combines in one person the terrorist, ward politician, clan leader, criminal warlord, and gang boss. To defeat such an adversary requires an intimate knowledge of local conditions, exceptionally difficult for the "imperial police" to acquire. It may also demand commanders who themselves manifest the gang leader's mix of flexibility and utter ruthlessness—not qualities nurtured in the officer corps of the typical Western democracy. In the movie *Casablanca*, the character played by Humphrey Bogart taunted a German officer, "Major, there are parts of New York I wouldn't advise you to try and invade." In the decades since, New York may have been (partially) pacified, but Western nations contemplating intervention in quarters disordered by civil war, ethnic conflict, or massive violations of human rights would do well to heed Bogart's warning.

II

Viewed simply as a display of technological superiority, the punishment inflicted on Yugoslavia at the hands of NATO air forces compared to the inability of Yugoslav air defenses to retaliate recalls certain nineteenth-century campaigns. On November 3, 1839, the British frigates HMS *Volage* and HMS *Hyacinth* engaged the Chinese southern fleet off Chuenpi on the Pearl River, in the first major engagement of the First Opium War. The *Volage* and *Hyacinth* were small frigates, mounting only 28 and 18 guns respectively—ships already outclassed for more than 30 years by the modern heavy frigates pioneered by the U.S. and French navies. These two British warships faced 29 large Chinese war-junks under the command of one of China's bravest and most determined officers, Admiral Kuan T'ien-p'ei. Yet within a 45 minutes, the small British force sank four Chinese warships and damaged most of the rest so severely that they escaped only because the

British mercifully ceased fire. In this engagement, hundreds of Chinese were killed; on the British side, a single seaman was wounded.[2]

From the Chinese point of view, disaster had only just begun. The arrival of a British paddle-steamer, HMS *Nemesis*, armed with Congreve rockets, confronted China with a threat to which it could make no effective response whatsoever. On land, too, British regiments equipped with muskets (once again, verging on obsolescence in Europe) repeatedly defeated numerically superior Chinese forces defending some of the most formidable fortifications in the Chinese empire. For example, at the second battle of Chuenpi, on January 7, 1841, the British army killed some 400 Chinese without losing a single soldier.[3]

The First Opium War was perhaps the moment that established European and North American military dominance of non-Western states and societies of the nineteenth and early twentieth centuries. The technological overmatch evident in this conflict presaged other lopsided imperial victories such as Ulundi in 1879, when British regulars killed thousands of Zulus at the cost of ten killed, or Omdurman in 1896, where they imposed a similar loss ration on the followers of the Khalifa Abdullahi.

In contrast to the classic battles of the late imperial age, however, the technological disparity in the war for Kosovo led NATO ultimately to focus allied air power not against the Yugoslav army on the ground in Kosovo but against Serb society. In fact, when the war ended Yugoslav forces withdrew from Kosovo in good order, hardly suggesting an army that had been beaten in the field. Yugoslav military losses amounted to an estimated 500 dead, substantially fewer than NATO propaganda had claimed.[4]

Indubitable, however, is the effect of NATO's bombardment on Yugoslav infrastructure. NATO air forces (or rather American air power, modestly augmented by Europe) demonstrated persuasively that precision air weapons can destroy from a safe distance any large fixed target like a bridge, power station, oil refinery or factory. Given a sufficient stock of cruise missiles and "smart bombs," the United States at minimal cost in American lives can inflict acute damage on the economies of states much more powerful than Yugoslavia.

Any modern organized state, dependent on a modern economy and transport links, will have to take this threat very seriously indeed—just as coastal or riverine Asian states in the nineteenth century were obliged to take seriously the ability of Western squadrons to roam at will, strangling trade, landing raiding parties, and bombarding forts and cities into submission.

III

Yet if the First Opium War signaled the advantages that technology bestowed on the West in the wars for empire, it also included a number of incidents—perhaps less well known—that prefigured later Western vulnerabilities. One of these occurred at the end of May 1841 near Canton. Infuriated by the behavior of British troops who requisitioned food from local Chinese, engaged in occasional acts of rape and looting, and generally displayed a contempt for Chinese culture, thousands of local peasants took up arms intending to expel the British.

Wielding homemade weapons and led by smaller groups of "braves" — local hard men normally engaged in village and clan feuds or in criminal activity—the peasants succeeded in forcing the British troops to withdraw from the countryside into the town of San-yuan-li, their assault aided by an intense thunderstorm that soaked British muskets and ammunition. British losses were modest—one British Indian soldier killed and 15 wounded—but these amounted to more than the Chinese army and fleet succeeded in inflicting in most battles of that war.

The incident was also affected by the moral terms of the First Opium War. On the British side, this was a war that dared not speak its name (and as such highly reminiscent of our own day when Western states rarely acknowledge that in using force they are waging war). For all the Palmerstonian rhetoric about Chinese "barbarism" and "arbitrariness," the British public was painfully aware that this was a war in defense of an indefensible trade, which China morally and legally had every right to ban. In the press and parliament, the military expedition was roundly criticized. That criticism, in effect, constrained the actions of British forces in the field. Proceeding initially with great and uncharacteristic caution, they avoided battles with the Chinese and sought what would now be called a "political solution." At San-yuan-li, British soldiers seem to have hesitated about firing volleys into the crowds of Chinese peasants. By the time the British lost their inhibitions they were already in a precarious situation.

Meanwhile, the undefined character of the conflict, together with the element of genuine spontaneous mass mobilization, allowed Chinese authorities to deny responsibility for the peasant attacks and to continue talking to the British. Indeed, the incident at San-yuan-li may have been a harbinger of the "Taiping" rebellion a few years later. For much to Britain's dismay, the First Opium War so badly shook the prestige of the Manchu state that it became acutely vulnerable to attack by both bitterly anti-Western internal rebels and Britain's European rivals. Very soon, therefore, the British found themselves trying to prop up the regime that they had just defeated.[5]

Barely mentioned in British sources, the affray at San-yuan-li was vastly magnified in later Chinese nationalist and Communist lore as the moment when the masses removed from the palsied hands of the alien Manchu dynasty responsibility for China's defense. Although such propagandists may have exaggerated its actual importance, the incident at San-yuan-li did indeed provide an early warning that Western discipline and technological superiority did not necessarily guarantee military success.

IV

For a great power seeking to justify the imposition of a particular order on others (as the British did on the Manchus or as NATO did on Yugoslavia), having another state as adversary is of inestimable value. Today, however, the worst, or at least the most complicated dangers in the world exist where states have failed and where chaos, organized crime, and terrorism have supplanted the civil order. This problem of failed states poses a problem not only for the West but also for the inheritor states of the former Soviet Union—the fate of Chechnya from 1996 to 2000 being an awful warning of this possibility. Likewise, in the Middle East, the greatest threat to U.S. interests derives not from conventional conflict between regional powers—not even an attack by a resurgent Iraq—but from internal upheaval that might destabilize key allied regimes.

In this sense, NATO coerced Yugoslavia into surrendering Kosovo only because Yugoslavia retains the characteristics of a modern state, not least of all a disciplined army and police forces under the effective control of a semi-autocratic president, Slobodan Milosevic. NATO needed the Serb leader in order to claim its victory. When Milosevic decided to call the war off—not because Yugoslavia was unable to resist further, but for his own political reasons—Yugoslav forces obeyed, and promptly withdrew from Kosovo.

Had the Serb effort to ethnically purify Kosovo relied on a mass movement supported by autonomous militia groups under local warlords, bombing bridges, factories, and TV stations in Belgrade would not, in all likelihood, have produced decision. And once "strategic" bombing had failed, what options would NATO have had available? The laws of war prohibit the indiscriminate bombing of villages and concentrations of people or live-stock—although Western scruples in this regard may well prove short-lived when truly important national interests, or the lives of numerous Western soldiers are at stake. The only recourse for NATO in Kosovo under these circumstances would have been either political compromise involving the partition of Kosovo or all-out invasion. An invasion employing NATO ground troops would have been politically unpalatable. An invasion relying on the KLA as proxies would have made NATO morally complicit in the conduct of its partner. As with the U.S.-supported Croat army in 1995 or Israeli-supported Christian militias in Lebanon in 1982, a KLA bent on liberating Kosovo would have simultaneously engaged in atrocities against the Serb civilian population—of the kind which accompanied the actual NATO occupation, but on a much larger scale.

While NATO's victory in Kosovo undoubtedly qualifies as an impressive achievement in the history of warfare between states, it therefore provides no answers whatsoever therefore for two other forms of armed conflict: wars against peoples in arms and wars against decentralized, anarchical, or "tribal" societies. Nor, of course, does the Kosovo experience provide ready answers for the dilemmas involved in occupying, administering and policing recalcitrant areas.

An English wit once wrote that you should never trust a corporation, since it possesses "neither a body to be kicked, nor a soul to be damned." However great their apparent military advantage, Western nations will be hard-pressed to impose their will on nonstate actors that possess neither infrastructure to be destroyed nor economies to be strangled.

Thus, in a decade that began on a triumphal note with victory over Iraq and ended with another over Yugoslavia, it is the military event sandwiched between these two victories—the debacle of Somalia—that should command attention. During the urban fighting in Mogadishu, American tactics, weaponry, intelligence and above all political analysis proved wanting. Somalia also demonstrated the limits of Western humanitarian concern and military self-restraint in actual combat. In the famous firefight that cost the lives of 18 of their comrades, American troops killed a far greater number—at least 500—of Somali civilians, including many women and children.[6]

After the firefight, Ambassador Robert Oakley promised Somali leaders that failure to release a captured American pilot would mean that U.S. forces would obtain that release forcibly, "The minute the guns start again," Oakley threatened, "all restraint on the U.S. side goes. Just look at the stuff coming in here now. An aircraft carrier, tanks, gunships . . . the works. Once the fighting starts, all this pent-up anger is going to be released. This whole part of the city will be destroyed, men, women, children, camels, cats, dogs, goats, donkeys, everything. . . . That would be really tragic for all of us, but that's what will happen."[7]

The point is not to criticize the way in which the United States used or threatened to use firepower in Somalia. In the last resort soldiers, like any human beings faced with death, will fight with all the means available, and the second duty of commanders — after mission accomplishment — is to the lives of their own men. Rather the point is that the brutal fight in Mogadishu should be a most searing reminder that orderly, "sanitized," limited war such as the kind NATO fought over Kosovo has been very much the exception historically and is likely to remain the exception in the future.

To emphasize that Kosovo not Somalia is the anomaly, we need only note that other instructive failures both preceded and followed the victories of 1991 and 1999. American intervention in Lebanon in 1982, like Somalia, led to dangerous mission creep. This in turn alienated much of the local population, drew U.S. troops into local ethnic conflict, and finally exposed them to a devastating terrorist attack. In Kosovo, efforts by NATO peacekeepers since the war's end to protect the local Serbian minority and to create a democratic, let alone a multi-ethnic Kosovo, have failed. As of August 2001, NATO has only very partially succeeded in blocking armed Albanian attacks from Kosovo first into Serbia proper, and then, much more dangerously, into Macedonia. The KLA retains a major armed presence in northern Albania, which NATO can do nothing about. As a result, NATO will sooner or later be faced with a set of choices every one of which will involve a measure of moral disgrace and political humiliation.

V

The alternation between overall military dominance, local defeats, and permanent, intractable problems has prevailed throughout Western military history over the past 500 years. Indeed, in each of the three great military revolutions of this period, a similar pattern has repeated itself. Given sufficient technological superiority, Western powers can defeat non-Western states with relative ease. Once their leaders of those states accept defeat, the war ends. Perhaps even more importantly, the bureaucratic institutions and habits of mass obedience inculcated under the former order enable the conquerors to administer the defeated states to the West's advantage.

The situation is vastly different with tribal and semitribal societies whose social disciplines are not based on submission to state authority or laws given from above, but on forms of "ordered anarchy"—where no permanent centralized authority exists, and where no "army" that can surrender exists, only local volunteers without uniforms or regular units, fighting on the basis of blood, personal, or religious allegiance.

Not only have Western militaries found it far more difficult to defeat such societies (at least without slaughtering much of the "civilian" population in the process), but officers and officials of modern states often have the very greatest difficulty understanding how such societies work, and devising even theoretical means of dealing with them. This was true of the Russian officials who planned the intervention in Chechnya in December 1994—and no less true of the American officials in Somalia who devised the war to get Mohammed Farah Aidid. Although describing Somalia, the anthropologist I. M. Lewis makes a point applicable to many similar societies:

> Like many pastoral nomads who range far and wide with their herds, the Somali have no indigenous centralized government. And this lack of formal government and of instituted authority is strongly reflected in their extreme independence and individualism. Few writers have failed to notice the formidable pride of the Somali nomad, his extraordinary sense of superiority as an individual, and his firm conviction that he is sole master of his actions and subject to no authority save that of God. If they have noticed it, however, they have for the most part been baffled by the shifting character of the nomad's political allegiance and puzzled by the fact that the political and jural unit with which he acts on one occasion, he opposes on another.[8]

When it comes to identifying the complex clan, family, religious, personal and opportunistic allegiances of ordinary Somali fighters, intelligence satellites or spy-planes are of limited utility.

A striking passage by the Russian anthropologist Sergei Arutiunov about Chechen society runs on similar lines:

> Chechnya was and is a society of military democracy. Chechnya never had any kings, emirs, princes or barons. Unlike other Caucasian

nations, there was never feudalism in Chechnya. Traditionally, it was governed by a council of elders on the basis of consensus, but like all military democracies—like the Iroquois in America or the Zulu in southern Africa—Chechens retain the institution of military chief. In peacetime, they recognize no sovereign authority and may be fragmented into a hundred rival clans. However, in time of danger, when faced with aggression, the rival clans unite and elect a military leader. This leader may be known to everyone as an unpleasant personality, but is elected nonetheless for being a good general. While the war is on, this leader is obeyed.[9]

In the late eighteenth and early nineteenth centuries, the Russian imperial army had won a whole string of victories over the Turks and various European rivals. It even fought Napoleon to a standstill; but it took decades to subdue comparatively tiny numbers of Chechens and other tribesmen in the mountains of the Caucasus. Even today such societies retain a remarkable capacity to mobilize formidable powers of armed resistance, even though lacking the formal institutions and cadres of "classical," mid-twentieth-century insurgencies, as exemplified by the Viet Cong or the Algerian FLN. Thus, faced with Russian aggression in 1994, Chechens once again rose to the occasion with a war effort spontaneously generated by Chechen society.[10]

Such successful opposition could exist even very close to the most developed states of the day: the British state did not succeed in "pacifying" the Gaelic clans of Scotland until after the Jacobite revolt of 1745, and then only by repressive measures the savagery of which prefigured that of the antipartisan wars of the twentieth century. This long British failure was due not only to the rugged terrain of the Highlands, but equally importantly to the clans' mixture of highly decentralized authority with fanatical loyalty to the clan chiefs. As a result, British authorities could rarely be entirely sure that an apparent ally would not change sides at a crucial moment; nor without massive repression could they force the highlanders to accept the authority of the new British state.

Similarly, in sixteenth-century Ireland, the establishment of British state authority was made extremely difficult not just by Irish resistance, the growing religious divide between Irish and English, and the wildness of the country, but also by the division of Irish authority into clans (or "septs"). Moreover, according to Irish tradition, the leadership of these clans did not pass from father to eldest son. The new head of the clan was elected by the clan's leading men.

In many ways, this was a curse for Irish society, sparking endless conflicts and feuds and undermining the resistance to the English. However, it was also a curse for the authorities in London and Dublin, who would extract allegiance from one chieftain only to find later that the clan had rejected the chieftain's son as successor and had renounced the treaty. British and American authorities faced this same problem in their dealings with Native American tribes. In both cases it contributed to their perception of Irish and Indian "treachery."[11]

In all these cases, nominally backward societies gained strengthen not just from ethnic and cultural loyalties but also from a profound attachment to an ancient way of life menaced by modernizing forces. When I first went into Afghanistan with the anti-Soviet Mujahedin in the late 1980s (as a journalist for the *Times* of London, based in neighboring Pakistan), the first thing to strike me in the "liberated areas" was the complete absence of all the institutions and visible symbols of the state: not a policeman, not a telephone or power line, not a court, not an office, not a doctor. As I wrote in the *Times* in February 1989, from the province of Nangrahar:

> In the Afghan countryside, the state and its symbols have vanished with a completeness almost inconceivable to the Western mind. There are no civil servants of any kind—not even a postman—and their symbol, the astrakhan fur hat, seems unlikely ever to return . . .
>
> With the Russians gone, the conflict will slip back to what it was before they intervened—a war by the bulk of the Afghan people against the modern Afghan state, as taken over by the Communists.
>
> Most people in the provinces always hated the modern and modernizing state . . . . It appeared to them chiefly in the guise of the conscripting officer, the ruthless bureaucrat, the brutal policeman, and the corrupt, savage, incomprehensible and atheistical legal system. It represented an assault on their religious and tribal traditions and on their idea of freedom. And unlike in Europe, it brought them very little of prosperity or progress and even on occasions destroyed what little they had.
>
> In return, the people have swept the state away, with all its works, and all its empty promises.[12]

VI

Afghanistan in its time brought both British and Soviet armies to grief. Almost simultaneously with the beginning of the First Opium War, a British army entered Afghanistan to install its own preferred claimant to the throne of Kabul and to create a bulwark against the Russian expansionism into Central Asia. But unlike China, where the defeat of the emperor's army and navy led to a settlement with the imperial government and an end to war, in Afghanistan—in the 1840s as in the 1980s—the multi-headed tribal and religious resistance could not be defeated in this way. There was, in fact, no unified enemy authority with whom to arrange a peace. And unlike the unarmed and generally passive Chinese peasantry, the Afghan tribesmen—like Somalis and Chechens, among others—were (and are) fierce fighters. Honoring warfare, they were trained from an early age to fight without mercy and equipped with weapons that (like the kalashnikovs and rocket-propelled grenades employed by partisan forces today) may not have been the most modern but were eminently well-suited for the preferred Afghan style of warfare.

In China, British officers at the time recognized the complete impossibility of invading and occupying the inland provinces, given the huge size of their territories and populations and the very small size of the British army and its Indian auxiliary troops. Fortunately, there was no need to do so. Once the British demonstrated their ability to move at will down China's rivers, and menaced the capitol, Beijing, the will of the Chinese government collapsed.

In Afghanistan too, the British did not have remotely enough troops to garrison the whole country. By late 1841, the force based in Kabul consisted of only one British and three British Indian infantry battalions and a single cavalry regiment, with other "armies" in Kandahar and Jalalabad. Although the British attempted to recruit local Afghan allies, relying on financial subsidies and allegiance to the local British puppet, Shah Sujah-ul-Mulk, the attempt failed. The presence of "infidel" troops in Muslim Afghanistan whipped religious leaders and their followers into a frenzy. As so often in such situations—one thinks of U.S. support for the Shah of Iran—British support for Shah Sujah undermined rather than enhanced his standing in the eyes of his own people. The British could not check atrocities by Shah Sujah's followers against their personal and political enemies. Liaisons between British officers and Afghan women infuriated the (male) population of Kabul. The British alienated a key ally—the Khan of Khelat—by holding him responsible for acts of banditry by his followers that he could not have prevented even had he wanted to, and ended by deposing and killing him. And finally the British government of India—under pressure from the government and parliament in London to economize—refused funds necessary to strengthen the British camp at Kabul and cut the subsidy to the tribes who controlled the British lines of communication.

The result of all this was the defection of the British allies, a general rising, an appallingly bungled attempt to retreat from Kabul across the mountains in midwinter, and the destruction of the entire British force. In addition to all their other failings, the British army had encumbered itself with an immense train of camp-followers, servants, and officers' luxuries— resembling the present-day U.S. Army in its insistence on deploying with all the comforts of home.[13]

Later that year, 1842, a much stronger British army returned to recapture Kabul and wreak revenge on its inhabitants: but the larger lesson had been learned. Never again did Great Britain permanently station troops in Afghanistan, or attempt to reduce its rulers to the completely subservient condition of the British Indian princes. Instead, the British exerted its influence over Afghanistan through "indirect" means. This approach saved the British from further disasters and the draining financial and human costs of an endless war of occupation; but it also meant that throughout the entire period of the British Empire in India, Afghanistan remained a constant security problem.

Although British authorities worried about Afghanistan providing a corridor for a Russian invasion of India, the real threat was quite different. As a practical matter, the security problem emanating from Afghanistan was twofold: It took the form of anti-British jihads stoked by local Muslim religious leaders (like the "Fakir of Ipi") and raids launched into British territory by tribal "bandits." British troops guarding the Afghan frontier tried various different responses to these dangers: the use of elite, locally-recruited troops (the famous Scouts and Guides) to seize individual troublemakers, the aerial bombardment of villages and flocks, and even full-scale punitive expeditions. The impact of all these responses—few of which were constrained by concerns about human rights—tended to be limited and above all temporary.[14]

In dealing with Afghanistan, British authorities found that it was largely pointless to pressure the government in Kabul to play a helpful role—for the simple reason that the government did not control its own territory and its own subjects in the frontier areas.

This same problem exists today. Chechnya provides an example. When Moscow pulled its troops out of Chechnya in 1996, the Yeltsin government decided to withdraw completely rather than leaving a security force along the Terek River. The government based that decision on the expectation that General Aslan Maskhadov, the former Soviet artillery colonel turned Chechen commander with whom Russia had negotiated, would prove to be a moderate and effective leader—someone who would keep order and with whom Moscow could deal on a pragmatic basis.

Unfortunately, while Maskhadov did indeed win presidential elections in January 1997, the destruction, militarization and brutalization caused by the war, together with the traditional Chechen aversion to authority, made it impossible to create an effective Chechen state. Instead, Chechnya became the base not only for international Islamic revolutionaries, but also for a great wave of kidnapping and raiding into surrounding Russian territory that claimed more than 1300 victims among Russians, Daghestanis and Ingush as well as a variety of Westerners.

In August 1999, Chechen and Islamist fighters launched a major incursion into the neighboring republic of Daghestan aimed at driving Russia from the region and creating a larger Islamic state. Russian pressure on Maskhadov to act proved ineffective since he did not in fact control the situation within Chechnya. That fall, Russia once again invaded.[15]

Even if, as appears likely, Russia succeeds in reconquering and occupying Chechnya, Moscow will find itself presiding over a bitterly discontented region and forced to deal with a long-running terrorist threat. The casualties inflicted by Russian bombardment of Chechen towns have alienated even Chechens who were thoroughly fed up with the anarchy and religious extremism of the years between 1996 and 1999—just as the civilian casualties inflicted by U.S. troops in Mogadishu infuriated even Somalis who loathed General Farah Aidid.

Because thousands of miles of ocean separate Somalia from the territory of the United States, the Americans at least had the option of abandoning Somalia. For Russia in Chechnya that option does not exist.

VII

If one of the lessons of Chechnya is the difficulty a modern state faces in dealing with an anarchic society that works by different rules, the other is the crucial importance of terrain. This lesson is, as already noted, a very old one.

Today, however, this lesson has taken on a new and sinister importance. For while in the nineteenth century Chechen fighters would hole up in the forested foothills, in the latest wars the key battles took place in the city of Grozny. As the Russians—and the Americans in Mogadishu—have learned at great cost, urban environments are the most difficult and dangerous of all battlefields even for modern armies with overwhelming firepower. Faced with brave, determined enemies armed with relatively primitive weapons, even modern tanks and armored personnel carriers can easily become death traps for their crews.[16]

Fighting in cities almost inevitably exacts a heavy toll in civilian casualties—around 100 for every U.S. military casualty during the battle for Manila in 1945, for example.[17] Even though U.S. doctrine now in theory at least eschews the kind of massive bombardment to which Manila was subjected, the sheer killing power of even small contemporary weapons platforms suggests the likelihood of similar civilian casualties in urban battles today—with Mogadishu a case in point. Writing about the Korean War, David Rees summed up the Western tradition this way: "At the heart of the West's military thought lies the belief that machines must be used to save its men's lives; Korea would become a horrific illustration of the effects of a limited war where one side possessed the firepower and the other the manpower."[18]

The Israeli army faced this dilemma when it invaded Lebanon in 1982. The PLO could not face them in the open field or even in the mountains, and instead retreated to Beirut and other cities. When the Israelis' heavy firepower caused heavy civilian casualties, they drew international condemnation. When they used infantry and suffered comparatively heavy casualties of their own, the result was domestic criticism and demoralization.[19]

Yet no army—least of all that of the world's hegemonic superpower—can assume that it will not have to fight in cities. Whereas in 1950, there were only 50 cities in the world with more than 1,000,000 people, today there are more than 300, with 25 cities claiming a population that exceeds 10,000,000. By 2025, 60 percent of the world's population will live in large cities, according to recent projections. As Stephen Metz has written, "The Army must be prepared to deter or defeat a cross-border invasion by another state, but if that is all it can do, it risks becoming the twenty-first-century equivalent of a sixteenth-century armored knight."[20] Today, as an ever increasing proportion of the world's population lives in ever larger cities, it would be simply ludicrous to draw up any military strategy that did not include urban warfare as a major component.

In January and February 1995, I witnessed the Russian assault on Grozny from both sides of the lines, and gained a vivid impression of the extreme difficulty and ugliness of urban warfare. At a lower intensity of violence, this had already struck me when I reported on ethnic violence in Karachi in 1989, and the way in which the Pakistani troops were swallowed up in the giant, featureless slums. During the Soviet occupation of Afghanistan, as I learned during my visits there, the Russians and their Afghan Communist allies never did succeed in controlling large areas of the suburbs of Kandahar and Herat. Their only recourse was to destroy these areas with artillery—after which Mujahedin sniped at them from the ruins.

In particular, what struck home in all these places was the huge number of troops needed to isolate, attack, and establish even a semblance of control over even a medium sized city like Grozny (which in 1989 had a population of just under 400,000)—unless, that is, the attacking troops are ready to accept the kind of casualties suffered in World War II by German troops attacking Stalingrad or Soviet units attacking Berlin.

A young Russian private named Valery Kukayev gave me a vivid picture of urban warfare conducted by armies trained for maneuver warfare. Describing the fate of his company of the 65th Motorized Infantry during the initial Russian attack on Grozny, he said:

> The commanders gave us no map, no briefing, just told us to follow the BMP in front, but it got lost and ended up following us. By morning, we were completely lost and separated from the other units. I asked our officer where we were, he said he didn't know—somewhere near the railway station. No, he didn't have a map either. We were told to take up defensive positions, but it was hopeless—the Chechens were all around us and firing. There was nowhere to take cover, because they were everywhere. I asked for orders from our company commander, Lt. Chernychenko, and they told me he'd already run for it. Then we tried to escape. That was when I was wounded, by a sniper—I'd got out of the BMP to try to find a way out.

Before mocking Russian incompetence and unpreparedness, it is worth remembering that in October 1993 in Mogadishu, the U.S. reaction force trying to locate the crew of one of the downed helicopters also got lost several times, despite being guided by a command-and-control helicopter above.[21]

The realities of urban warfare mean that the fog of war remains to a considerable degree impenetrable even to the latest technology. This is especially true in the shambolic, faceless, endlessly repetitive cities of the "Third World," where often no street names (and certainly no street signs) exist. Anyone who has experienced the frustration of spending hours searching for a house or flat at night in Delhi or Karachi understands this—and that is without the added strain of people shooting at you.

To the extent that the U.S. military is attempting to learn the lessons of Grozny and Mogadishu, that effort has taken the form of a search for technological fixes that will, in the words of one senior American officer with whom I spoke, make urban warfare "fast, clean and painless, just like current U.S. military operations on open terrain."

Thus, the Army and Marine Corps' Joint Advanced Concept Technology Demonstration has identified the following capabilities (among others) as ones towards which U.S. forces should be working in the field of urban warfare:

1) the ability to identify and discriminate between combatants and noncombatants at greater ranges and during all conditions;

2) the possession of vision equipment allowing all soldiers to see at all times (day, night, in basements/tunnels, through smoke, etc.);

3) the ability to produce maps and distribute them down to at least squad level within 6 to 12 hours of notification;

4) the possession of a soldier-portable, intelligence collection and dissemination tool to conduct remote, route/area/building reconnaissance, ideally incorporating through wall and countersniper sensors;

5) the possession of recoilless, hand-held projectiles capable of piercing walls and armor (a "bunkerbuster");

6) the possession of thermal, electronic and visual "badges" to mark all friendly soldiers;

7) the possession of nonlethal weapons for use in peacekeeping and police operations, and for storming buildings that may contain civilians.[22]

An Integrated Helmet Assembly Subsystem (IHAS) already exists, allowing the individual soldier to see computer-generated data, maps, and im-
agery, including pictures from a camera. This will enable the soldier to see
and fire around corners. Much thinking is also going into the creation of
small robots both for intelligence and fighting in urban terrain.

Whatever the utility of individual items that emerge from this project,
the overall approach displays a dangerous degree of wishful thinking. To
begin with, there is a real risk that a mixture of the strain of combat and the
sheer complexity of the equipment will overwhelm the ordinary soldier. In
the words of one British officer with urban combat experience, "They'll be
so busy looking into the computer screens in their helmets that they won't
notice when someone creeps up behind them and hits them on the head."
He pointed out that commanders of armored vehicles have long been
equipped with numerous vision and sensory devices—and in the British
case, still prefer to take the risk of sticking their heads out of the hatch to
see what is happening. Talk of this kind also ignores the way that commanders too can be overwhelmed by sheer volume of information. If, as is
often the case, the chain of command has also become disrupted, the result
can be a confusion that, because it has its roots in essentially human limitations, technology cannot remedy. Episodes during the Rangers' fight in
Mogadishu illustrate this to perfection.

Secondly, the technology that aims to distinguish between combatants
and non-combatants is very much at the wish-list stage. From this point of
view, the introduction of robotic devices could represent a step backwards,
since it is not clear how these could be prevented from killing everything in
their path, or even—if they malfunction—turning on their own side, electronic "recognition devices" notwithstanding. Moreover, the technology for
these is in fact still embryonic.

Above all, much of the U.S. military literature on future urban warfare
seems to assume two things. The first is a really remarkable level of leadership ability and courage on the part of junior officers, non-commissioned
officers, and even privates. The courage expected is both physical and in a
sense moral—the courage to operate in near-physical isolation or in very
small groups.[23]

This has indeed always been a feature of urban warfare. In the words of
Marshal Vasily Chuikov, commander of the defense of Stalingrad, "In street
fighting a soldier is on occasion his own general." A critical failing of the
Russians in Grozny in 1995 was the poor quality of their junior leadership,

and the acute demoralization of their individual soldiers. These, however, are essentially traditional military qualities, not provided for under the heading of technological or robotic development.

The other assumption pervading U.S. literature on urban warfare is the tendency to underestimate the potential tactical skill of the enemy while greatly exaggerating the capacity of U.S. troops on the ground. Thus the principles set out by Marine analysts for the Active Urban Defense of a city by U.S. troops are very close to those actually employed by the Chechens in Grozny. This assumes a hardly credible level of local knowledge, fanatical determination, and courage among the U.S. troops concerned. Such qualities might be forthcoming in the unlikely event that like the Chechens, U.S. troops were fighting an invader of their country, in the streets of Los Angeles or Chicago. These qualities are unlikely to be present to the same degree in U.S. soldiers fighting in Baghdad or Kabul.

Finally, U.S. planners are in my view hopelessly overoptimistic about the prospects for minimizing civilian casualties by the use of "nonlethal" weapons. As Major John Schmitt has written, "The idea of using nonlethals to incapacitate everyone and then sorting things out once everyone is "down for the count" greatly oversimplifies the problem and betrays an imperialistic high-handedness that will be politically unviable in many situations." On the whole, the U.S. approaches to future urban warfare are characterized— if only unconsciously—by what has been called "Technological Superiority Theory" rather than "Mental Agility Theory."[24]

VIII

Urban combat against well-armed and fiercely committed, but politically amorphous bands constitutes the kind of warfare that over the next two generations will pose the greatest challenge to Western armed forces. By contrast, major wars between the West and large opposing states are less likely. The drubbing administered to the Iraqi and Yugoslav national infrastructures will have had their effect. Unless the United States hopelessly mismanages relations with Russia, China or both, it is difficult to see why these or other states would risk directly confronting U.S. military power.

For a long time to come, the enormous superiority of American technology and military spending will, in this limited sense, make conventional war "obsolete." Despite Chinese alarm over the demonstration of American military prowess in Kosovo, China for a long time to come will possess neither the technological nor the financial resources to exploit the "Revolution in Military Affairs" so as to pose a really serious challenge to the United States in high-tech warfare.[25]

Failing some truly absurd American provocation—for example, supporting full independence for Taiwan or a Ukrainian move to expel Russia's Black Sea Fleet from Sevastopol—Chinese and Russian national elites are unlikely to risk their national infrastructures, and no less importantly, their own positions and wealth on so hazardous a gamble as war against the United States. On the American side, ever since Vietnam the inclination to court a major war has been limited by a fear of casualties and well-founded doubts about the American public's ability to stomach operations in which the United States itself has not been directly attacked and vital U.S. interests are not at stake. For years to come, the more immediate threat to the U.S. military will come not directly from existing states, but from within states, as those groups who have failed to benefit from the new world economy express their frustration by rising up against their own rulers, venting their anger against ethnic neighbors, or trying to create a radical new order.

At times, the United States will find itself drawn into these conflicts because of regional sensitivities—in Central America and the Caribbean, for example. At other times, it will intervene because critical interests are at stake, as for example, with the oil-producing states of the Persian Gulf. In other instances, intangibles may propel the U.S. to intervene—to shore up American credibility or to sustain U.S. claims to global leadership.

Critics will say that the United States can always avoid such conflicts by simply refusing to get involved.[26] But to assume that this will always be possible suggests an attitude of profound complacency. In the eyes of future generations, a nation willing to spend tens of billions of dollars to create a missile shield that saves North Korea from committing suicide, while failing to prepare for urban and partisan warfare, is likely to be regarded as at least irresponsible if not altogether paranoid. Apart from anything else, such a view assumes that our leaders will exercise unerring judgment and never engage in seemingly safe and limited military deployments that turn out to have unforeseen consequences—a naive assumption, given the historical record.

The further spread of terrorism will only serve to increase the likelihood of such interventions, especially if—as seems all too possible—at some stage terrorists gain access to weapons of mass destruction. The existence of states acting as bases for terrorism has already led the United States in the last two decades to bombard Libya, Afghanistan, and Sudan. This is the underside of the "global village": it spawns universal threats, thereby creating the requirement for universal policing.

As the brutal, chaotic, and menacing aftermath of the war in Kosovo suggests, the possession of superior air power does not necessarily equip a nation to keep order in that global village. In that regard, the intellectual and cultural weaknesses of Western armed forces in general, and U.S. forces in particular, are acutely relevant, whether they are the reluctance to suffer casualties among ground troops or to use ground troops to inflict heavy casualties on civilians—as may well be unavoidable on occasions.[27]

At the very least, some pretty tough, consistent and lengthy policing may be necessary. Where a tradition of socially sanctioned violence and theft is present in both parts of an ethnically mixed society, the only way of containing this in a moderately equitable way is sustained policing by an outside power. But for this to work, a whole series of factors have to be present, which the United States seems unwilling to countenance.

In the first place, the outside power has to be actually in control of the police forces and other authorities concerned and capable of handing out real rewards and punishments. It needs to maintain a sufficient number of its own men on the ground, speaking a local language and understanding local society. Given the general U.S. assumption that globalization means that the rest of the world is gradually becoming more American, U.S. forces are not likely to make the effort to become sufficiently conversant with other cultures.

Secondly, the presence of the outside power has to appear pretty much eternal—or at least it must appear that way to the local population. The mere discussion of "exit strategies"—much less publicly declared deadlines for withdrawal—signals to adversaries that they need simply bide their time.

Thirdly, the outside policing force, to be effective, will have to adopt methods very different from those common to modern Western societies. In circumstances where criminality is ethnicised and enjoys communal protection, pursuing individual perpetrators may be worse than useless. It may therefore in the end be both more effective and less provocative to resort to collective punishment; not mass executions or the burning of villages, but fines, confiscations, and restrictions on movement.

For obvious reasons, it is extremely difficult for U.S. (or European) armed forces of today to fulfill such requirements.

IX

The remarkable American reliance on air power stems at least in part from a determination *not* to become bogged down in such situations—to police the world but to do so on the cheap. This is not a new phenomenon. In the days of empire, whenever possible, European colonial powers used professionals—drawn from the expendable underclass and led by a largely hereditary caste of officers—rather than conscripts in their colonial campaigns. The determination to sustain the empire at minimum cost to the nation explains the creation of the French Foreign Legion in the nineteenth century and the retention of the British Gurkhas into the twenty-first. There was always a strong feeling that conscripts could only legitimately be used close to home and in wars for the defense of the homeland. It helps explains why despite much saber-rattling, no major European powers ever went to war with each other over colonial possessions in Asia or Africa (with the partial exception of the Crimean War). As a reflection of Western social, political, and cultural reality, the aversion to casualties in distant operations is nearly inevitable. The only difference today is that the aversion to losses in far-off operations now applies to professional soldiers as well (though less so in Britain than America).

But the concentration on aerial warfare suggests trends that go beyond and are more worrisome than the fear of casualties alone. One such trend is an aversion to combat itself, reflected in the belief that judiciously administered punishment (or even the prospect of punishment) along with skillful diplomatic signaling can bring an adversary to terms. Hence, the expectations in Brussels and Washington that three or four days of NATO bombing would surely suffice to force the Serbs to evacuate Kosovo.

Even more significant is the desire to impose order on warfare—to bring precision, predictability, and control to the use of force. Many—perhaps most—soldiers have always resisted the notion that war *by its very nature* is chaotic, filled with chance, and, at a certain level, unfathomable. For while this truth is acceptable to the freelance warrior, it goes against the entire spirit of the organized, "rational" military machine. Today, the age of the computer and so-called information revolution combines with these traditional bureaucratic and hierarchical elements of Western military culture to foster expectations that war can now at long last be tamed. This tendency may well be particularly pronounced among American officers, and is likely to get worse as more and more of the senior ones are drawn from the ranks of the technicians rather than the units "at the sharp end." For example, former U.S. Air Force Chief of Staff General Ronald Fogleman has declared that "in the first quarter of the twenty-first century you will be able to find, fix or track, and target—in near-real time—anything of consequence that moves upon or is located on the face of the Earth."[28]

But while a career spent ascending the ranks of the military bureaucracy in peacetime may equip a man for the technical and organizational aspects of warfare, it does not provide adequate psychological and intellectual preparation for command in the Mogadishus or Groznys that define much of the future of warfare. Such a career path tends to diminish a capacity for flexibility and improvisation, and to encourage a preference for what Andrew Bacevich has called "stylized warfare." While such warfare may make its appearance every generation or so—as in the Gulf War of 1991—the record of military history *since* Desert Storm, to include the war over Kosovo, suggests that other contingencies are far more commonplace as well as more perplexing.[29]

X

This then would seem the greatest threat: not major battles in the open field, where electronic intelligence and accurate firepower will give the United State huge advantages; but the America's global aspirations leading to the commitment of U.S. forces to occupy territories, and above all great cities, in the face of a bitterly hostile population and amidst a mixture of cultural ignorance, poor intelligence, racist hostility, brutality, and demoralization that affect its own forces and civilian population. Such conflicts could not in themselves lead to major physical defeats for U.S. forces, nor are they alone likely to destroy American global hegemony. But moral defeats like Somalia, and the losses and the moral squalor of such conflicts could over time undermine the will of the American people to play a global role. And if anger at a bungled and brutal American occupation encouraged massive terrorist attacks on the continental United States, it could inflict terrible harm on the American people.

Most of the thinking being done by the U.S. armed forces is wholly irrelevant to such conflicts, and the lessons learned from Kosovo have been entirely the wrong ones. The chief result, as evidenced by the 2000 military budget and the proposed reforms of Defense Secretary Donald Rumsfeld, appears to have been even more spending on the airforce and high technology. This spending has gone in part to "smart" weapons, which however useful against enemy armor in the open field, are next to useless in cities and in partisan warfare. The "lesson" of Kosovo has also translated into further development of the joint strike fighter, a weapon designed to fight above all against sophisticated, well-trained, large scale enemy air forces of a kind which simply do not exist in the world today.

Meanwhile, the limited contingent of U.S. troops on the ground in Kosovo are discovering that they lack both the numbers and the determination to prevent ethnic cleansing by the victorious Albanian majority, or even adequately to patrol Kosovo's border with Serbia proper and, even more importantly, with Macedonia. To accomplish the tasks those soldiers actually face, horses and mules would be more useful than additional smart weapons, fighters, and main battle tanks.[30]

At the time of writing, there are several potential scenarios in Kosovo and the wider Balkans that could lead either to a humiliating and disastrous NATO withdrawal or a dangerously increased NATO presence in the whole region: Relations with the Albanian majority could breakdown entirely, leading to attacks on NATO forces supported by segments of the local population. KLA incursions into neighboring Macedonia have spurred an Albanian revolt there and may lead to the collapse and partition of Macedonia. Bloody Serbian terrorist attacks on U.S. troops could prompt either a hasty Somalia-style pullout or a U.S.-led invasion of Serbia proper. A unilateral Montenegrin declaration of independence could provoke a Serb intervention there, leading to civil war and a NATO military invasion and occupation undertaken in the midst of a largely hostile Montenegrin Serb population.

Such conflicts are exactly the kind that will pose the greatest threat to Western armed forces in the decades to come. They are unlikely, even theoretically, to end in American victory through new technology or the adoption of grand new strategic theories. They will demand stamina, casualties, ruthlessness and adaptability. In the end the lessons most useful in such conflicts are likely to be ancient ones: know thy enemy, despise not thy enemy, and pick thy battles with care. Or in the words of Ecclesiastes, the preacher who was also a king and military leader: "I returned, and saw under the sun, that the race is not to the swift, nor the battle to the strong . . . but time and chance happeneth to them all. For man also knoweth not his time: as the fishes that are taken in an evil net, and as the birds that are caught in the snare; so are the sons of man snared in an evil time, when it falleth suddenly upon them."[31]

Notes

An abridged version of this chapter appeared in the winter 2000–2001 issue of *The National Interest.*

1.   John Keegan, "How We Beat Milosevic," *Daily Telegraph* (London), 12 July 1999. For a more skeptical view, see Alexander Nicoll, "The Lingering Question," *The Financial Times* (London), 1 July 1999.

2.   See Edgar Holt, *The Opium Wars in China* (London: Putnam, 1964), p. 91, and Maurice Collis, *Foreign Mud* (London: Faber and Faber, 1946), pp. 253–61.

3.   Holt, p. 111; Lieutenant John Ouchterlony, *The Chinese War* (London: Saunders and Otley, 1844), pp. 98–99.

4.   Moreover, there is strong evidence to suggest that Yugoslav ground forces in Kosovo suffered most of their losses when the Kosovo Liberation Army (KLA) launched an offensive over the mountains from Albania. They forced the Yugoslavs to concentrate against them and thereby expose themselves to NATO fire. In other words, to the extent that NATO did defeat the Yugoslav army as such, the victory was not due to airpower alone. Lieutenant Colonel Price T. Bingham, "Rapidly Stopping an Invasion," *Strategic Review*, Fall 1998.

5.   For San-yuan-li, see Frederic Wakeman Jr, *Strangers at the Gate: Social Disorder in South China, 1839–61* (Berkeley: University of California Press, 1966), pp. 11–21. For Chinese accounts, see Arthur Waley, *The Opium War Through Chinese Eyes* (London: Allen and Unwin, 1958).

6.   Captain Kevin W. Brown, "The Urban Warfare Dilemma," *Marine Corps Gazette*, January 1997.

7.   Mark Bowden, *Black Hawk Down* (New York: Atlantic Monthly Press, 1999), pp. 327–28. A less colorful account in reported speech is to be found in Oakley's own description of developments in Somalia: John L. Hirsch and Robert B. Oakley, *Somalia and Operation Restore Hope: Reflections on Peacemaking and Peacekeeping* (Washington, D.C.: United States Institute of Peace, 1995), p. 131. See also Patrick J. Sloyan, "How the Warlord Outwitted Clinton's Spooks," *Washington Post*, 3 April 1994.

8.   I. M. Lewis, *Understanding Somalia: Guide to Culture, History and Social Institutions* (London: HAAN Associates, 1993). Quoted in Hirsch and Oakley, p. 4.

9.   Sergei Arutiunov, "Ethnicity and Conflict in the Caucasus," in *Ethnic Conflict and Russian Intervention in the Caucasus*, ed. Fred Wahling (Institute for the Study of Global Conflict and Cooperation, University of California, San Diego), p. 17.

10. This is not simply an "Old World" phenomenon. The Spanish conquistadors managed in a very few years to subjugate the great Aztec and Inca empires — and then spent several centuries attempting to subdue comparatively tiny numbers of primitive Yaquis, Apaches, and Araucanians in the deserts of northern Mexico and the freezing wastes of southern Chile.

11. For a recent survey of European wars with "primitive" peoples, portrayed as far as possible from the side of the resistance, see Mark Cocker, *Rivers of Blood, Rivers of Gold: Europe's Conflict with Tribal Peoples* (London: J. Cape, 1998); for the "Indian wars" in North America, see Armstrong Stanley, *European and Native American Warfare, 1675–1815* (London: UCL Press, 1998).

12. *Times* (London), 7 February 1989.

13. Patrick Macrory, *Signal Catastrophe: The Story of a Disastrous Retreat from Kabul, 1842* (London: Hodder and Stoughton, 1966); Lady Sale, *A Journal of the Disasters in Affghanistan, 1841–2* (London: Murray, 1844). For the general background of British Afghan policy, see Malcolm Yapp, *Strategies of British India: Britain, Iran and Afghanistan, 1798–1850* (Oxford: Clarendon Press, 1980), and David Gillard, *The Struggle for Asia, 1828–1914: A Study in British and Russian Imperialism* (London: Methuen, 1977).

14. For a late-nineteenth-century British campaign against a religiously inspired tribal rising by a young officer who participated, see Winston S. Churchill, "The Malakand Field Force," in his *Frontiers and Wars* (New York: Harcourt, Brace and World, 1962), pp. 17–130.

15. For the background to the invasion, see Anatol Lieven, "Nightmare in the Caucasus," *The Washington Quarterly* (winter 1999).

16. For a description of the battle for Grozny in January 1995, see Anatol Lieven, *Chechnya: Tombstone of Russian Power* (New Haven: Yale University Press, 1998), pp. 108–17, and Carlotta Gall and Thomas de Waal, *Chechnya: calamity in the Caucasus* (New York: New York University Press, 1998), pp. 204–27.

17. See Keith William Nolan, *Battle for Hue: Tet, 1968* (Novato, Calif.: Presidio Press, 1983).

18. David Rees, ed., *The Korean War: History and Tactics* (London: Orbis, 1984).

19. Mark Hewish and Rupert Pengelley, "Warfare in the Global City," *Jane's International Defense Review*, June 1998.

20. Stephen Metz, "The American Army in the 21st Century," *Strategic Review* (fall 1999).

21. Bowden, *Black Hawk Down*, pp. 160–64.

22. See International Institute for Strategic Studies, "The Future of Urban War-fare," *Strategic Comments* 5, no. 2 (March 1999); "Non-Lethal Weapons Bestow Particular Advantages in MOUT," *Jane's International Defense Review*, June 1998; and "MISER Permits Engagement from Confined Space," *Jane's International Defense Review*, September 1998.

23. See Lieutenant General Paul K. Van Riper, USMC, "A Concept for Future Military Operations on Urbanized Terrain," *Marine Corps Gazette*, October 1997 (special supplement), and Colonel Randolph A. Gangle, "The Foundation for 'Urban Warrior,'" *Marine Corps Gazette*, July 1998.

24. Major John F. Schmitt, USMCR, "A Critique of the Hunter Warrior Concept," *Marine Corps Gazette*, June 1998.

25. Paul Dibb, "The Revolution in Military Affairs and Asian Security," *Survival* 39, no.4 (winter 1997–98).

26. David Tucker, "Fighting Barbarians," *Parameters* (summer 1998).

27. See John A. Gentry, "Military Force in an Age of Cowardice," *The Washington Quarterly* (autumn 1998).

28. Quoted in Michael O'Hanlon, "Can High Technology Bring US Troops Home?" *Foreign Policy* (winter 1998–99).

29. Andrew J. Bacevich, "Preserving the Well-Bred Horse," *The National Interest* (fall 1994).

30. Indeed, in 1946 a British officer attempting to prevent rural massacres by Hindus and Muslims in India expressed regret that the British Indian army had scrapped its horse cavalry units.

31. Ecclesiastes 9:11–12.

5   Kosovo and the Moral Burdens of Power

Alberto R. Coll

Beyond its military and political dimensions, the war in Kosovo was filled with large and daunting moral complexities. The purpose of
this essay is to examine these in light of the responsibilities the United States
faces today as the world's preeminent power. The essay will analyze the
moral ends for which United States and its allies carried out the Kosovo
operation, the means by which they conducted it, and the war's consequences for the international system and its evolving norms of state behavior.
The essay also will explore the degree to which the Kosovo operation yields
insights for future statesmen committed to using American power in a morally responsible fashion. While this writer agreed with the decision to intervene militarily in Kosovo, the other side of the debate will be presented in
this essay in order to give readers the opportunity to reach their own conclusions.

We must begin, as future historians no doubt will, by noting the strategic
context in which the United States and its allies undertook the Kosovo operation. In 1999 the United States stood at the apex of its military, economic,
and political power. At no time before in its history had the United States
found itself so strong, in both absolute and relative terms, and so unopposed
by any potential rival or challenger. The American economy, in the midst
of an unprecedented expansion powered by huge productivity increases,
generated by the revolution in information technologies, was the envy of the
world. American society was recording 30-year lows in crime and unem-
ployment. Militarily, the United States was outspending Russia, China,

Great Britain, France, Italy and Spain combined, and U.S. military forces were unmatched in their capabilities, technological sophistication, and global reach. Politically, the United States was acknowledged by all, and feared by some, as the world's hegemon. The United States either controlled outright or exercised decisive influence over all of the world's leading political and financial institutions, including the United Nations, NATO, the World Bank, and the International Monetary Fund. The only power that historically would have had the ability and the inclination to frustrate NATO's actions in Kosovo, Russia, was politically and economically weak and ultimately dependent on Western goodwill. Throughout the crisis, it could play no more than a mildly obstructionist role and, in the end, it encouraged Serbia to give in to Western demands.

American primacy in the 1990s gave free rein and heightened impetus to a series of long-held American beliefs about the historical role of the United States in the world. These beliefs, commonly grouped in recent decades under the rubric of Wilsonianism, have been an important strand of the American political psyche since the country's earliest days. In its barest outlines, Wilsonianism holds that the United States is a unique society destined by Providence to lead the rest of the world to a future of freedom, democratic equality, and harmony.[1] Wilsonianism is exceptionalist, universalist, and messianic. It is exceptionalist to the degree that it posits that the United States is different from other nations, and that it has a unique historical mission. It is universalist in that it maintains that the liberal Western understanding of liberty, democracy, and equality, notions of what constitutes a legitimate polity, and definitions of human rights are desirable across the entire range of global cultural and religious differences. And it is messianic in that it holds that America's historical mission is to promote, not only by example but also by energetic action, these values around the world. A vibrant force in American foreign policy for much of the twentieth century, Wilsonianism entered a particularly vigorous phase during the years of the Clinton presidency.

Several developments illustrate the resurgence of Wilsonianism in the 1990s and the degree to which it helped to set the stage for the Kosovo intervention. First, Wilsonian rhetoric found renewed favor among American leaders, with frequent references by President Clinton and Secretary of State Albright to the United States as "the indispensable nation." National Security directives and State Department documents became steeped in grandiose language about America's responsibilities to promote global democratization and human rights. The State Department established an "Assistant Secretary of State for Democracy," and the creation of a similar office within the Department of Defense was averted only by the narrowest of margins after a tough bureaucratic fight. Second, within the executive and legislative branches there was a massive urge to impose diplomatic and economic sanctions, or strengthen existing ones, on many countries. While in a handful of cases, such as Iraq, North Korea, and Libya, the sanctions were related to national security concerns, most were imposed on the basis of human-rights violations. As of early 2001, the United States maintained diplomatic and economic sanctions on some 75 countries, compared to fewer than a dozen countries subject to sanctions by the United Nations. Almost half of the 125 unilateral economic sanctions imposed by the United States since World War I took effect between 1993 and 1998.[2]

The revival in Wilsonian rhetoric and the use of sanctions as a foreign policy instrument were coupled with several major interventions in which the United States deployed military power to restore order and to promote Wilsonian goals. The most notable of these were in Somalia (1992–93), Haiti (1994) and Bosnia (1996–the present). Like the subsequent intervention in Kosovo, the interventions in Haiti and in Bosnia combined security and humanitarian objectives, whereas the Somalia operation was almost purely humanitarian in character. It is impossible to understand the context of the Kosovo operation without some discussion of the three major interventions that preceded it.

When the Bush administration launched the Somalia operation in its last days in office, it conceived it as a narrow humanitarian intervention to end the famine scourging the country, and was intent on withdrawing U.S. forces as soon as it achieved this objective. The Clinton administration, prodded by its then Ambassador to the United Nations, Madeleine Albright, broadened the mission's goal to include supporting the United Nations agenda for rebuilding the country's political and economic institutions and creating a more democratic and prosperous Somali society. This expansion of the original objectives brought the United Nations and the American government into conflict with Somali warlord and political leader Mohammed Farah Aidid, who sought to take control of the country. For several months in the summer and fall of 1993, American military forces were openly at war with Aidid and his partisans. In October of that year, after a violent clash in which U.S. forces killed several hundred Somalis and suffered 18 killed in action, the Clinton administration, under pressure from Congress and the American public, abruptly terminated U.S. participation in Somalia and shortly thereafter withdrew all U.S. forces.

Several key facts stand out about the Somalia episode. First, even though there were no important U.S strategic interests at stake, the Clinton Administration embarked on an ambitious "nation-building" mission from which it withdrew only in the face of strong U.S. domestic opposition. Second, although one of the intervention's declared goals was to improve the lives of the Somali people, it encountered fierce resistance from significant elements of the Somali population and its political elites, and in due course UN and U.S. forces wound up taking the lives of several thousand Somalis and inflicting considerable material damage. While it is also true that, thanks to the U.S.-UN intervention, the Somali famine came to an end and some 10,000 lives were saved, the overall moral picture was one of considerable ambiguity.[3] Ironically, smarting from criticism of its handling of Somalia, the Clinton administration refrained the following year from intervening in Rwanda, where again there were no security interests at stake, but where a modest U.S.-European military involvement might have stopped a genocide that took more than half a million lives.

Next on the road to Kosovo came Haiti, which, in the wake of a military coup against the elected government of President Jean Bertrand Aristide, verged on political and economic chaos. With the Haitian economy in 1994 groaning under the weight of U.S.-imposed "pro-democracy" economic sanctions, violence between security forces and pro-Aristide elements escalating, and the number of Haitians fleeing their homeland mounting daily, the Clinton administration decided to intervene militarily on both security and humanitarian grounds. Internal unrest, accentuated by the military junta's illegitimacy and its authoritarian and corrupt practices, was provoking an exodus of Haitian migrants to American shores. The Clinton administration considered this exodus destabilizing for the Caribbean region and for the southern United States, especially for the populous and politically influential state of Florida. To this security-related concern was joined the Wilsonian goal of promoting Haitian democracy and a more prosperous and equitable Haitian society. In contrast to the U.S. operation in Somalia, the U.S. occupation of Haiti generated no opposition, but the results were equally ambiguous, politically and morally. When the last American troops left in 1999, Haiti was no closer to true democracy, social stability, or economic prosperity than it had been five years earlier.

In Bosnia, the United States carried out another military intervention in which security goals were joined to humanitarian ones. The Bosnia intervention had two principal objectives: to strengthen NATO and European security through the enforcement of the 1995 Dayton Accords settling the war in Bosnia-Herzegovina, and to promote order and stability within Bosnia by preventing further human-rights violations, including acts of war and genocide against any ethnic or religious minority groups. The Clinton administration persuaded Congress to support the intervention, at least half-heartedly, with the rationale that the American effort would enhance U.S. influence in NATO and Europe at a time of growing reassertion of European independence, and that it would stop the massacres of innocent Bosnians dominating the evening news. The intervention appealed to large numbers of internationalists of all stripes: conservatives and liberals, idealists and realists, Cold War warriors and Wilsonian crusaders, many of whom saw it as an instrument for promoting American security interests while accomplishing worthy humanitarian ends.

As of this writing, a large contingent of U.S. troops remains in Bosnia and progress in the implementation of the peace settlement has been glacially slow. Yet, under the shadow of the American peacekeepers, human-rights violations have ceased; a semblance of order, stability, and normal economic activity has returned to the country, and there is a glimmer of hope that over time a durable peace may emerge. In Bosnia, as in Haiti, the American military entered the country with the approval of the relevant political authorities and major political factions, and this helped to insure little violent opposition to the American presence and thus hardly any U.S. casualties. This also meant that, in both cases, the American intervention, even if it did not accomplish the wholesale restructuring of society hoped for by some of its more ardent Wilsonian advocates, at least had the salutary effect of ratcheting down the overall levels of violence.

To what degree did the Kosovo intervention differ morally from those that had occurred in the Clinton years? While Haiti and Bosnia resemble Kosovo in their underlying mix of security and humanitarian objectives, neither Bosnia nor Haiti took the form of a full-fledged war against an established government and its military forces, as was the case in Kosovo. In fact, Kosovo can be considered the first war of humanitarian intervention ever carried out by the Western liberal powers. This is its salient characteristic, and the main reason its moral complexities were numerous, and its implications for the future exercise of American power in a morally responsible manner so significant. Looking over the course of the last hundred years, never before had the Western powers used force for ostensibly humanitarian purposes, whether in Katanga in 1961 or in China's Boxer Rebellion of 1908, *except* for the purpose of rescuing nationals. Never before had the West carried out a full-scale war against an established state, as it did in Kosovo, for the sake of protecting the rights of a foreign people with whom it had no ethnic, religious, or political ties.

Ius ad Bellum: Was it Right to Undertake the Kosovo Intervention?

An analysis of Kosovo's moral complexities and their long-term implications for the morally responsible use of American power must begin by asking whether the United States and its allies were morally justified in undertaking the intervention. Was it right for NATO to unleash a full, violent war against Serbia? To address this question requires, in turn, asking a series of related subquestions that are part of common moral reasoning and intrinsic to the Western philosophical and political tradition within which American public life and discourse continue to be embedded. They are questions that seem to come naturally to anyone inquiring into the rightness of a decision to resort to the highly destructive instruments of war. In the West's history these questions have come to be known collectively as "just war theory." This term is perhaps misleading because the word "theory" implies a high degree of abstraction, an artificial flight from natural human moral reasoning and discourse into the realm of formalism. But the questions at the heart of just-war theory are neither artificial nor abstract. They are quite "natural" questions that a reasonable human observer would ask when placed in the position of having to analyze the moral rightness of the resort to war.[4]

Just-war theory evaluates the rightness of a war by examining two dimensions: the rightness of the decision to wage war (*ius ad bellum*), and the rightness of the means by which the war is conducted (*ius in bello*). We will examine these two in order, first looking at the rightness of NATO's decision to employ force as an instrument of policy to compel Serbia to stop its massive human-rights violations against the Albanian Kosovars. The related subquestions that come naturally to mind, and that are also part of just-war theory are as follows. First, was there sufficient cause to justify NATO's resort to force—in other words, were the evils being perpetrated by Serbia in its province substantial enough to justify the violence, deaths, and destruction entailed in war? One way of putting this question is to ask whether the object of the intervention was of sufficient moral worth to outweigh the evils likely to be generated by the use of force. Second, did NATO have lawful authority to engage in war against Serbia, and what was the source of that authority? Third, was there a reasonable chance of success? Fourth, did NATO exhaust all reasonable peaceful alternatives prior to waging war — in other words, was war truly the last resort?

One word of caution is necessary at this point. This writer does not see the just-war tradition as a simple formula that consistently provides clear-cut answers to the moral dilemmas posed by the use of force. Even though some writers treat just-war reasoning this way, others see it instead as a series of broad guidelines or principles that help policymakers discern the moral rea- sonableness of a particular resort to war but never provide the equivalent of scientific certainty or precision. Under this latter view, the just-war tradition is useful, not so much because it supplies definitive answers, but because it forces decision makers to ask a series of tough questions and to engage in the kind of careful deliberation that can clarify the moral costs and benefits of alternative policy choices and, in some cases, lessen the likelihood that some terrible crimes will be committed. Applying just-war criteria to the use of force in Kosovo may not tell us beyond a shadow of a doubt whether NATO was right or wrong in doing what it did, but it will clarify the issues that demand attention in order to reach one's own conclusions.

Was There Just Cause?

Were Serbia's acts against the Albanian Kosovars on such a scale as to justify NATO's use of force? The immediate justification for the war was the recrudescence in 1998 and 1999 of Serb violence against the ethnic Alba- nians, apparently calculated to drive most of them out of Kosovo into Al- bania. It was similar to the "ethnic cleansing" that the Bosnian Serbs, with the full backing of Slobodan Milosevic, had carried out against the Muslims in Bosnia. In 1989, aware that Yugoslavia was on the verge of breaking up along ethnic lines, Milosevic had reversed Marshal Tito's policy of granting considerable autonomy to the Kosovars and opted for a policy of centrali- zation and tighter control. The Albanian Kosovars resisted this new policy. Milosevic's policies spurred the rise of several new Kosovar nationalist groups, the more moderate ones insisting on a return to autonomy, the more radical ones such as the Kosovo Liberation Army (KLA) agitating for full independence. As Slovenia and Croatia broke away from Yugoslavia in 1990 and the war in Bosnia broke out, Milosevic's energies became focused away from Kosovo, where an uneasy calm punctured by sporadic low-level violence prevailed. In its closing days, the administration of George H. W. Bush warned Serbia that "in the event of conflict in Kosovo caused by Serbian action, the United States will be prepared to employ military force against the Serbs in Kosovo and in Serbia proper."[5] It is not altogether clear why the elder President Bush chose to draw the line in Kosovo when he failed to do so earlier in Bosnia. But there was a belated recognition that Milosevic had to be stopped from further depredations, coupled with fear that a Serb-Kosovar war would destabilize the Balkans beyond the breaking point and draw into the conflict Greece, Bulgaria and Turkey with potentially devastating consequences for European peace and NATO's continued viability.

When in 1999 President Bill Clinton made good his predecessor's threat, the chief NATO powers—the United States, Great Britain, France, and Germany—offered several reasons for their military intervention in Kosovo. First, NATO sought to stop ongoing human-rights violations against the ethnic Albanians, including ethnic cleansing and killings of those who resisted or were considered KLA sympathizers. These human-rights violations were significant in their number and severity, and they had increased throughout 1998 and early 1999. Second, NATO feared the destabilization of southeastern Europe if the situation in Kosovo further deteriorated. The flow of refugees from Kosovo into Albania, Bosnia, and Macedonia was rising sharply, affecting the internal stability of those states. If the strife in Kosovo continued to worsen, outside powers might step in, provoking a wider conflict. From the time Milosevic stepped up repression against the ethnic Albanians in 1998 to the end of hostilities following NATO's intervention, approximately one million refugees fled Kosovo, and another 300,000 to 500,000 remained as internally displaced persons within Kosovo.[6] Third, NATO members wanted to avoid a repetition of the earlier events in Croatia and Bosnia, and were eager to establish a precedent by indicating to Milosevic that they would not tolerate his policy of fanning ethnic strife to establish a Greater Serbia. The NATO powers also claimed to be establishing the broader precedent that such aggressive behavior would not be tolerated anywhere in Europe.

Thus, a cluster of three reasons supported the intervention, all of them adding up supposedly to sufficient justification. The first cause was *humanitarian*, the second one was grounded in regional *security*, and the third one could be called *normative,* that is, related to upholding the norms and precedents necessary to maintain a humane and peaceful international order. Did all these justify the war? Did they outweigh all the evils and disorders that a war was likely to set in motion? This writer believes that they did. The scale of human-rights violations was sufficiently high, the regional security problem generated by these violations sufficiently severe, and the need to uphold normative standards compelling enough to add up to a justification for military action.

Yet debate on this critical question has not stopped, and it is useful to consider some of the arguments against NATO intervention. Critics maintain that none of the justifications given, either individually or combined, amounted to a just cause for war. First, the comparative scale of repression in Kosovo did not differ appreciably from other cases—for example, Turkey's treatment of the Kurds and Guatemala's abuse of its own indigenous peoples—where it never occurred to the United States government to carry out a military intervention on behalf of the victims. Moreover, critics argue that in Kosovo some of the acts of violence classified as Serb human-rights violations were either legitimate acts of war against the violent terrorist KLA paramilitary forces, or else unfortunate and unavoidable by-products of the war with the KLA.

Second, critics argue that the Kosovo conflict posed no real threat to regional security. In fact, not only was there no serious risk of the war spreading, but it was NATO's military intervention that raised such risks dramatically by antagonizing Russia in an area of great sensitivity to Russian interests and prestige, by raising the tempo of ethnic cleansing and overall violence, by increasing refugee flows, and finally through the bombing of the Chinese embassy. While the ongoing conflict between Serbs and Albanians in Kosovo posed a risk of escalation, the best way to contain the conflict was not to turn it into a full multistate war but through diplomacy.

Critics likewise dismiss the normative justification for intervention. They argue that the Serb-Albanian conflict in Kosovo did not affect the normative foundations of international order because it was a domestic conflict within a recognized nation-state. Encouraging further negotiations among the concerned parties, perhaps under the auspices of the United Nations, was the appropriate course of action. Moreover, the NATO intervention established several morally and legally noxious precedents. First, internal strife in a weak and isolated country such as Serbia can be a handy excuse for meddling by outsiders, using humanitarianism as a pretext. Under this precedent, dozens of countries around the world could find themselves at the receiving end of a humanitarian intervention by more powerful, self-interested neighbors. Second, by acting militarily without UN authorization, NATO undermined the United Nations's credibility and authority and created a precedent giving regional organizations wide latitude to intervene militarily. This undermines international order and morality because regional organizations such as NATO and the OAS are generally less impartial than the United Nations— they tend to be dominated by the stronger regional powers that belong to them. Far from strengthening the normative pillars of international order and morality, the Kosovo intervention visibly weakened them by pushing the world in the direction of the rule of the weak by the strong.[7]

It is hardly surprising that the issue of whether there was sufficient cause to intervene provoked controversy. This has been the case with most wars throughout history, even many that in retrospect appear to have been clear-cut cases of justifiable wars. While the Kosovo military intervention garnered the support of many countries, it did not attract the more solid international consensus the Persian Gulf War enjoyed. This, too, should not be surprising. The principle that no country should be allowed to invade and occupy another sovereign state unless attacked is deeply rooted in international law and morality as one of the basic safeguards of international order. States perceive this principle as clearly in their interests, as an indispensable guide to survival in an anarchic world. On the other hand, states are highly suspicious of the concept of humanitarian intervention. There are few countries in the world, including the United States, which at some point in their history have not committed serious acts of violence against minorities in their midst. Whereas the principle at stake in the Gulf War was supportive of state power, and hence enjoys the support of most states in the international system, the principle of humanitarian intervention is threatening to many states and is viewed skeptically by most governments.

The inherent suspicion with which most governments view humanitarian intervention explains why the concept disappeared from the practice of international law at the end of the seventeenth century and did not enjoy a revival again until the last decade of the twentieth. What international law theorists of the nineteenth and early twentieth century called "the right of humanitarian intervention" was a desiccated, shrunken version of the real thing; it referred only to the right of states to rescue their own nationals. The idea that states had a right to rescue other peoples from the depredations of their own rulers, advocated by such early international legal theorists as Aquinas, Vitoria, Suarez, and Grotius, ceased to be a living element of international law and practice by the late seventeenth century in tandem with the end of the wars of religion and the consolidation of the secular nation-state system.[8] It was roundly dismissed by Vattel and his positivist successors in the nineteenth century, and remained an unfashionable viewpoint for most of the twentieth.[9]

There were two main reasons why the almost absolute ban on humanitarian intervention that dominated international law throughout the twentieth century crumbled over the last decade. First, there was the collapse of the Soviet Union and the emergence of an international system in which the United States and its allies hold a preeminent position, together with great freedom of action to carry out such interventions as their interests dictate or their publics demand. Second, the conceptions of state sovereignty underlying the older absolutist position are no longer as credible. In our crowded, highly interdependent planet, certain human-rights outrages that decades ago could be coldly ignored as a state's domestic matter no longer are truly domestic because they affect the stability and welfare of neighboring

coun   ociety. A number
of hu   BAKING PAPER   e end of the Cold
War   by the forces of
globa   new world order
that s   os against govern-
men   ction against Iraq
in 19   nd Shiites in that
coun   a, and Kosovo as
flawe   l order in which
the c   those of a global
com   ligations.

B   arian intervention
has   al opinion today
rang   rian intervention,
with   a handful of powerful   opposition to, the
conc   articular case and

on the strategic interests of each state. At one end of the spectrum are the United States and Tony Blair's United Kingdom, eager to reserve as much freedom of action as possible for future interventions, especially if carried out by NATO. Strategically, the United States sees itself as the guarantor of

international order, the great power that must be ready to intervene anywhere, anytime, when others cannot or will not do so. A muscular Wilsonianism demands this freedom of action, as also does a calculated realpolitik.
Meanwhile, Great Britain sees its strategic interests as closely bound with
those of the United States and with an activist NATO role that enables the
British to play one of their strongest cards in Europe: their robust military
capabilities relative to those of other European states. Next on the intervention spectrum are states such as France and Germany. The French are suspicious of excessively elastic pro-intervention criteria that might legitimize
what they see as American hegemonic pretensions. For their part, the Germans want to avoid situations in which Germany will act militarily outside
its borders without a clear international mandate.

At the other end of the spectrum are the most vocal opponents of loos-
ening the crtieria for humanitarian intervention. As one might expect, these
include some of the weakest states in today's international system or those
that have the most to lose from a resurgent American Wilsonianism. Cuba
fits the first category, China and Russia the latter. For the Cubans, NATO's
intervention in Kosovo, devoid as it was of a Security Council mandate,
opened the door for bolder U.S. action around the world, including the
Western hemisphere and someday, possibly even Cuba. Russia and China
have large minorities in their midst, such as the Chechens and Tibetans,
against whom they are prepared to use force on a massive scale in order to
preserve national territorial integrity. They have nothing to gain and much
to lose from more flexible standards for humanitarian intervention.

In the end, the arguments for or against a broader concept of humanitarian intervention seem to be dictated, not so much by their legal or moral
persuasiveness, as by the strategic perspective and self-interest of each state.
This also means that no solid consensus is likely to emerge. For the foresee-
able future, the five Security Council members will remain divided, with
the Western powers far more willing to countenance a more activist position
than either Russia or China will support. Like the other four powers on the
Council, the United States will focus first on its specific strategic responsibilities as it decides which interpretation of the rules to support, rather than
its responsibilities to international law in the abstract or even to international
morality.

Thus, the answer to the question whether there exists a new right of
humanitarian intervention is complex. The Western powers insist that such
a right is indeed beginning to emerge, while China, India, Russia, and much

of the developing world reject the notion. Undoubtedly, the conviction that such a right exists is much stronger today than at any previous time in the last three centuries. If the international distribution of political, economic, and military power continues to favor the United States, Europe, and Japan, the right of humanitarian intervention will continue to enjoy its current resurgence. But any future assertions of this right will be resisted by a large number of states, including some with substantial military clout. If a prospective humanitarian intervention threatens to escalate into a serious conflict with a large- or medium-size military power, the odds are that the Western powers will not undertake it. If, on the other hand, the intervention is directed against a weak or isolated state such as Serbia that is unable to defend itself or to call upon a powerful ally to do so, the Western powers will be more likely to intervene.

Did NATO Have Lawful Authority?

Did NATO have lawful authority to engage in war against Serbia, and what was the source of that authority? In light of the preceding discussion, it is clear why those states that oppose the revival of humanitarian intervention will insist that, even in the most egregious cases of human-rights violations, a humanitarian intervention against a sovereign state requires the full backing of the international community, meaning, at a minimum, authorization from the United Nations Security Council. According to this viewpoint, only the United Nations commands sufficient legitimacy, universality, and impartiality to legitimize an act so extreme as the resort to war. While regional organizations carry enough authority to promote the peaceful settlement of disputes, they are not sufficiently impartial to authorize the use of force because they tend to be dominated by the strongest regional powers, and they lack mechanisms to protect weaker member states.

The opposing viewpoint, with which this writer agrees, contends that in the real world United Nations consensus is extremely difficult to achieve. No matter how hideous its human-rights violations, a state will almost always be able to find a patron in the Security Council willing to cast its veto on that state's behalf to protect it against a humanitarian intervention. In the case of Kosovo, Serbia found two such friends in Russia and China, both of which would have vetoed any United Nations resolution authorizing the use of force. If we are not prepared to acknowledge the legitimacy of humanitarian intervention by regional organizations or even individual states in cases of extreme human-rights violations, we will have a world in which such violations will take place with impunity while the international community stands by helplessly. Such an outcome is highly subversive of world order and human decency. Princeton philosopher Michael Walzer has put the case for this viewpoint eloquently:

> It was the Vietnamese who stopped Pol Pot in Cambodia, the Tanzanians who stopped Idi Amin in Uganda, the Indians who ended the killing in East Pakistan, the Nigerians who went into Liberia. Some of these were unilateral military acts, some (the Nigerian intervention, for example, and now the campaign in Kosovo) were authorized by regional alliances. Many people on the left yearn for a world where the United Nations, and only the United Nations, would act in all such cases. But given the oligarchic structure of the Security Council, it's not possible to count on this kind of action: in most cases on my list, UN intervention would have been vetoed by one of the oligarchs. Nor am I convinced that the world would be improved by having only one agent of international rescue. The men and women in the burning building are probably better served if they can appeal to more than a single set of firefighters.[10]

NATO argued that it had lawful authority to intervene on the basis of several grounds. First, the conflict's refugee flows, interethnic violence, and human-rights violations seriously affected regional stability in an area immediately adjacent to NATO. European security, broadly defined to include economic and social stability and containing the risk of conflict escalation, was at stake. In the face of likely United Nations inaction, NATO had the right to address this security threat. Second, NATO had lawful authority because it was sufficiently impartial. The NATO powers insisted that they were not pursuing an anti-Serbian crusade. They offered to take into account legitimate Serbian interests by specifying at the Rambouillet conference that Kosovar autonomy, not independence, would be the basis of any settlement; that the KLA and other Kosovar factions would have to disarm; and that Serb historical and religious shrines in Kosovo would be fully protected and controlled by Serbia under any autonomy scheme. The NATO powers also argued that they were willing to let Russia play a constructive role in their dealings with Serbia, though they also made it clear that they would not allow Russia to obstruct a humanitarian intervention. Third, NATO claimed that it had lawful authority because it was intervening on behalf of principles of human rights and international order fully compatible with those of the United Nations Charter. NATO's action would strengthen those principles, not only in southeastern Europe, an area of vital concern to NATO, but elsewhere in the world.

As with the debate on whether there was sufficient justification to intervene, the debate on whether NATO had lawful authority has remained inconclusive, shaped more by the interests and perspectives of the state making the argument than by the intrinsic legal and moral foundations of the argument itself. While NATO members and most Western authors are convinced that NATO had lawful authority, a large body of opinion in much of the non-Western world led by China and India strongly disagrees. This divergence of viewpoints seems unavoidable, if unfortunate. From the perspective of creating a more humane international order, it would be best if a solid consensus developed legitimating humanitarian intervention in cases of outrageous human-rights abuses. Two key elements of such a consensus would be *standards of impartiality* and *practical mechanisms for implementation*. These standards are unlikely to emerge anytime soon. UN Secretary General Kofi Annan has described the problem at the heart of the debate:

> Kosovo has cast in stark relief the dilemma of what has been called humanitarian intervention: on the one side, the question of the legitimacy of an action taken by a regional organization without a UN mandate; on the other, the universally recognized imperative of effectively halting violations of human rights with grave humanitarian consequences. The inability in the case of Kosovo to unify these two equally compelling interests of the international community—universal legitimacy and effectiveness in defense of human rights—can only be viewed as a tragedy.[11]

Was There a Reasonable Chance of Success?

The use of power in a morally responsible manner requires that close attention be paid, not just to one's good intentions, but also to the practical realities of acting on them. Good intentions that are carried out ineptly, or that result in evil consequences, are morally questionable. In the real world, of course, these are precisely the kinds of situations that even well-intentioned statesmen have to deal with most of the time: either policies that are difficult to implement well or actions that, no matter how skillfully implemented, will produce, along with some good, a great deal of evil as well. How did NATO and its key military power, the United States, do in Kosovo with regard to this calculus?

From the outset, the question was not whether NATO would prevail militarily but whether it would achieve its political objectives at a reasonable cost. These objectives were to stop the ongoing human-rights violations, end all violence in Kosovo, and facilitate a settlement of the conflict along the lines of the Rambouillet conference. In the end, NATO achieved these only partly, and at a much higher cost than anticipated. The question presenting itself is whether the alliance's leaders should have foreseen the difficulties they would encounter in achieving their objectives and, if so, whether they still should have gone forward with the military intervention.

First, did NATO's leaders err strategically and morally by failing to anticipate that the commencement of military operations against Serbia would lead the Serbs to step up the pace of ethnic cleansing, thereby increasing violence and human suffering dramatically? It was reasonable to expect that, in a conflict as charged with hatred as that between Serbs and ethnic Albanians, an effort to help the latter would also trigger massive reprisals against them, especially because the Serbs could not strike back at NATO itself.[12] And if there was a reasonable possibility that this would happen, the problem was compounded by NATO's obvious inability to respond, unless the Alliance was willing to use ground forces, something which would carry its own set of serious risks and disadvantages. Thus, the moral score is mixed. On the one hand, it is fair to charge NATO with a degree of strategic and moral turpitude to the extent that its intervention worsened considerably the very outrages it was meant to halt. But on the other hand, NATO eventually did put a stop to Serbian depredations against the ethnic Albanians.

NATO only partially achieved its two other objectives: to end all violence in Kosovo and to facilitate a settlement of the conflict along the lines of the Rambouillet conference. Following the withdrawal of Serbian forces from Kosovo in the wake of NATO's victory, a wave of violence by ethnic Albanians against Serbs broke out, and NATO proved unable to control it for a period of time. Though not on the same scale as Serb abuses against the Albanians, the abuses suffered by the Serbs were massive and resulted in the flight of 250,000 Serbs and Gypsies from Kosovo.[13] Eventually, NATO asserted its control and an uneasy peace ensued, although to this day sporadic acts of violence against Serbs continue in spite of NATO's best efforts to suppress them.

Two years after the NATO intervention, the Kosovo conflict remains far from settled. Intransigent ethnic Albanians, spearheaded by the KLA, insist on independence, while the Serbs vow never to accept such an outcome. The democratic election in the fall of 2000 of Vojislav Kostunica to the presidency of Yugoslavia, and the advent to power of a noncommunist Serbian government, may open up some space for a peaceful compromise between the more moderate elements on both sides. But one should not be too optimistic. In the wake of the atrocities committed prior to, during, and after the war, NATO's objective of an autonomous Kosovo that remains part of Serbia, where Albanians and Serbs can live together peacefully, seems increasingly elusive. Yet, for now, NATO has no option but to maintain its occupation force in Kosovo, including the large American contingent. To withdraw it in the absence of a settlement agreed to by all the major parties would mean a return to civil strife.

In retrospect, NATO underestimated the difficulty of achieving a lasting settlement of the Kosovo conflict through military means. Stopping the anti-Albanian human-rights abuses, and even most of the open violence between both sides, was something that military force could achieve, however slowly. But force has not been able to bring all the enemies to the peace table to agree on a comprehensive solution to the Kosovo problem. Political and religious animosities are too strong, and historical memories too long. While this could have been foreseen prior to the war, it was a probability that NATO's leaders chose to ignore given how morally and politically unpalatable it seemed to them to refrain from intervening altogether. In light of Milosevic's intransigence and the quickening pace of ethnic cleansing by early 1999, the choices facing NATO were less than perfect. Had NATO chosen not to act, the Serbs would have succeeded in driving a large proportion of Albanians from Kosovo permanently, at a high cost in human lives and suffering. In acting militarily, NATO could at least stop human-rights violations, level the playing field within Kosovo itself between the Serb and Albanian factions, and create the conditions for a reasonably humane settlement of the conflict down the road.

Was War the Last Resort?

Did NATO exhaust all realistic peaceful alternatives prior to unleashing its military might? NATO imposed stringent economic sanctions on Serbia and put enormous diplomatic and political pressure on it to alter its policy in Kosovo. It appears that Serbian leader Slobodan Milosevic miscalculated NATO's resolve to use force and decided he could ignore NATO's non-military measures. By the time Milosevic realized that the NATO powers meant business, it was too late for him to compromise without forfeiting his domestic political credibility. This in turn suggests that Milosevic's authoritarian personality, his inability to assess realistically his chances, and the closed nature of his regime may have left NATO no reasonable alternative by early 1999 but to go to war. It is always plausible to argue that NATO could have persisted longer in using non-military means, and that perhaps Milosevic eventually would have given in, at least on the demand of protecting the human rights of the Albanian Kosovars. But this argument ignores the fact that, while the NATO powers waited, the onslaught in Kosovo would have continued. While the resort to war entailed human costs, so did inaction. In the end, one is left with as much ambiguity on this issue as with the previous ones. While the critics insist that NATO acted too fast and hard, NATO's defenders argue, with considerable plausibility, that the alliance had exhausted all realistic options short of force to achieve its humanitarian and security objectives.

Ius in Bello: Did NATO Use the Right Means in the Conduct of its War?

No matter how worthwhile the cause, states also have an obligation to use the right means in waging war. They have a moral obligation to wage war consistent with certain principles, and to refrain from certain practices. A just war must be fought justly. In the Western tradition, this dimension of the moral rightness of fighting a war is known as *ius in bello*. The two key elements of *ius in bello* are *proportionality* and *discrimination*. Proportionality is not "tit-for-tat." It is a subtler calculus that requires that the means employed, and the violence they generate, be roughly proportional to the evils the war sets out to eradicate. To take one example: Serbia's acts against the ethnic Albanians would not have justified Dresden-type terror bombing raids on Belgrade costing tens of thousands of lives. Even less would it have justified NATO's resort to nuclear weapons.

Discrimination is the requirement that military forces refrain from targeting noncombatants. In most wars, discrimination is more honored in the breach than in actual practice. Yet, tenuous as its hold is, and as contrary as it is to the claims of military necessity, discrimination is a vital barrier that helps to keep wars from pushing to the outer limits of barbarism to which they naturally tend. The foremost problem in applying the principle of discrimination is what is known as *collateral damage*, the harm that ensues to non-combatants as a result of military operations directed against seemingly legitimate military, industrial, and economic targets. Even in the age of precision weapons, smart bombs stray on hospitals, schools, and foreign embassies. Attacks on military installations and war-related factories kill innocent civilians who live and work nearby.

Worse yet, given the nature of modern warfare and its close dependence on economic, industrial, transportation, communications, and energy infrastructure, many of the targets that a belligerent will attack because of their close relationship to the war effort are also targets the destruction of which will cause untold suffering to the adversary's civilian population. A key example in both the Gulf War and the Kosovo intervention was the electrical grid, considered essential to the effectiveness of the Iraqi and Yugoslav military and therefore a legitimate military target. In both cases, attacks on the electrical grid caused enormous harm to the civilian population by hampering the functioning of hospitals, public utilities, and water-purification systems.

NATO's difficulties in fighting a proportionate and discriminate war against Serbia were compounded by several factors, all of them related to the democratic character of NATO's societies. Chief among these problems was the aversion to casualties. Democratic societies are willing to endure high numbers of casualties if the interests at stake are significant, especially if they confront a serious threat to their survival or to major tangible economic or strategic interests that the public can readily understand. But when it comes to interventions that the public perceives as mostly humanitarian, and only indirectly related to security interests, public tolerance for casualties is minimal. It took the loss of 18 U.S. soldiers in Somalia to convince the American government to end its intervention. In the subsequent interventions in Haiti and Bosnia, even though the security interests involved were more apparent than in Somalia, the Clinton administration still conducted its military operations with extreme care to avoid American casualties. In Kosovo, the same administration feared that even minimal losses would cause public support for the operation to crumble. President Clinton's situation was not helped by the fact that the opposition party controlled the

Senate and the House, and that a number of prominent congressmen immediately went on record to question and oppose the intervention. Among the various candidates for the Republican presidential nomination, only two, George W. Bush and John McCain, spoke in support of the administration's decision to intervene. A number of commentators have noted the discrepancy between NATO's lofty rhetoric justifying the Kosovo intervention and the unwillingness of NATO leaders to ask even the smallest sacrifices of their peoples.

The United States's aversion to casualties, shared in varying degrees by all of its NATO partners, complicated allied efforts to fight the war proportionately and discriminately.[14] Several examples illustrate this. From the outset, the NATO commander made it clear that this would be exclusively an air operation. When bombing alone proved inadequate to stop the ethnic cleansing, critics began to clamor for the introduction of Apache attack helicopters and ground troops. The debate continues to this day on whether this would have been a wise thing to do. Assuming that the forces could have deployed in a timely fashion (not an easy thing to do given the Cold War characteristics of the U.S. Army), ground troops would have put an end to Serbian atrocities more quickly and would have sent a powerful signal to Milosevic regarding NATO's will to prevail. But there would have been two serious drawbacks. First, sending in ground troops would have antagonized Russia, potentially destabilizing the government of Boris Yeltsin and fraying Russia's ties to the West. Second, in ground combat, NATO would inevitably have suffered casualties.

The Clinton administration, along with the rest of the allies, decided after a great deal of intra-allied debate and skirmishing, to persevere in the use of air power alone. While one may disagree with this decision, it is possible to see why reasonable people could have arrived at it. The grave error was to announce the decision in public, and to insist that under no circumstances would NATO change its strategy in the future. Doing so gave Milosevic a green light to continue Kosovo's accelerated ethnic cleansing, and led him to hope, mistakenly as it turned out, that the alliance, unwilling as it was to incur any serious costs for its campaign, might give up if the Serbs hung on long enough. Yet the reason President Clinton made the public announcement, and insisted on the unchangeable character of allied strategy, was to reassure the U.S. public and prevent Congressional opposition to the intervention from gathering momentum. Thus did an aversion to casualties lead the NATO powers to conduct the war in a way that undermined the allied objectives of a swift end to the violence and human-rights abuses in Kosovo. The announcement also lengthened the war itself by feeding Milosevic's intransigence and his erroneous assessment of Western political will. The cost of maintaining public support for the war within the NATO powers was to increase innocent suffering in Kosovo and Serbia proper as the war dragged on longer than necessary.

There was another unfortunate consequence of the aversion to casualties. Reliance on air power alone meant that for NATO to compel Milosevic to accept its terms it had to attack targets of value to the general civilian population, and it had to conduct those attacks in a way that placed non-combatants at risk. For example, even though the most appropriate targets would have been the Serbian military and security forces in Kosovo providing the support for ethnic cleansing, NATO found itself able to do little damage to these forces. Its air campaign failed, for example, to destroy Serbian armor or infantry units. Not only did NATO limit itself to air attacks, but to avoid casualties commanders restricted their missions to high altitudes. The Serbs took advantage of this by hiding their forces, complicating NATO's efforts to hit them. After several weeks of the most intensive bombing campaign recorded in Europe since the Second World War, NATO had managed to destroy only a small handful of tanks and had inflicted minimal casualties on Yugoslav infantry and paramilitary units.

Thus, the alliance turned its attention to Serbia's overall economic, industrial, transportation, communications, and utilities infrastructure. Targeting them just might put sufficient pressure on Milosevic to give up. Moreover, attacking the civilian infrastructure became NATO's only option given its unwillingness to use ground forces, Apache helicopters, or low-altitude bombing missions. Yet, these attacks also ran counter to, and severely undermined, NATO's political objectives of ending the war in Kosovo quickly, facilitating a long-term peace settlement, and encouraging Milosevic's replacement by a democratic Yugoslav government. At the same time that NATO was urging Serbs to overthrow Milosevic and opt for Western-style democracy, the alliance was raining bombs on Belgrade and making life miserable for millions of innocents. Although the attacks hurt the civilian population, they did not do much damage to the Milosevic regime. In some ways, they strengthened Milosevic by giving him nationalist, patriotic ammunition while leaving his forces in Kosovo with impunity to continue their ethnic cleansing campaign. Far from shortening the war, the NATO strategy lengthened it unnecessarily. Moreover, the destruction of civilian infrastructure will slow down considerably future efforts to build an economically prosperous, democratic Serbia.

Morally, one of the great contradictions involved in NATO's conduct of the war was its tacit decision to value the lives of its soldiers above those of the enemy's non-combatants, including even those ethnic Albanians on behalf of whom NATO launched its humanitarian intervention. Yet this is not altogether new. Governments at war routinely design military operations to reduce casualties among their own forces at the expense of increasing non-combatant deaths and suffering on the enemy side. In the Kosovo War, however, this otherwise routine practice seemed jarring given the supposedly humanitarian nature of the intervention. Speaking in their own defense, NATO leaders argued that the bombing campaign against Serbia's infrastructure was carried out with as much precision as possible, with the objective of destroying material targets but sparing human lives. It was the best they could do, they claimed, to avoid the collapse of public support that would have ensued had NATO itself suffered casualties.

Finally, one of the more tantalizing moral questions NATO faced as it fought the war was whether it should target President Milosevic with a view to killing him. There were those who argued at the war's outset that Milosevic, as commander in chief of the Yugoslav military, was a legitimate target. They also pointed out that Milosevic was the main culprit of the war and the chief obstacle to its settlement; hence, targeting Milosevic seemed more justifiable than targeting thousands of innocent Serbs.

Proposals to target Milosevic ran counter to a centuries-long Western tradition that has looked askance at killing heads of state during wartime. Only during that bitterest of total wars, World War II, did this tradition weaken when Allied leaders contemplated assassinating Adolf Hitler.[15] At the height of the Cold War, neither the Americans nor the Soviets attempted to kill the other side's political leaders, though they did not apply this prohibition to political leaders of smaller countries that might defect to the rival alliance. In the early 1960s, the U.S. government attempted several times to assassinate Fidel Castro, and the Soviet Union murdered Imre Nagy, who was acting as head of the Hungarian government following the November 1956 revolution. In 1975 President Ford signed an executive order forbidding any U.S. government agency from carrying out assassination attempts against foreign heads of state, thereby vindicating the honored tradition of refraining from such acts. The tradition, however, suffered setbacks subsequently when the United States targeted Libya's Muammar Ghaddafi in 1986 and Iraq's Saddam Hussein in 1991, in both cases unsuccessfully.

On balance, the traditional prohibition on killing heads of state is still strong. During the early stages of the Kosovo intervention NATO rejected calls to target Milosevic. But as the ethnic cleansing campaign in Kosovo intensified and Milosevic showed no signs of giving up, NATO decided to step up its air attacks against high-profile political targets. Eventually, NATO attacked the key government-controlled television station in Belgrade as well as one of Milosevic's better known residences. By then Milosevic knew that he was likely to be targeted and was careful about his whereabouts. NATO never succeeded in killing him, and it appears that NATO never really tried—the attack on his residence was more symbolic than substantive. It was not intended to kill him but to let him know that NATO was serious about achieving its objectives, and that in the end NATO would hold him personally responsible for war crimes in Kosovo.

The Kosovo War raises the question of whether the new kinds of weapons associated with the "Revolution in Military Affairs" impose a qualitatively new set of moral obligations. The availability of precision weapons has raised expectations about the feasibility of minimizing collateral damage. And with those higher expectations has come a higher moral standard, with the more technologically sophisticated Western powers expected to use high precision weaponry in such a way as to keep civilian casualties to a minimum. At the same time, however, Western public opinion has come to expect that the new kinds of weapons also make it possible to avoid casualties among one's own soldiers. Thus, two new sets of moral expectations are at play: a reduction in enemy civilian casualties, and a reduction in casualties among one's own military forces. These two sets of expectations are not easy to reconcile. In Kosovo, the tension was resolved in favor of minimizing losses among one's military forces. This implied refraining from using ground troops or Apache helicopters, flying bombing missions at high altitudes, and focusing on the destruction of military-industrial-infrastructure targets most susceptible to air attack.

One should not read too much into the ostensible requirement to keep enemy civilian casualties low. That requirement is likely to hold only so long as the war is short, its objectives limited, and the enemy unable or unwilling to deliver a major blow to U.S. and allied forces. If any one of those three conditions were to change, public opinion in Western countries would likely support less discriminate strategies that might increase the pressure on the enemy to give up. Had Milosevic persisted longer, or had he used missiles or weapons of mass destruction against NATO forces, there would have been considerable pressure within NATO countries for an even more intense bombing campaign even if it meant larger numbers of Serb civilian casualties.

Implications for the Morally Responsible Use of American Power

America's unchallenged global power at the opening of the twenty-first century has prompted many to argue that the United States today enjoys a unique opportunity to fulfill the Wilsonian dream of remaking the world in America's image. Among conservatives, the argument has been made most forcefully by William Kristol and Robert Kagan of the Project for the New American Century, and among liberals by former Secretary of State Madeleine Albright. As they see it, the United States and its allies are strong, the enemies of liberalism are on the defensive, and there are plenty of opportunities where a limited investment of American resources can make a substantial difference. The world may never again be so pliable, and action now may help to move at least some regions of the world in directions more congruent with long-term American interests and values.

Assuming that this is, indeed, a historic opportunity for the United States to advance liberal democratic values, how can the United States do so in a morally responsible fashion? Thucydides' *History of the Peloponnesian War* poignantly reminds us of the follies and hubris of which even the greatest, most exalted democracies are capable in peace and war. Like Athens in its golden heyday of the Periclean Era, the United States today faces great dangers as well as great opportunities. The opportunities to use its power to accomplish good are matched by the dangers that the United States will wield its power irresponsibly, thereby diminishing its credibility and undermining the very values it seeks to spread. The Kosovo intervention amply illustrates this quandary.

The Kosovo intervention highlighted some of the political and moral complications that an overly passionate embrace of Wilsonianism can produce. By supporting and leading NATO's intervention in Kosovo, the United States went on record in favor of a world of dissolving sovereignty barriers, a world in which notions of an international moral consensus can override the claims of individual nation-states. This development is a double-edged sword. On the one hand, American statesmen cite the world's growing interdependence and the decline of state sovereignty when they push the American agenda on trade, democratization, and human rights, especially in places where doing so serves the interests of the United States or involves minimal costs. But the Wilsonian appeals seem hypocritical, and undermine American credibility, when the United States resists the Wilsonian logic on issues where its application does not serve America's own interests.

President George H. W. Bush's rhetoric about a "New World Order" and his successor's humanitarian interventions have raised expectations that the United States will strengthen the norms of an international community. But recent American decisions to vote against an International Criminal Court, to refuse to ratify the Comprehensive Ban Treaty, and to maintain sanctions on Cuba with the support of only two other UN members send a different message. They suggest that the United States brandishes Wilsonianism selectively, on the basis of considerations as pragmatic or cynical as those of any other country in the world. This would not be so bad if American leaders in the Wilsonian tradition were not also insisting so earnestly that America is not just another great power, but a uniquely benevolent nation destined by history to lead the rest of the world toward a new moral order. What damages American credibility is not that the United States acts in accordance with its interests, but that it claims to be more disinterested than anyone else. There is a marked discrepancy, for example, between the vigorous American demands that Milosevic be tried by the Hague Tribunal for his crimes in Bosnia and Kosovo, and the equally dogged U.S. refusal to accede to the creation of an International Crimes Tribunal.

The Kosovo intervention also provided reminders that humanitarian interventions are not risk-free. The costs of Kosovo easily could have been much higher. Assume that Slobodan Milosevic, whose military forces were not being seriously damaged by NATO's air campaign, had decided not to yield. Eventually, NATO would have had to use ground troops. In spite of mounting casualties, NATO would have had to persevere, even as domestic opposition to the intervention increased. Assume also that Russia, seeing its credibility at stake, had dispatched forces to create a "cordon sanitaire" on the Kosovo-Serbia border, or within Kosovo itself, to prevent NATO forces from pushing far into either Kosovo or Serbia. These developments were well within the realm of the possible and suggest how quickly the Kosovo intervention could have escalated into a broader conflict that, at a minimum, would have done lasting damage to Russia's relations with Europe and the United States.

Kosovo also suggests that, although Wilsonianism and the concept of humanitarian intervention bound up with it seem attractive options for a powerful United States, their practical application can be morally troubling. As pointed out earlier, the advanced military technologies associated with the "Revolution in Military Affairs" gave NATO the unusual option of fighting the war solely from the air without having to put combat troops on the ground. This had several regrettable consequences. First, because NATO was not incurring any significant risks or losses, it was difficult for the public to appreciate what was really at stake in the conflict. The public, in fact, was prepared to "cut and run" at any moment if the military operations did not go well. There was a morally absurd contrast between the high-sounding rhetoric of Western leaders about the mission's idealistic goals, and the costs they and their peoples were willing to pay to attain these goals.

Second, the alluring prospect of fighting without casualties meant that NATO was willing to proceed deliberately, thereby permitting the Serbs ample time to complete their campaign of ethnic cleansing. During the long weeks of the air campaign, the Serbs moved ruthlessly to uproot as many ethnic Albanians as possible. Along with the ethnic cleansing went an unprecedented degree of rape, looting, and murder. In initiating force against Serbia, NATO should have contemplated the possibility that, with their backs against the wall and little to lose, the Serbs would be tempted to destroy the Albanian presence in Kosovo once and for all so as to make an Albanian-free Kosovo an irreversible fait accompli. NATO's failure to anticipate this development, and even worse, its failure to act once it became apparent that it was happening, was morally irresponsible to a high degree.

Third, the seemingly "cheap" option of fighting a war without casualties may have profound long-term systemic consequences, as Carl Cavanagh Hodge persuasively has argued.[16] The notion of "war without casualties" has chipped away at the firewall laboriously built up throughout the twentieth century against the casual use of military force. To the extent that they view Kosovo as a "success," political leaders may come to view the use of force through air power as a sanitized instrument of statecraft requiring few moral scruples and no international sanctioning.

The breakdown of the firewall poses long-term dangers to the stability of the international system. Any use of force, no matter how sanitized, carries a high risk of escalation. It was Clausewitz who, almost two centuries ago, recognized that even limited wars, those conflicts in which "the statesman seeks to turn the terrible two-handed sword that is war into the lightest rapier, fit only for thrusts and parries," can degenerate into bitter, all-out general war as the passions of the people are aroused and outside parties intervene.[17] While the risk of such escalation may have been low in Kosovo, it will not always be so. Inevitably, as enthusiasm for "casual war" or "sanitized war" spreads, some statesman somewhere is bound to miscalculate its consequences, and what was conceived as a self-contained conflict will escalate and draw in great power antagonists. The Viennese statesmen who contemplated a limited punitive strike against Serbia in 1914 had no idea of the global conflagration they were about to kindle.

At a higher level of analysis, Kosovo offers us some general reminders for the United States at a time when its power, and therefore its moral obligations, have never been greater. The exercise of power in this broken world, even for the noblest values, is bound to be a messy affair, full of paradoxes, unintended consequences, ample doses of inconsistency and hypocrisy, and ultimately falling considerably short of expectations. That said, hopes that the United States will use its power responsibly should entail several things.

First, a restoration of rhetorical modesty is necessary. There is no escaping that the United States, exceptional as it is in some ways, is still a fallen, sinful society, to use the language of Christian realism with which readers of Reinhold Niebuhr and Herbert Butterfield are familiar. We are as eager to put our interests at the center of our global agenda as any other state, and as easily able as anyone else to deceive ourselves about the extent to which our interests correspond with those of the rest of the world. One problem with Wilsonianism is that its proponents tend to forget this and become seduced by their own rhetoric. Our allies and friends are prepared to respect us when we make a case for policies that benefit us as well as them, but our sanctimony erodes our credibility and elicits their resentment when we speak as if our actions are guided entirely by disinterestedness. The language with which a great power speaks, as Theodore Roosevelt well understood, is central to its leadership. More often than not, Wilsonian rhetoric weakens rather than enhances our leadership through its hubris and self-righteousness, though this is far more obvious to the rest of the world than it is to us. A sense of modesty would help to counteract this weakness.

Second, in future humanitarian interventions American statesmen will need to consider more rigorously whether the ends to be achieved are worth the destruction caused by war, and whether the constraints of "sanitized war"—war fought solely through long-range precision strikes—are suitable to the war's particular political objectives. Even if one agrees that NATO was right to fight the Kosovo War exactly as it did, on future occasions, given the nature of the enemy's strategy or U.S. political objectives, the United States will not always have the option of fighting a "casualty-free" war. On those occasions, it will be incumbent upon American leaders to understand the limits of "sanitized wars," lest they employ means that are inappropriate, impossible, or counterproductive to the moral goals and political objectives being pursued.

Does NATO's Kosovo War of 1999 suggest the creation of a new set of international norms? It is difficult to determine the extent to which Kosovo may be a harbinger of future humanitarian wars as opposed to being an isolated incident. Two or three decades from now, Kosovo may appear as a significant milestone in the evolution of international politics, law and morality in the post–Cold War world. Or it may be seen instead as an aberration, an episode that, controversial though it was, remains unique. Only time will tell. In either case, Kosovo will claim significance because of the moral and political debates surrounding it, debates about what kind of international society the United States and its allies ought to nurture, who should make its rules, and how the rules should be enforced.[18]

The debate generated by the Kosovo intervention revolves around two conceptions of international order, each of which has profound implications for future American foreign policy. One side of the debate argues that Kosovo embodies a new trend in international politics, in which a few states, often led by the United States, will undertake joint military action to prevent aggression and extreme human-rights violations. Intrinsic to America's moral responsibilities as a great power is the obligation to shape the norms of international society. This obligation includes the use of American economic, political and military power to help move international society in the direction of greater security and respect for human rights. Occasionally, a humanitarian intervention supported by America's full military might will be necessary to uphold these values.[19]

On the other side of this debate are those who view the Kosovo War as bad news. These critics divide into two camps. Among American conservatives, there are critics who insist that Kosovo, insofar as it is a precedent, is an insidious one. The United States should be careful not to associate itself with the notion of a world of dissolving sovereignty barriers, lest this notion come back to haunt it in the form of future restraints on American unilateralism. According to this argument, humanitarian interventions such as those in Kosovo are not only wasteful and distracting from America's core strategic priorities. They also give the misguided impression that the United States supports the establishment of some form of transnational normative system, under UN or NATO sponsorship, that will ultimately trump American sovereignty and hem in American power.[20]

A second camp of critics make a different set of arguments. On the American left are those who claim that Kosovo's precedent is bad, precisely because it endows America with dangerous prerogatives. In this view, the Kosovo intervention gives the United States wide latitude to interfere in the internal affairs of other states and the excuse to maintain the world's mightiest military establishment.[21] According to these critics, Kosovo also feeds American exceptionalism and perpetuates the bogus notion of the United States as a uniquely benevolent, disinterested power. For these critics, the Kosovo intervention was tainted because it was led by the United States; a humanitarian intervention sanctioned by the United Nations could well have been legitimate and appropriate.

Whether Kosovo turns out to be an aberration or the start of a powerful new trend in world politics, the United States and its allies will confront future humanitarian crises that invite intervention. As they ponder such situations, American statesmen would do well to keep in mind the moral complexities surrounding Kosovo. The key will be not to draw simple lessons from NATO's apparent success, but to reflect soberly on the risks, ambiguities, and shortcomings. Great care will be necessary in determining whether military force is the best instrument to right the evils in question. Much deliberation will be needed to calculate whether the good produced by the forcible intervention will outweigh the totality of human, moral, and economic costs. In addition, American leaders will confront the conundrum of fighting with due regard to the principles of proportionality and discrimination while treating the avoidance of friendly casualties as an important goal but never an absolute one. As the chief provider of forces for such an operation, the United States will exercise decisive influence on the type of strategy that is adopted. One of America's responsibilities will to avoid a repetition of some of the more unfortunate aspects of the Kosovo campaign. Good intentions are not enough. Equally important will be competence, foresight, avoiding the hubris to which our technology makes us so vulnerable, and not underestimating the adversary. In other words, those who claim to use military force for good ends have a moral responsibility to use force wisely, and this includes taking into account the irrationality, unpredictability, and the Clausewitzian fog and friction that make war a less than perfect instrument of politics. This kind of strategic humility will be essential to the morally responsible use of American power in a new century.

Notes

1. For discussions of the intellectual origins of Wilsonianism, see David M. Fitzsimons, "Tom Paine's New World Order: Idealistic Internationalism in the Ideology of Early American Foreign Relations," *Diplomatic* History 19, no. 4 (fall 1995): 569–82; and Walter MacDougall, *Promised Land, Crusader State: The American Encounter with the World Since 1776* (Boston, Mass.: Houghton Mifflin, 1997).

2. "Powell Intends to Curb US Use of Diplomatic Sanctions," *Los Angeles Times*, 22 January 2001, p. 1.

3. For the controversy surrounding the estimates of lives actually saved, see Coll, *The Problems of Doing Good: Somalia as a Case Study in Humanitarian Intervention* (New York: Carnegie Council on Ethics and International Affairs, 1997).

4. For two classic discussions of "just war theory" and the just-war tradition, see Paul Ramsey, *The Just War: Force and Political Responsibility* (Princeton, N.J.: Princeton University Press, 1968) and Michael Walzer, *Just and Unjust Wars* (Cambridge, Mass.: Harvard University Press, 1977).

5. "Bush Warns Serbs Not to Widen War," *New York Times*, 28 December 1992.

6. William Joseph Buckley, ed., *Kosovo: Contending Voices on Balkan Interventions* (Grand Rapids, Mich.: William B. Eerdmans, 2000), p. 4.

7. See the Melian Dialogue at the end of Book 5 of Thucydides' *History of the Peloponnesian War*.

8. For a discussion of the classic theory of humanitarian intervention as developed by Vitoria and Suarez in the sixteenth century, see Alberto R. Coll, *The Western Heritage and American Values: Law, Theology and History* (Lanham, Md.: University Press of America, 1982).

9. For a comprehensive discussion of the question of humanitarian intervention from different historical and philosophical perspectives, see Laura W. Reed and Carl Kaysen, *Emerging Norms of Justified Intervention* (Cambridge, Mass.: American Academy of Arts and Sciences, 1993). The ethical issues in the contemporary debate over the place of humanitarian intervention in American foreign policy are reviewed most lucidly in Michael J. Smith, "Humanitarian Intervention: An Overview of the Ethical Issues," *Ethics and International Affairs* (1998): 63–79.

10. Michael Walzer, "Kosovo," *Dissent* (Summer 1999), reprinted in William Joseph Buckley, ed., *Kosovo: Contending Voices on Balkan Interventions* (Grand Rapids, Mich.: William B. Eerdmans, 2000), p. 335.

11. "Secretary-General Presents His Annual Report to General Assembly," UN Press Release SG/SM/7136, GA/9596, 20 September 20 1999, cited in Richard J. Goldstone, *Kosovo: An Assessment in the Context of International Law*, Nineteenth Morgenthau Memorial Lecture on Ethics and Foreign Policy (New York: Carnegie Council on Ethics and International Affairs, 2000).

12. See Craig R. Whitney (with Eric Schmitt), "NATO Had Signs Its Strategy Would Fail Kosovars," *New York Times*, 1 April 1999, p. A1.

13. Buckley, *Kosovo*, p. 9.

14. Among the NATO powers there was a "spectrum of hawkishness" regarding their willingness to suffer casualties, with the British government being the most outspoken in favor of the use of ground troops, and the United States and Germany at the other end of the spectrum opposing any measures that might raise the risks. For an interesting study on the issue of casualties and public opinion, see Charles K. Hyde, "Casualty Aversion: Implications for Policymakers and Senior Military Officers," *Essays 2000: Chairman of the Joint Chiefs of Staff Strategy Essay Competition* (Washington, D.C.: National Defense University Press, 2000), pp. 1–16.

15. The successful American plan to kill Admiral Yamamoto in 1943 did not violate the taboo against killing heads of state. Yamamoto was a senior military commander, not Japan's political leader.

16. Carl Cavanagh Hodge, "Casual War: NATO's Intervention in Kosovo," *Ethics and International Affairs* 14 (2000): 39–54. See also the interesting discussion by Martin Cook in the same volume, "'Immaculate War': Constraints on Humanitarian Intervention," 55–66.

17. Carl von Clausewitz, *On War*, Book 8, ed. and trans. Michael Howard and Peter Paret (Princeton, N.J.: Princeton University Press, 1976), p. 606.

18. For a discussion of this debate in the context of the views of the new Bush Administration, see James Traub, "Downsizing Foreign Policy," *New York Times Magazine*, 14 January 2001, pp. 28–34.

19. For articulate presentations of this viewpoint, see Richard N. Haass, *The Reluctant Sheriff: The United States After the Cold War* (New York: Brookings Institution Press, 1997); Chester Crocker, "The Lessons of Somalia," *Foreign Affairs* (May–June 1995); and Andrew Natsios, "Humanitarian Emergencies and Moral Choice," *American Purpose* (Winter 2000).

20. For an exponent of this viewpoint, see Marc A. Thiessen, "When Worlds Collide," *Foreign Policy* (March–April 2001): 64–74.

21. Noam Chomsky, *The New Military Humanism: Lessons from Kosovo* (Monroe, Maine: Common Courage Press, 1999).

6   Neglected Trinity: Kosovo and the Crisis in U.S. Civil-Military Relations

Andrew J. Bacevich

I

In the annals of U.S. military history the war for Kosovo stands out as a singularly peculiar episode. Among other things, the war produced more than its share of "firsts." It was, famously, the first war that U.S. forces fought to its conclusion without sustaining a single combat casualty. Indeed, for the policymakers who conceived Operation Allied Force and the commanders who directed it, minimizing the risk to allied soldiers seemingly took precedence over both their obligation to safeguard Serb noncombatants and their interest in protecting the ethnic Albanians whose plight provided the ostensible rationale for intervention.[1] American officials described that intervention as a *moral* imperative. Yet before the conflict had even ended observers were wondering if the United States had turned moral tradition on its head, with combatants rather than noncombatants provided immunity from the effects of fighting.[2]

Reflecting in part this pronounced sensitivity to casualties, Kosovo was also the first American conflict in which the commander in chief at the very outset offered public assurances that the adversary need not fear suffering the full weight of U.S. military power. As the bombing commenced, President Bill Clinton on March 24, 1999 told the nation and the world, "I do not intend to put our troops in Kosovo to fight a war." By foreclosing the option of introducing ground troops, the president made it unmistakably clear that NATO would restrict itself to conducting a standoff war. Hallowed bits of military doctrine—for example, the supposed requirement to "close with and destroy the enemy"—did not apply.

The overriding priority assigned to force protection inevitably called into question other presidential statements, namely, that crucial U.S. interests were at stake in Kosovo and that the United States and its allies were determined to "persist until we prevail."[3] The circumspect language employed to explain NATO's military objectives did little to help. "Our goal is to exact a very high price for Mr. Milosevic's policy of repression," Mr. Clinton announced during the war's first days, "and to seriously diminish his military capacity to maintain that policy."[4] Commanding the world's most capable military machine, backed by a formidable array of allies, the president studiously refrained from suggesting that NATO sought anything so definitive as the actual "defeat" of Yugoslavia.

Such radical departures from military convention—renouncing the most ordinary instruments of combat, reviving the long-discredited principle of gradual escalation, avoiding any mention of victory as an objective, indeed, avoiding the term "war" altogether—distressed senior American military officers, already leery of deepening the U.S. involvement in the Balkans. So the war for Kosovo also broke new ground in the swiftness with which it exposed rifts between senior soldiers and their civilian masters. As soon as it became apparent that the campaign would last beyond the four or five days initially expected, leaks emanating from the Pentagon were signaling the military's extreme dissatisfaction with the way that civilians were orchestrating the war against Yugoslavia.[5]

Even the campaign's ultimately successful outcome did not restore civil-military comity. Indeed, Kosovo prompted complaints of civilian interference—voiced openly by serving officers—not heard since Vietnam. A widely circulated postmortem prepared by Admiral James O. Ellis, commanding U.S. naval forces in Europe, lamented that an otherwise well-executed air campaign had been "politically constrained." Among the adverse effects, according to Ellis, were a tendency toward "incremental war" and excessive concerns about collateral damage. Political considerations had also needlessly complicated efforts to implement "NATO out-of-charter operations."[6] Similarly, in a postwar interview, Lieutenant General Michael C. Short, who directed the air war, complained of being "constrained in this particular conflict to an extraordinary degree." Political restrictions had prevented Short "from conducting an air campaign as professional airmen would have wanted to conduct it."[7]

In fairness to Short, civilian intrusion into operational matters did, in certain respects, recall Vietnam. Before striking targets in Serbia deemed especially sensitive, military commanders found themselves obliged to gain clearance from high-ranking civilian officials, including in some instances Clinton himself. Throughout the campaign, according to the *Washington Post*, "Generals raced across the Potomac River with satchels of targets to get the White House to approve the next night's work." Among senior military officers, the perception of civilian meddling roused unhappy memories. Short, himself a veteran of the Vietnam War, worried about getting "into something like the Rolling Thunder campaign, pecking away indefinitely" while public support gradually ebbed away.[8]

Whether or not civilians were guilty of inappropriate meddling, senior officers could justifiably conclude that in the Clinton White House their own professional counsel was not in high demand. Whatever their actual opinion of the advice rendered, every president since World War II has made a point in times of crisis of "consulting" with the Joint Chiefs of Staff. Throughout the Cold War, the image of a grim-faced commander in chief surrounded by beribboned four-stars as he announced some portentous new decision had been a stock part of American political theater. Here too Kosovo marked a departure, ringing down the curtain on this hoary old tradition.

Rather than consulting the Joint Chiefs collectively, Bill Clinton relied for professional advice (as he had in lesser military contingencies throughout his presidency) almost exclusively on the chairman of the Joint Chiefs of Staff—in 1999, General Henry H. Shelton. A seasoned and dutiful soldier, Shelton is by all reports not the type to make waves. Described by one newspaper as "the general who speaks when spoken to," he possesses little of the flair, political savvy, or media presence of a Colin Powell—indeed, the Clinton administration may well have appointed him for that very reason. With a compliant Joint Chiefs of Staff chairman reportedly "unwilling—or unable—to air the Pentagon's misgivings about the war," the White House managed the campaign according to its own lights.[9]

Kosovo may well have sealed the demise of another tradition as well, one stretching across a bloody century in which Americans frequently found themselves called upon to fight, but in which the United States itself was spared the direct experience of war. As a matter of course, throughout that century, whenever American soldiers ventured into harm's way American journalists went with them, not infrequently at considerable personal risk. Charged with explaining war to readers largely insulated from its impact, the very best reporters did so by documenting the experience of their fellow citizens in military service—flesh-and-blood Americans with actual names and real hometowns. On behalf of a worthy cause, the vivid and intimate reporting of an Ernie Pyle or an A. J. Liebling helped sustain popular support for the war effort, forging a bond between citizens and soldiers. In the case of a more dubious enterprise, press coverage could undermine that support, as Pyle's successors did in bearing witness to the experience of American soldiers in Vietnam. In every case, however, by reporting the war from the field, journalists made it next to impossible for those on the home front to ignore or take for granted the sacrifices of those actually doing the fighting.

Not so with the war for Kosovo. In this conflict, citing security concerns, senior commanders restricted the journalistic coverage of the war, thereby erecting a barrier between those serving in the combat zone and those following the war from the comfort of their living room.[10] Interviews with pilots flying combat missions over Yugoslavia were kept to a bare minimum. Personal information such as names and hometowns was off-limits. This did not mean that the war went unreported. But instead of American soldiers themselves framing the story, attention shifted to the relentlessly upbeat news briefings conducted in Washington or Brussels and to the suffering of ethnic Albanian refugees or of Serb civilians victimized by errant allied bombs (neither of which corroborated official claims that all was well).

To the extent that journalists were permitted to glimpse American servicemembers "in action," their reports did little to promote understanding, much less empathy. A revealing wartime dispatch in the *New York Times* typifies the result. Visiting the destroyer *Gonzales*, periodically lobbing cruise missiles toward Serbia from its station in the Adriatic, the *Times* reporter discovers there "the face of modern warfare: antiseptic, distant, impersonal." A montage of accompanying photos shows various American sailors—all of them nameless—"pumping iron" in the ship's exercise room, taking a smoke break below decks, posing in dress uniform for cruise-book portraits, and gazing at "a buffet that could be in Las Vegas as easily as the Adriatic."[11] Who are these people? Where do they come from? What precisely are they contributing either to preserving U.S. national security or to the eradication of ethnic cleansing? Why should we care about them? On these matters, the reader—and perhaps the reporter as well—remains unenlightened.

Another factor further complicated the average citizen's efforts to make sense of Kosovo. Signposts of sound thinking once deemed authoritative, whatever one's political persuasion, now pointed every which way. In the

overlapping worlds of intellectuals, pundits, and political ideologues, disagreement over the most fundamental questions—whether the war was
moral or immoral, necessary or unnecessary, a success or a failure—demolished longstanding alignments and overturned views once deemed sacrosanct. The result was not simply that hawks and doves reversed their usual
roles. The war for Kosovo scrambled the political line-up, creating odd alliances between figures who had stood for decades on opposite sides of the
barricades. Old radicals like Tom Hayden, archconservatives like Patrick
Buchanan, and libertarians like Ted Galen Carpenter all railed against "liberal humanitarian imperialism run amok." On the Right, Trent Lott, the
Senate Majority Leader, called on President Clinton to "Give peace a
chance." On the Left, Todd Gitlin, veteran of the 1960s antiwar movement,
enthused about the potential uses of American military power. "Just wars are
not only possible, but legion," he proclaimed.[12] Meanwhile, David Rieff, a
journalist of impeccably Left liberal pedigree, could be found doing a pass-
able imitation of Henry Kissinger: "you send your F-15 to help the Kosovars
and what it does is it blows up a bunch of children in a hospital. It is
inevitable. That's what war is. We've made a lot of claims for ourselves, for
our societies and for our moral aspirations. But without force or the threat
of force, they're hollow ideas."[13]

By the time the war finally wound down in June, Americans had effectively decided that it no longer merited their attention. When in the weeks
following the end of hostilities the air squadrons that carried the brunt of
the fight rotated back from the war zone, their return failed to cross the
threshold of newsworthiness. If newspapers reported the troops' homecom-
ing at all, they did so via brief, colorless wire service dispatches, buried in
the inside pages. Sports teams that *lose* the Super Bowl or the NCAA bas-
ketball championship receive a warmer welcome upon returning home than
did the Americans who *won* the war for Kosovo. In present-day America,
even the runner-up in a major sports competition qualifies as a celebrity. In
contrast, the aviators who conducted—and won—the air campaign against
Yugoslavia remain even today shrouded in anonymity. Indeed, the war for
Kosovo also broke new ground by being the first American conflict not to
produce a single bona fide hero.[14]

Even the campaign's chief architects reaped few of the accolades that
normally accompany victory. Publishers suppressed any impulse to pony up
a Schwarzkopf- or Powell-style advance for the wartime recollections of
General Wesley K. Clark, the officer commanding all NATO forces. In-

deed, when in the war's immediate aftermath General Clark appeared in Washington, he found himself not basking in the adulation proffered by a joint session of Congress but being grilled by notably frosty members of the Senate Armed Services Committee.[15] Soon thereafter, Clark was, if not exactly sacked, shoved unceremoniously into early retirement. Voices protesting the ingratitude implied by his treatment were notable by their absence. As for the triumphant commander in chief, far from being rewarded with a "bounce" in the polls, Bill Clinton actually saw his approval rating dip.[16]

In the end, Kosovo qualifies as peculiar because as "a war waged from 15,000 feet and fought mainly for humanitarian principles" it failed to engage the passions of the people.[17] For most Americans, Kosovo was a *distraction* and not really a very important one at that. In the 1990s, the nation's real business lay precisely where Calvin Coolidge had located it in the 1920s. As if to emphasize that point, during the 78-day campaign the Dow Jones industrial average not only broke 10,000 points for the first time, but continued to advance through the 11,000 point barrier. Thus, when the war finally concluded, the nation showed no inclination to organize tickertape parades to celebrate "V-K Day." Befuddled, impatient, and slightly embarrassed, Americans instead gave a sigh of relief, purged from memory the odd bits of knowledge acquired about Serbia and its history, and gratefully turned their attention back to more important things.

II

Yet however peculiar Kosovo appears when contrasted with previous episodes in American military history, it is not simply a momentary aberration, a lapse never to be repeated. Nor does it signify an abrupt departure from established practice. On the contrary, for all of its apparent novelty, the war for Kosovo offers the fullest expression yet of changes in U.S. national security policy that had been underway throughout the decade following the end of the Cold War.

As Eliot A. Cohen suggests elsewhere in this volume, the campaign waged for Kosovo reveals the outlines of a "new American way of war," heralding the role of U.S. military power in the aftermath of the Cold War. The purpose of this essay, which builds on Cohen's thesis, is threefold. First, it identifies the origins of this new style of warfare, attributing it to a seemingly incompatible mix of large strategic aspirations and formidable domestic constraints, largely cultural in nature. Second, it argues that efforts to reconcile this disparity between strategy and culture have necessitated a profound realignment in the relationship between the state, the military, and the American people. That is, instituting a new way of war has entailed a commensurate transformation of civil-military relations. Finally, it suggests that national security policies based on this new civil-military paradigm are inherently flawed and are likely to prove unsustainable if not downright pernicious.

More broadly, the essay takes issue with the tendency, increasingly prevalent since Operation Desert Storm, to neglect the nontechnological dimensions of war. If anything, the war for Kosovo—reputedly won by air power alone—has reinforced this inclination to see armed conflict largely as the application of advanced technology. Americans take comfort from such a view: sustaining the nation's technological edge—in intelligence collection and analysis, command and control, strategic mobility, and long-range precision strike—will seemingly guarantee continuing U.S. military supremacy with minimal exertion and sacrifice. But such expectations are dangerously misleading.

Such, at least, is the view implied by the greatest Western philosopher of war, Carl von Clausewitz. In his classic work *On War*, Clausewitz all but ignored technological considerations, identifying instead three distinct but intertwined "tendencies" that govern armed conflict. Together, according to Clausewitz, these three tendencies—reason, primordial violence, and chance—comprise a "remarkable trinity." Conceiving through careful deliberation the ends that necessarily guide the conduct of war is, according to Clausewitz, the province of the *state* and its political leadership. War implies the use of force in pursuit of those ends. Force derives its efficacy from the passions of the *people*. The creativity required to harness that violence to policy—and to do so despite the physically and psychologically daunting reality of combat—defines the realm of the *army* and its commander. To wage war effectively—and by extension to create sound military institutions—the elements of this trinity must exist in harmony with one another. According to Clausewitz, students of warfare who disregard any of the three or who impose a fixed and arbitrary relationship between them misconstrue the nature of their subject. A military policy that neglects the relationships embodied in Clausewitz's trinity courts disaster.[18]

Formulated in an age when kings and emperors still dominated politics, Clausewitz's insight becomes even more pertinent in an age of democracy and for a democratic superpower such as the United States. Indeed, far more than any other factor, the changing nature of this coupling of state, people, and army accounts for the rise and fall and restoration of American military power during the momentous half-century that began when Germany invaded Poland and ended with the fall of the Berlin Wall. During the first decade of the new era that began with the end of the Cold War, further changes in that relationship—largely unnoted—are reshaping the character of U.S. military power.

To understand the significance of those changes requires a basic understanding of the history of American civil-military relations.

The theme of the earliest (and longest) chapter of that history was anti-militarism. A suspicion of things military formed part of the American birth-right, predating even the founding of the republic. Among the Founders, the belief that standing armies were antithetical to liberty was commonplace, hence, the preference for relying chiefly on politically reliable *citizen*-sol-diers rather than regulars to defend the nation. That belief persisted for generations. Among Americans generally—pragmatic, individualistic, and (to a degree) egalitarian—the professional soldier's taste for pomp, hierarchy, and iron discipline was anathema. The approach to civil-military relations devised in response to these considerations was based on the principles of wariness and strict supervision. The objective was less to provide for effective military policy than to guarantee absolute civilian control. Consistent with the terms of this model, the United States had habitually maintained in peacetime the smallest possible regular army, confined the officer corps to the periphery of public life, and relied on a militia of dubious military value as the chief instrument for national defense. To the extent that officers oc-cupied themselves with activities related to national development—explor-ing the West, building canals, and developing railroads and harbors—they earned the gratitude of their fellow citizens. But gratitude was not to be confused with status or clout. This republican model of civil-military rela-tions served the United States well through 1898 and survived even during the period following World War I.

The coming of World War II spelled the demise of this republican model. A relationship based on an instinctive aversion to all things military did not suit the needs of an industrialized democracy compelled to raise a massive military establishment. Even before the United States entered the war, states-men like Henry L. Stimson and generals like George C. Marshall were collaborating in the creation of a new liberal democratic model of civil-military relations. The guiding principles of this new model were respect and reciprocity. The new compact served purposes that extended well beyond the immediate needs of national defense: It succeeded because it worked to the mutual benefit of all three elements of Clausewitz's trinity.

For example, the "way of war" to which the United States subscribed throughout the conflict not only provided a suitable means to achieve victory, but also meshed precisely with the important political and social priorities. To defeat Nazi Germany and imperial Japan, the United States created military forces suited for decision-oriented, machine-age warfare—campaigns and battles waged by vast fleets of tanks, warships, and combat aircraft. Fielding armies and fleets large enough to permit the United States to fight on several fronts simultaneously demanded an unprecedented mobilization of the nation's industrial and human resources. Notably, to satisfy the services' enormous manpower needs, that mobilization relied on conscription, initiated well before U.S. entry into the war and endorsed by the people with only the barest hesitation.

Adhering to a strategy of abundance (when possible equipping other nations to shoulder the brunt of the actual fighting), the United States achieved victory with relatively few casualties. No less important, the transformation of the United States into the "arsenal of democracy," from which there flowed a torrent of weapons, munitions, and supplies needed to fight, fueled an economic boom. On the American home front, military Keynesianism restored prosperity.

By 1945, its enemies crushed, its allies exhausted, the United States had ascended to a position of dominance rare in recorded history. This marked an astonishing turnaround. During the decade prior to war, the Great Depression had threatened the legitimacy of the political order in the United States. Bolshevism on the Left and fascism on the Right posed ideological challenges that called into question the viability of liberal democracy. Although Franklin Roosevelt's New Deal had stanched the economy's downward spiral, it had not produced recovery. As a result, the government that led the nation into war in December 1941 did not enjoy an excess of credibility. Within four years, wartime achievements—not only in battle, but also on the factory floor—had restored confidence in American institutions and in the American elite that presided over those institutions.

In this and other ways, the methods chosen to conduct World War II found favor with the American people. That was hardly an accident. In crafting the policies that would guide the war effort, senior leaders, both civilian and military, did so with one eye fixed on public opinion. The problem was to keep the people engaged in supporting the war without exacting more from them than they were prepared to offer. "A democracy cannot fight a Thirty Years War," General Marshall warned.[19] Like Roosevelt himself, Marshall understood the imperative of ending the war quickly and decisively while sparing Americans unnecessary sacrifice for what was, after all, a "foreign" war.

Among other things, those directing the war effort reassured the majority that military necessity would not become a pretext for radical social experiments. The world's greatest democracy, the United States in the 1940s was also a society in which white male Protestants wielded power and in which distinctions, especially those based on race and gender, mattered. Although the war did generate demands for change, political and military authorities did their best to preserve the social status quo ante bellum. By 1940, the era of reform had ended, Roosevelt himself offering his assurance that "Dr. New Deal" had retired in favor of "Dr. Win-the-War." Apart from creating a handful of Negro combat units, the army resisted the efforts of those hoping to use the war to advance the cause of civil rights. The armed services remained rigidly segregated, with African Americans largely relegated to menial service support duties. Notwithstanding unprecedented wartime opportunities for women both in and out of uniform, men at least understood these to be emergency measures, not a permanent transformation of gender roles. And indeed, when the war ended, women for the most part reverted to their traditional status. Millions of returning male vets reclaimed the best jobs and, propelled by the G.I. Bill's generous educational benefits, joined the expanding ranks of the upwardly mobile, white-collar, suburban-bound middle class.

Because it had satisfied the disparate interests of the state, the people, *and* the military during World War II, this new civil-military compact endured beyond 1945. Underpinning that compact was a tax that before 1940 Americans would have found inconceivable and unacceptable: a permanent peacetime draft.

Restored following the war after only the briefest interruption, conscription provided the foundation of postwar U.S. national security policy. It also extended through the first decades of the postwar era the liberal democratic model of civil-military relations forged during the war. As was the case during the war, the reciprocal relationship worked to the mutual benefit of all parties concerned.

From the point of view of the officer corps, the draft imparted predictability and stability to the military's connection to state and people. Assuring the armed services that they could draw as needed on the pool of the nation's best and brightest young men, conscription also provided a hedge against misuse by a reckless government or abandonment by a feckless polity. From the point of view of those formulating U.S. strategy, the draft provided the muscle to pursue the ambitious policies of the immediate postwar and early Cold War eras—and it implied popular support for those policies.

But in acceding to this arrangement, the people exacted a price. Included in that price were several expectations. First, Americans assumed that these citizen-soldiers would be used sparingly. Their primary purpose was to prevent the occurrence of war, not to engage in constant campaigning. Second, if U.S. interests required those soldiers actually to fight, the people expected that the war would be brief, decisive, and conducted far from America's shores. Third, in anticipation of such contingencies, government was to amass weapons and materiel sufficient to insure that the next war, whenever it occurred, would be fought with the same emphasis on avoiding unnecessary American casualties that had characterized the U.S. approach to World War II. Not incidentally, this requirement to stockpile and modernize a great arsenal would also reduce the danger of returning to the hard times of the 1930s—defense spending continuously priming the pump of economic expansion.

The arrangement did not survive without missteps or without its critics. In its eagerness to bring the Korean War to neat and rapid conclusion— consistent with popular expectations and past military practice—the Truman administration in the fall of 1950 permitted an overconfident Douglas Mac-Arthur to push beyond the 38th parallel toward the Yalu. The result was a war larger, longer, and bloodier than Americans were prepared to accept. Truman's miscalculation earned Democrats a sharp rebuke. In 1952, the people elected the first Republican president in two decades—a general who promised to extract the U.S. from a war that promised to continue without end.

Calculating but prudent in his approach to statecraft, Dwight D. Eisenhower hewed closely to the terms of the civil-military compact. There would be no more Koreas on his watch. Nor, as a result, would there be any demands by a people exhausted by war for the United States to revert to isolationism. Gratified that the new president had promptly ended the fighting in Korea, Americans acceded to Eisenhower's determination to maintain

U.S. commitments abroad. Throughout his two terms, without complaint or controversy, a continuous flow of draftees — even Elvis — rotated to Europe and the Far East, pulled their hitch, and came home. Meanwhile, defense plants from Long Island to southern California churned out a never-ending stream of fighters, bombers, tanks, and guided missiles. With defense priorities dictating the allocation of research dollars, institutions of higher learning happily crowded around the bountiful government trough. Among the few who worried about the potentially insidious consequences of this cozy arrangement for American democracy was Eisenhower himself. Two terms as commander in chief had convinced the former general that the United States was at some risk of becoming, whether due to malice or inadvertence, a garrison state. In his farewell address to the nation, Eisenhower warned his fellow citizens about the dangers of a "military-industrial complex." But few heeded his words. The immediate and tangible benefits for all concerned — corporations, labor unions, universities, the entire national security apparatus — trumped the concerns of the outgoing president.

III

Despite its apparent durability, the civil-military equilibrium bred of the Second World War and sustained through the 1950s collapsed soon thereafter. The implications for American military power and policy were catastrophic.

The proximate cause of that collapse was Vietnam. Cast in terms of Clausewitz's trinity, Vietnam was a conflict in which the state flagrantly violated its covenant with both people and army. Civilian officials responsible for formulating policy, abetted by ineffectual military advisers, perpetrated a crisis in U.S. civil-military relations without precedent. By the end of the 1960s, the trinity lay in shambles.

Vietnam became the "Thirty Years War" that George Marshall had warned against, an amorphous, protracted war of attrition, conducted with little immediate prospect of achieving a decisive outcome. Lyndon Johnson and his advisers concluded that the best way to wage a conflict of indeterminate length was to *avoid* rousing the passions of the people. To the maximum extent possible, they wanted to disguise the realty of the war by insulating the home front from it effects. Hence, the administration rejected Pentagon recommendations in favor of mobilization, refusing to call up the reserves and placing the entire burden for fighting the war on active duty forces.

In the combat zone, campaigns orchestrated by commanders schooled in the arts of conventional warfare relied on the abundance of materiel (and firepower) that had become an American hallmark. But the enemy refused to fight on American terms, shrewdly exploited the self-imposed restrictions to which U.S. forces adhered, and exacted a gruesome toll in casualties, both American and Vietnamese.

At home, defense contractors worked overtime to replace the fighter-bombers and helicopters lost in combat, but instead of promoting prosperity, increased military spending—combined with Johnson's refusal to choose between guns and butter—produced by the early 1970s deficits, inflation, and economic stagnation. To the manifest unhappiness of the American people, Vietnam brought the postwar boom to an abrupt end. Nor did the administration even succeed in keeping war away from America's shores: By 1968, opposition to Vietnam had fueled a level of civil unrest, frequently violent, not seen in a century.

For the military itself, as the war dragged on from one year to the next, Vietnam became a nightmare. The United States Army, with the largest contingent engaged, suffered the most acutely. By the early 1970s, the Army teetered on the verge of disintegration. In Vietnam itself, combat refusals and attacks by soldiers on their own leaders ("fraggings") became common-place. Throughout the service, problems of drug abuse and racial animosity raged all but out of control. Basic discipline broke down.

Even with conscription still in place, the people began severing their links to the military. Avoiding the draft lost its stigma; subverting it acquired a certain fashionability. By implication, only the morally inert or the politically unenlightened would submit to the directives of the selective service system in support of a pointless war. Thus, by the time Vietnam was winding down, the great American middle class had all but opted out of military service—a process acknowledged and affirmed in 1970 when President Richard Nixon announced plans to terminate the draft altogether. Henceforth, the United States would rely for its defense not on citizen-soldiers drawn from throughout American society, but on an "All Volunteer"—that is, professional—force.

Yet for all the stresses induced by Vietnam, the war alone cannot explain the full extent of the civil-military estrangement symbolized by Nixon's decision to terminate the draft. The story had another dimension. Unlike Korea—the so-called "Forgotten War" that even now appears historically dis-embodied—the Vietnam war occurred in the midst of (and itself helped to spur) a cultural revolution of extraordinary scope and intensity. Beginning in the mid-1960s, that revolution transformed manners, morals, and mores throughout the West but most particularly in the United States. That up-heaval also provoked resistance, touching off a fiercely contested "culture war." At the heart of the culture war were (and are) two radically divergent views of what "The Sixties" signified. To some, the period fostered a new spirit of liberation, exposing the repressive underpinnings of American life and promising justice to oppressed minorities, especially blacks and women. To others, it meant, as Gertrude Himmelfarb recently observed, "the collapse of ethical principles and habits, the loss of respect for authorities and insti-tutions, the breakdown of the family, the decline of civility, the vulgarization of high culture, and the degradation of popular culture."[20]

Already reeling from the war itself, the United States military found itself battered further still by this cultural revolution. For partisans on both sides of the cultural divide, the soldier became an invaluable symbol and military policy a battleground in which to fight out their differences.

For the Left, the military provided a palpable representation of all that they scorned. Military institutions were impersonal, uptight, authoritarian, bureaucratic, and resolutely male. They served as instruments of American imperialism abroad and government oppression at home. Military life itself—implying the loss of individual identity and the submission to authority—was the polar opposite of cool.

In the eyes of the Right, the military represented a last bastion of order, tradition, patriotism, and respect for basic national institutions—all of which the 1960s had seemingly swept away. Conservatives saw in the sol-dier's calling the best hope of preserving from complete extinction virtues like honor, courage, self-discipline, and self-sacrifice. Inveterate cold war-riors understood (correctly) that attacks on the military were attacks on the anti-Communist crusade, to which they remained passionately committed.

Thus did the military become an object of intensely partisan struggle. After Vietnam, the old pretense that matters pertaining to national defense remained above mere politics now became a complete fiction: Henceforth, everybody knew that controversies revolving around nominally military ques-tions contained a political subtext. Deciphering that subtext was impossible without reference to the ongoing culture war.

In this environment, preliminary efforts to reconstitute a viable trinity foundered. Moving beyond the war was not just a matter of soldiers knocking the mud off their boots and getting back to work. The task at hand was to rebuild U.S. military institutions from the bottom up and to do so in the teeth of the barely disguised hostility of American elites and despite the bone-deep weariness of the American people who were sick and tired of Vietnam and all its works. And despite, too, the fact that the officer corps came home from Vietnam nursing its own feelings of resentment and alienation.

Recruiting jingles proclaimed that "The Army Wants to Join You." But the sort of people the army wanted couldn't imagine wanting to join the army or any of the other services, for that matter. In the 1970s, those who did enlist tended to be those with few other options. The military effectively found itself the employer of last resort.

Yet despite such troubles—today largely eradicated from national memory—the seeds of recovery were being planted. Ignored by the media, unnoticed by their fellow citizens, a counterrevolution of sorts, instigated by soldiers, was laying the foundation for the revival of American military power. The aim of this counterrevolution was to *restore* what Vietnam had destroyed. By returning to the old strategy of containment and by redirecting its attention to a more familiar form of war, the military sought to regain a semblance of institutional stability and to reestablish its relevance. Ultimately, soldiers sought to repair their estrangement from American society, which had been a by-product of Vietnam.

Having had a bellyful of fighting guerrillas, military leaders after Vietnam reconfigured the services into instruments for large-scale, mechanized conventional conflict. Their intent was by no means to raise forces that reckless policymakers could then expend in further Third World crusades. Rather, they proposed to revert to the core mission of the Cold War: deterring Soviet aggression in "the Central Region." The Pentagon consciously designed the post-Vietnam force structure so that active duty forces would depend on the reserves for certain critical support functions, thereby making it next to impossible for a president to order any large-scale intervention without at least partial mobilization. Soldiers calculated that such a mobilization would proceed only if the intervention itself enjoyed popular support, thereby reducing the danger of being abandoned as they had been (in their own view) in Vietnam.

All of these preliminaries occurred before Ronald Reagan became president. Indeed, all of the major reforms of the post-Vietnam era—the overhaul of operational doctrine, the innovations in training, the design of new weapons like the Abrams tank—predate the Reagan era, as does reversing the post-Vietnam decline in military spending. It nonetheless remains true that but for the contribution of President Reagan himself, efforts to revive American military power may well have come to naught.

Without doubt, Reagan facilitated that revival by boosting defense spending to unprecedented peacetime levels. Yet his most important contribution was to restore to reasonable health the civil-military relationship that Vietnam had ruptured. Reagan repaired the bond between the military and society. Exuding optimism, he lifted the country out of its post-Vietnam funk. Lavishing soldiers with affection and entrusting to them the task of thwarting Soviet aggression, Reagan validated the Pentagon's determination to redefine its raison d'être: standing athwart the Fulda Gap rather than vainly chasing pajama-clad guerrillas. The people, still harboring their visceral dislike for communism and rankled by Vietnam era scapegoating of soldiers, applauded. More substantively, their sons (and now increasingly their daughters) found reason to serve in uniform: by the mid-1980s, the shaky experiment in creating an all volunteer force appeared headed for success. Patriotism had become respectable again. Being a soldier became hip.

Even without conscription, Reagan reactivated the liberal-democratic civil-military compact that had governed the immediate postwar era. Apart from the single, disastrous lapse of Beirut, he was careful to abide by its conventions. There would be no Vietnams on Reagan's watch. On that score, both citizens and soldiers could rest easy. The Reagan administration publicly committed itself to a demanding set of prerequisites—codified in the Weinberger doctrine—that would govern its use of force. Meanwhile, as had been the case in World War II, a revival of military Keynesianism energized the economy and fostered a renewed sense of national well being.

In short, bountiful defense budgets alone did not produce American military preeminence in the 1980s. Military power in a democracy is not simply a product of money or technology. Whether through instinct, reasoning, or the advice of wise counselors, Reagan grasped that nurturing sound military institutions and using military power effectively demanded the active engagement of the people. He secured the people's support by restating with conviction simple truths: that communism was a great evil, that the Soviet Union threatened American security and values, and that the United States was not condemned to inevitable and irreversible decline. To these—which until the deluge of the sixties had seemed self-evident—he added one notion that was uniquely his: that the Cold War was not something to be managed, but to be won.

To be sure, Reagan could not repeal the cultural revolution. As a result, his views did not go down well among the sophisticates in the prestige media or in faculty lounges. But throughout his presidency—that revolution's Thermidor—they resonated on Main Street.

Reagan's own election to a second term, the election of George Bush as his designated successor, and victory in the Cold War all seemingly validated Reagan's achievement. The result—demonstrated most vividly, after Reagan had left office, in the Persian Gulf War—was a Clausewitzian trinity of surpassing robustness. For a brief moment, the policy objectives of the state and the capabilities of the military appeared to align precisely. And the new professional military establishment to which the United States had committed itself—its members now universally referred to as "the troops"—became also at one and the same time a people's army.

IV

But the Reagan restoration has proven to be strikingly ephemeral. In the comparatively brief interval between Operation Desert Storm in 1991 and Operation Allied Force in 1999, the liberal democratic covenant between state, people, and military has once again come unglued, this time in all likelihood for good. A new civil-military arrangement has evolved, one that reflects the prevailing values of a different time—the age not of Ronald Reagan but of William Jefferson Clinton.

The geopolitical upheaval caused by the end of the Cold War, a redefinition of U.S. grand strategy, and a novel conception of warfare that itself is a product of powerful technological and cultural influences have all contributed to this transformation. Whereas the old liberal democratic covenant operated on the principle of reciprocity, the new arrangement adheres to the nostrums of a new age, one that is postliberal, postindustrial, postmodern, and postheroic. In Kosovo this new "trinity" was fully on display for the first time.

Devising this new postliberal model of civil-military relations ranks among the least recognized accomplishments of the Clinton presidency. But the achievement, if not necessarily salubrious, is a genuine one.

Clinton the master politician accurately gauged—indeed, in his own personal conduct, exemplified—the temper of his times. Better than any other player on the national political stage, he understood what Americans want, how much they will pay, and what they will put up with.

Meanwhile, Clinton the statesman—schooled in his duties through intensive on-the-job training—recast the nation's strategic purposes. Contrary to the assertions of critics who complained of a decade of drift, the president outlined an ambitious project that both departs from the obsolete pattern of the Cold War and yet maintains continuity with the underlying thrust of twentieth-century U.S. foreign policy. He articulated a clear vision of what the world of the twenty-first century should look like and within that vision allotted to the United States a role worthy of a superpower. Moreover, speaking from his Bully Pulpit, he explained with almost mind-numbing frequency the assumptions and principles that underlie that grand strategy.

Finally, Clinton the commander in chief fashioned a doctrine for employing American military power that bridges the gap between his grand strategic objectives and the public's limited willingness to exert itself on behalf of those objectives. The military component of Clinton's strategy requires minimal blood and only modest treasure—indeed, the cash flow on balance may be positive. And it does not unduly tax the nation's attention span. Finessing the deficit between ends and means, the new postliberal civil-military relationship that Clinton ushered into existence seemingly reconciles the irreconcilable. For this achievement, Bill Clinton, in his own way, deserves to rank alongside FDR and Reagan as one of the most influential commanders in chief in modern American history.

This achievement is not without considerable irony. Indeed, at the outset of his first term, as evidenced by the fiasco over gays in the military, Bill Clinton seemed oblivious to the very concept of civil-military relations. Tone-deaf to military culture and unimpressed by the military's longstanding exercise of professional autonomy, the newly inaugurated Clinton apparently took for granted that as commander in chief his authority was absolute. He issued orders. Soldiers obeyed. Although the Pentagon signaled frantically the officer corps' unwillingness to accept a repeal of the ban on gays serving openly in the military, the newly inaugurated president ignored that warning. The upshot was a public spectacle in which Clinton and the top brass came precariously close to toppling the carefully erected edifice of constitutional precepts, traditional prerogatives, and mutual self-restraint that sustains civilian control. Embarrassed, Clinton cut a deal and acceded to the phony "don't ask, don't tell" policy.

Clinton's first year in the White House provided a similar education regarding the use of force. The president had been in office less than five months when he first ordered U.S. troops into action—a cruise missile attack against Baghdad in June 1993. Yet in many respects, his (vicarious) baptism of fire occurred later that year. In the same month that he pummeled Baghdad with missiles, Clinton quietly launched a quasi-covert war against the Somali warlord Mohamed Farah Aidid. In October of that year, Clinton's war careened out of control. A bungled raid in downtown Mogadishu resulted in a fierce firefight between U.S. forces and Somali militias. By the time it ended, American helicopters had been shot down, a pilot was being paraded in captivity, and 18 U.S. Army rangers lay dead. The political outcry in Washington was immediate and deafening.

In responding to this crisis, Clinton displayed all of the instincts for self-preservation for which he became rightly known. He assigned primary blame for the debacle to the United Nations. To placate an infuriated Congress, he offered up as sacrificial lamb his own secretary of defense, Les Aspin. And he wisely cut his losses, ordering U.S. forces to terminate their mission in Somalia and come home. Being bloodied by General Aidid did not diminish the president's propensity to employ coercion, as subsequent events in Haiti, Bosnia, Iraq, Sudan, Afghanistan, and Kosovo would show. But there would be no more Mogadishus on his watch.

From the gays-in-the-military debacle and the bloody encounter with General Aidid, Clinton took away important lessons. He would, henceforth, avoid ruffling the military's feathers and give wide berth to African warlords. But conclusions drawn from those two episodes also contributed directly to the larger task that he faced as commander in chief, namely to adapt U.S. national security policy more generally to the perplexing conditions that he encountered as the first genuine post–Cold War president. On that score, Clinton's critics fail to give him the credit he deserves.

In the eyes of his admirers, Ronald Reagan won the Cold War. By extension, in bringing about the downfall of communism, Reagan gets credit for furthering the global spread of market principles. But Reagan did not succeed in winning the culture war or even in rolling back the torrent of cultural change unleashed by the sixties. Indeed, the fact that the electorate in 1992 chose (in the formulation of a U.S. Air Force major general) a dope-smoking, skirt-chasing draft dodger to lead the nation illustrates that the values of the cultural revolution emerged unscathed from the ostensibly conservative decade of the 1980s. In short, the situation that Clinton inherited from his Republican predecessors was one in which the Right had won decisively the argument over economics and in which the Left had prevailed in matters of culture. Free enterprise and the politics of personal liberation had both triumphed.

This result was a new zeitgeist, one that the Cold War had kept in check but that sprang loose as Bill and Hillary proudly marched down Pennsylvania Avenue at their first inaugural. Profit, lifestyle, and radical individualism became the dominant values of Bill Clinton's America. Exploiting a revolution in information technology, more Americans made more money than ever before. It was money they intended to enjoy. Autonomy, extravagance, self-gratification, and tolerance were in. Accountability, austerity, self-denial, and being judgmental were definitely out. Rights proliferated. Responsibilities shrunk. As postmodern precepts such as deconstruction and multiculturalism seeped from the academy into the public square, old distinctions blurred: between men and women, good and evil, reality and fiction, truth and falsity, freedom and responsibility, art and exhibitionism. As the president himself suggested, even the meaning of the word *is* could no longer be taken for granted.

All of this provoked dismay and even outrage in some quarters. So-called "virtuecrats" worried about the collapse of American civilization and grew apoplectic at the lubricious antics of Clinton himself. But the American people — at least the dwindling proportion of the electorate able to motivate itself to go to the polls — expressed their approval of Clinton's stewardship, awarding him in 1996 a second term. Despite evidence of the most egregious presidential misconduct, efforts to remove Clinton from office in 1999 left the majority of Americans unmoved.

In the age of Clinton, the traditional martial virtues — honor, courage, and self-discipline — were notable by their absence, both in the culture at large and in the person of the commander in chief. This shortfall would not matter if the United States were a small nation comparable, say, to Switzerland or if the end of the Cold War had prompted it to become once again a "normal nation," chiefly preoccupied with cultivating its vast North American homeland.

But returning to the normalcy of pre-1940 America was simply out of the question. The foreign policy establishment that greeted Clinton when he arrived in Washington in 1993 refused categorically to accept any diminution of the global role to which the United States had become accustomed during the Cold War. Although the former Arkansas governor did not claim prior membership in that establishment, he could not afford — or was unwilling—to ignore its requirements, any more than he could ignore those of teachers' unions or the Black Caucus.

From the perspective of the foreign policy elite, Clinton's chief responsibility as president was to formulate a strategy of sufficient grandeur to justify America's continuing status as the World's Only Superpower—something to replace the outmoded concept of containment. Always a quick study, Clinton gamely rose to the occasion and soon enough was mouthing phrases about America's indispensability and its inescapable obligation to lead, codewords signaling his support for activist policies aimed at perpetuating U.S. global preeminence.

A handful of skeptics suggested that the cultural fabric of postliberal America seemed rather poor stuff with which to sustain such a policy.[21] Such concerns did not deter the majority of foreign policy experts, whatever their political inclination. Operation Desert Storm and the collapse of communism had convinced the Left and the Right of the superiority of American power. But Clinton understood that the skeptics were on to something. He knew—or during his first painful year in office had learned—that if the United States would not return to normalcy neither did it possess the capacity to engage in any great crusades: Neither the people nor the military had the stomach for the sacrifices that such crusades would entail. If the Clinton years have produced a broad domestic consensus in favor of a quasi-imperial role, a tacit corollary of that consensus was that the United States must gain and maintain its global hegemony without tears.

V

The twin phenomena identified by the Clinton administration as the cornerstones of its post–Cold War grand strategy reflect this requirement. Amidst all the confusing welter of change, the president and his chief lieutenants identified two developments that really matter: the information revolution and the process of globalization. These two all but inseparable factors, the administration believed, were transforming the international order. As such, they were creating vast new opportunities while imposing on the United States new responsibilities to exercise leadership.

The defining quality of the order resulting from this transformation is openness. Under the impact of technological change, according to Mr. Clinton, "the blocks, the barriers, the borders that defined the world for our parents and grandparents are giving way."[22] As they fall, there is emerging, in the words of Madeleine Albright, a world of "open markets, open invest-ment, open communications and open trade."[23]

Openness will permit—indeed, is already permitting—the creation of wealth on a scale hitherto unimaginable. In explaining the stakes in Kosovo, the president described "a new century and a new millennium where the people in poor countries all over the world, because of technology and the Internet and the spread of information, will have unprecedented opportu-nities to share prosperity."[24] Indeed, thanks to the information revolution, "we clearly have it within our means to lift billions and billions of people around the world into a global middle class and into participation in global democracy."[25] As that remark suggests, a more prosperous world points in-evitably toward a more democratic world. Given the administration's belief that "democracies do not go to war with one another," a more democratic world will in turn be more peaceful as well.[26]

For all of its apparent novelty, little of this strategy of openness was sub-stantively new. Certainly, the foreign policy pronouncements issuing from the Clinton administration would be of little surprise to Charles Beard, eminent historian of an earlier generation, or William Appleman Williams, his intellectual heir. Both had identified the quest for a world open to U.S. economic activity as the overarching theme of American diplomacy.[27] The strategy of openness revives that theme.

Yet much as Beard and Williams had both argued, American enthusiasm for openness is by no means an exercise in altruism. In the eyes of the Clinton administration, globalization became, for the United States itself, an impera-tive. A failure to create an open order would imperil America's own well being. According to Albright, "our own prosperity depends on having partners that are open to our exports, investment, and ideas."[28] Or as Clinton himself bluntly put it, "Growth at home depends on growth abroad."[29] Indeed, given "the inexorable logic of globalization," as the president declared just prior to the war for Kosovo, "everything, from the strength of our economy to the safety of our cities, to the health of our people, depends on events not only within our borders, but half a world away."[30] With so much at stake, insuring the success of globalization became a vital U.S. interest.

According to administration spokesmen, "the President's strategy for har-nessing the forces of globalization" aimed to make the promise of a peaceful, prosperous world a reality.[31] Topping the agenda of that strategy was trade liberalization—hence, the priority assigned to the North Atlantic Free Trade Agreement, the World Trade Organization, economic engagement with China, and the 200-plus trade agreements that the administration touted among its proudest achievements.

But the strategy has an important political aspect as well. Openness does not imply anarchy. As the chief proponent of globalization, the United States is also its midwife, responsible for insuring adherence to established norms of behavior and for comporting itself such that no nation questions its prerogative to do so. As Secretary Albright remarked, the United States must serve as the "organizing principal [sic]" of the new global system.[32]

Yet as events obliged Mr. Clinton to admit, "globalization is not an unmixed blessing."[33] The prospect of joining a global middle class—saturated with American pop culture, American tastes, and the American preoccupation with lifestyle—does not elicit universal delight. Globalization has evoked backlash by "forces of destruction"—terrorists, rogue states, drug cartels, and religious extremists who "find opportunity in the very openness, freedom and progress we cherish."[34] The result is conflict, amorphous, protracted, and bitter. Thus, according to the president, as it entered the new millennium, the United States found itself engaged in "a great battle between the forces of integration and the forces of disintegration; the forces of globalism and the forces of tribalism; of oppression against empowerment."[35] Kosovo became only the latest skirmish in that larger struggle.

As the U.S.-led intervention in Kosovo suggests, for all of the administration's emphasis on international economics, its strategy contained a vital security component. American military power is essential to the prospects of globalization. Without it, the misguided and the malicious will wreak havoc. Stability will erode. Progress toward openness will stall. Barriers will go back up. Assertions by American officials that the United States alone is equipped to preside over the global order will ring hollow.

Thus, whereas in former times wariness of becoming entangled in foreign wars was a hallmark of American statecraft, in an age of globalization, any disturbance anywhere demands the attention of the United States. As one senior Clinton administration official admitted in a moment of candor, "I am not sure there is such a thing as a foreign war anymore."[36]

The operational implications of converting the American military into an adjunct to globalization loom large. Soldiers themselves have obscured those implications by clinging to an identity that has long since become anachronistic. Although soldiers insist that they remain "warriors" who exist to

"fight and win the nation's wars," the frenetic military history of the 1990s—
a single, brief, prematurely terminated war followed by a nearly continuous
stream of "operations other than war"—tells a different story. Today's G.I.
functions in practice as a member of an armed constabulary that exists to
nudge others into conformity with the American vision of a well-ordered
planet and to punish (usually from a safe distance) those with the temerity
to challenge that vision.

Indeed, the principles governing the Clinton administration's use of force
had little to do with war as traditionally conceived: Globalization is, after
all, making war as such obsolete. Under the terms of the Clinton doctrine,
the United States wields military power not to defeat adversaries but as part
of an effort to "shape" the international environment.[37] Policing and punishment have supplanted the pursuit of victory as the primary purpose of
military action. Publicly announced objectives that are intentionally spa-
cious (obliging transgressors to "pay a price" has become a favorite) permit
maximum creativity when evaluating the outcome of any military operation.[38] Vaguely defined objectives also permit political leaders to extricate
themselves altogether at the first hint of quagmire—declaring success all the
while. When administering punishment—whether against rogue states like
Iraq and Yugoslavia or against alleged terrorists in Sudan or Afghanistan—
the Clinton doctrine eschewed full-fledged campaigns in favor of brief, measured ripostes. The idea was not to achieve decision, but to signal, warn,
contain, or punish, or at least to avoid the appearance of weakness and
inaction. Limited numbers of cruise missiles or air strikes with precision
guided munitions were usually deemed sufficient to make the point. When
policing—as, for example, in Haiti or the Balkans—the standard practice
was to intervene massively and to tailor the mission so as to minimize exposure and commitment. In all cases, casualty avoidance ranked as a para-
mount measure of success.

VI

The liberal democratic civil-military compact forged in World War II
reflected not only the requirements of war in an industrial age but also a
particular set of socioeconomic and cultural imperatives. The same holds
true for the postliberal covenant that has supplanted it: it manifests the new
American way of war. It also testifies to changes in the nation's aspirations
and character.

To the casual observer, the implications of the transformation may not be immediately self-evident. The survival—and skillful manipulation—of familiar symbols and rituals convey the impression that traditional civil-military arrangements remain intact. In the manner of his predecessors, President Clinton still placed wreaths at the Tomb of the Unknowns, visited U.S. troops abroad on Thanksgiving, and on occasions of state routinely praised their dedication and patriotism. Artifacts of military professionalism remain much in evidence. Distinctive uniforms, insignia of rank, service ribbons, recruiting slogans, and the presence of military color guards at football games all suggest continuity rather than change. As reflected in opinion polls, popular regard for "the troops" remains at or near Gulf War levels.

These vestiges of past practice conceal the extent to which a fundamentally new relationship has supplanted the "trinity" with which Americans are familiar. The connecting tissue in the old liberal democratic relationship—underpinning policy and essential to the actual conduct of war—was popular support. During World War II and through the Cold War, the engagement of the people lent credibility to the policies devised by the state—or, as in the case of Vietnam, undermined that credibility. The people provided the human and material resources that created effective military institutions—or, as was the case during the years immediately following Vietnam, withheld those resources with severely adverse consequences. In contrast, the new postliberal relationship obviates the need for popular support altogether, insulating both U.S. policy and American military power from the vagaries of a fickle and moody public. Decoupling the people from military affairs is its primary purpose.

Its primary purpose but not its sole one: The postliberal system of civil-military relations also seeks to reduce the influence of soldiers. Having long since concluded that "diplomacy and force are two sides of the same coin," President Clinton knows that coercion is integral to his efforts to pry open the world.[39] The flowering of American aspirations to global hegemony no longer permits the United States to turn a blind eye to crises that in an earlier era would have been dismissed as not our affair. Instead, political elites persuade themselves that the nation has essentially no choice but to become involved, if only to demonstrate leadership or prevent the erosion of American credibility.

But coercion is not to be confused with waging war, which entails huge risks and all too often produces unintended and highly disruptive consequences. As envisioned by Mr. Clinton and his advisers, the use of force was to be calibrated, judicious, and precise. Above all, whereas war implies a sharing of authority between policymaker and generals, force as an instrument of diplomacy would become exclusively the province of the statesman, with soldiers reduced to the role of mere ordnance deliverers.

The essential ingredient in the new civil-military relationship—rendering both popular support and professional military advice moot—is technology.

Much as information technology fuels hopes for globalization and expectations of continuing U.S. economic dominance, so too does technology infuse the Clinton doctrine for the use of force and the civil-military relationship that supports that doctrine. High-tech military capabilities—to strike with accuracy and impunity, to anticipate and parry attack—reduce the uncertainty formerly inherent in the use of force. Technology largely obviates the need for sacrifice. It seemingly permits the United States to pursue global policies without subjecting the home front to the unwelcome dislocations of large-scale armed conflict—political protest or economic instability, for example. In short, technology enables the United States to use its military power to sustain American hegemony without the necessity of fighting messy old-fashioned wars. As a bonus, technology even facilitates efforts to align American military institutions more closely with advanced thinking on sensitive issues such as gender and sexual orientation.

The best illustration of the postliberal civil-military relationship in action is the Clinton administration's *other* war of 1999, the yearlong bombing of Iraq.

What war? In the administration's view, needless to say, the ongoing hostilities against Iraq, launched in December 1998 with a four-day air offensive known as Operation Desert Fox, failed to qualify as actual war. Indeed, the White House barely acknowledged that military action continued thereafter. This, despite the fact that, in the twelve months *after* Desert Fox, U.S. and British warplanes unloaded nearly 2,000 missiles and precision-guided bombs against several hundred targets scattered throughout Iraq.

According to administration officials, the aim of U.S. policy was to contain Iraq and prevent it from acquiring weapons of mass destruction, while ultimately removing Saddam Hussein from power. Observers might expect, therefore, that a year's worth of bombing would have pounded weapons research facilities, military headquarters, key government installations, and presidential palaces—in the jargon favored by air power advocates, "all that the regime holds dear."

Such was not the case. Principles of the schoolyard rather than principles of war governed the campaign: It was a game of tit-for-tat. Iraqi air defenses "painted" or otherwise challenged aircraft flying daily patrols in the Northern or Southern No-Fly Zone. Using this pretext, allied bombers flying at high altitudes retaliated against radar sites, surface-to-air missile batteries, and command centers, targets that shared one thing in common: They were all remote from Baghdad. The result testifies to the proficiency of American airmen—tens of thousands of sorties flown without a single loss—but there is no evidence that the attacks caused Saddam to lose sleep, literally or figuratively.

Yet as a demonstration of postliberal civil-military relations, the Persian Gulf conflict of 1999 was a rousing success. Administration officials labored assiduously to deflect scrutiny from Mr. Clinton's stealth bombing campaign. To their delight, Congress, the media, and the military all played along, permitting the administration a free hand.

As with every other U.S. military operation launched since the Persian Gulf conflict of 1990–1991, the Persian Gulf conflict of 1999 proceeded on executive authority alone, Congress tacitly accepting the administration's thesis that the clashes in the skies over Iraq did not require legislative sanction. The Republican majority did not even motivate itself to ask what the nation had gotten in return for the billion or so dollars expended in support of this operation.

News organizations likewise largely ignored the resumption of hostilities against Iraq. A brief report buried in the inside pages of the *New York Times* makes the point. The headline reads "Iraq: U.S. Bombs Again," that slightly weary "again" hinting at the incident's failure to qualify as genuinely newsworthy. The wire service dispatch that follows—barely a single column-inch in length—reinforces that interpretation. Repeating the mutually contradictory claims of the Iraqi News Agency (civilians attacked) and U.S. military spokesmen (military targets destroyed), it conveys the impression that the incident merits scant attention. Thus cued, the American people responded accordingly: They remained oblivious to what had become a stealth war.

Meanwhile, although the bombing of scattered Iraqi installations, by any standard measure of effectiveness, was pointless, senior military leaders themselves found no cause for complaint. Flying live-fire missions beyond the reach of Iraqi defenses provided American pilots with a welcome opportunity to enhance their skills. Commanders and staffs gained invaluable operational experience. Aging stocks of munitions were expended and then replenished with the latest that money can buy. Back in the Pentagon, arguments for additional force structure or for new weapons systems accrued.

Best of all, no one got hurt—at least not on our side. Even after Clnton had departed the White House, squadrons continued to deploy, rotate home, and prepare to deploy again, their movement like their operations all but unnoticed by the public.

In the skies over Iraq, the postliberal system of civil-military relations functioned precisely as intended. In the interest of freeing policymakers from constraints, the system delivered two essentials: acquiescent citizens and compliant soldiers. With the American people increasingly inured to the use of force, with American soldiers dutifully pushing the buttons that put bombs on target, this new "trinity" offers the prospect of compensating for the disparity between the nation's quasi-imperial grand strategy and its singularly nonimperial culture.

VII

A new strategic azimuth, a new doctrine for the use of American military power, a radically altered climate of civil-military relations: each of these, prominently on display during the war for Kosovo, deserves to be ranked among the foremost accomplishments of the Clinton presidency. To a far greater degree than the signature issues of the 1990s—health care, welfare reform, public education, the environment—they are likely to form an enduring part of the actual Clinton legacy.

None of the three has attracted the attention it deserves. For critics interested in scoring partisan points, bashing the administration for having failed to devise a coherent strategy is far more gratifying than tracing the connections (and noting the contradictions) between American actions and the rationale for those actions offered by the White House or the State Department. Similarly, lambasting Bill Clinton for amateurism or incompetence in his various military adventures is easier than identifying the patterns of behavior that constitute, for better or worse, a new American doctrine for the use of force. Thus, the failure of most commentators in the aftermath of Kosovo to gauge its true importance as a watershed in U.S. military history. No sooner had the last bomb fallen than Operation Allied Force faded into the crowded tableau of military adventures in which the United States had engaged since the end of the Cold War.

Given the habitual inclination of most Americans to take civil-military matters for granted, it comes as no surprise that this dimension of the story likewise escaped notice. Yet for a democratic superpower, reconfiguring the connection between state, people, and army must inevitably have profound consequences. Indeed, as Kosovo suggested, the postliberal model of civil-military relations is deeply flawed. It is incompatible with traditional military professionalism and it poses an unacceptable risk to democratic practice.

As noted above, President Clinton's grand strategy of hegemony through globalization requires coercion but has no place for real war. But the ob-solescence of war portends the obsolescence of officership as a profession. Indeed, with the end of the Cold War, the delegitimization of "the art of war"—begun in 1914, seemingly validated by the events of August 1945, but then held in abeyance—has resumed with a vengeance. In a society in which the professions generally are suffering a loss of prestige and authority, the notion that the "management of violence" constitutes a distinctive field of endeavor to be mastered only through lifelong study no longer commands automatic assent.

Where does that leave soldiers?

With war no longer the chief reason for their existence, they are hard pressed to sustain the claim that the business of soldiering constitutes a unique calling, guided by its own values and nurturing its own culture. As a result, military service is in danger of becoming, as the distinguished so-ciologist Charles Moskos has suggested, just another job, subject to the so-cietal norms that govern other occupations.

Thanks to a long string of embarrassing incidents—beginning with the infamous Tailhook convention of 1991—the services themselves have man-aged to increase the pressures to adhere to those norms. Revelations about the predatory sex life of the Air Force's first woman B52 pilot, boorish drill sergeants hitting on female recruits at Aberdeen, the U.S. Army's top NCO hauled into the dock for sexual harassment, general officers being disci-plined for sleeping with the wives of their subordinates: These public rela-tions disasters not only demolished cherished images of the military as a repository of rectitude and propriety but undercut the Pentagon's efforts to sustain even minimal claims to autonomy.

For cultural progressives, these incidents have been a godsend. Forced onto the defensive, the services spent the 1990s appeasing their critics, in particular by striving to demonstrate enlightened attitudes regarding gen-der.[40] In the traditionalist camp of the culture war, such efforts triggered concerns about the "feminization" of the armed forces.

Although these concerns are not entirely misplaced, they miss the heart of the matter. The real problem is not the military's prospective emasculation but its inability to identify *any* persuasive rationale for maintaining a distinctive ethos. Adherents of the old school may still *recite* hallowed soldierly values—manliness, courage, discipline, sacrifice, self-abnegation—but the society from which the military fills its ranks no longer *assents* to those values. Certainly, most members of the elite, increasingly innocent of first-hand military experience, no longer connect such values to the actual role of present-day soldiers. A recent report in the *New York Times* makes the point. Struggling to explain the renewed popularity among soldiers of a Vietnam-era novel that is a tract on behalf of military traditionalism, the *Times* correspondent discounts the phenomenon as simply "nostalgia for simpler days with obvious heroes and villains . . . when 'duty, honor, and country' *really was* the soldier's calling."[41]

If indeed nostalgia is all that sustains the residual identification with the military ethic, then the profession's days are numbered. Young Americans of the current generation who choose to serve—themselves products of a culture that cherishes individual autonomy and lifestyle above all else—are not prone to nostalgia and differ little from their counterparts who stay back in the neighborhood. When today's soldiers deploy to keep the peace in Kosovo or to rebuild shattered nations like Bosnia-Herzegovina, they expect that the "neighborhood"—pizza places, video arcades, and cable television—will accompany them. The terms of the soldiers' implicit contract with their employer have changed accordingly.[42]

As traditional military culture erodes, other potentially perverse "values" fill the void. In the eyes of some analysts, the extraordinary sensitivity to casualties—so vividly on display during the Kosovo war and as prominent among senior officers as among their civilian counterparts—is itself "corrosive to the professional military ethic," endangering ancient principles such as the primacy of mission accomplishment.[43] The aversion to casualties may likewise reflect a growing aversion to risk of any kind. For those hoping to get ahead in today's military, "zero defects" is the rule—a precept more conducive to careerism than to leaders gutsy enough to ask tough questions of civilian officials inclined to view force as an all-purpose remedy to political predicaments.

Most troubling of all, the erosion of received values is also undermining old taboos that obliged soldiers to remain above politics. For generations, nonpartisanship formed an integral part of officership. Eminent soldiers like George Marshall thought it improper even to vote. Evidence suggests that such attitudes are on the wane. Today's officer corps has become consciously "conservative" in its outlook and identifies itself with the Republican Party.[44] This trend, if unchecked, suggests that the military may well become just another interest group like big business or big labor, wooed by opposing political factions and placing its own parochial concerns above the nation's.[45]

If the postliberal approach to civil-military relations weakens the second element of Clausewitz's trinity, by negating the traditional basis of military professionalism, it has had an equally damaging impact on the third element, excluding the people from a direct and active role in military affairs. The predictable result is a popular indifference that is manifesting itself in several ways. Members of Congress and their staffs are increasingly uninformed about and uninterested in military matters—except for hot button issues related to the culture war. Other institutions such as the prestige media or universities treat military subjects as hardly worthy of serious attention. (Again, the culture-war exception applies—the *New York Times* will interest itself in the rigor of boot camp only to the extent that it relates to the preservation of gender-integrated training).

For members of the elite, security, which in the liberal democratic era implied the citizen's obligation to contribute to the nation's defense, becomes in the postliberal age yet another function best satisfied by outsourcing. It is something that *they* do for *us*. Meanwhile, the plain folk, no fools, express their own indifference in a way that strikes directly at the very lifeblood of the armed services: They chose not to serve. As a result, the vaunted all volunteer force today faces the imminent prospect of running out of volunteers.[46]

Whether America's new technology-dependent way of war, vividly displayed in Kosovo, will suffice to create and maintain the global democratic imperium envisioned by Bill Clinton remains to be seen—although on that score the difficulties caused by an adversary as puny as Yugoslavia offer scant cause for optimism. No doubt the conduct of that war—at once pusillanimous and needlessly brutal—would have left Clausewitz for one appalled.

The thought of offending the sensibilities of a long-dead German soldier-intellectual is unlikely to trouble most Americans. When was the last time that Germany got a war right? Yet the trinitarian arrangement accompanying this new approach to employing American military power—a state with an appetite for empire, an exceedingly powerful army shorn of professional restraint, a self-absorbed and apathetic citizenry—would also likewise appall Americans whose views once commanded respect: soldiers like Washington, Marshall, and Eisenhower. That Americans have so casually discarded *their* views regarding the difficulty of balancing politics, military power, and liberty may yet prove our undoing.

Notes

1. In the end, according to estimates by journalists, "NATO killed about as many civilians as military personnel." Dana Priest, "France Played Skeptic on Kosovo Attacks," *Washington Post*, 20 September 1999, p. A1.
2. Jean Bethke Elshtain, "Whose Lives Are We Sparing?" *Washington Post*, 16 May 1999, p. B3.
3. Bill Clinton, "Statement by the President," 5 April 1999.
4. Quoted in Tim Weiner and Jane Perlez, "How Clinton Approved the Strikes on Capital," *New York Times*, 4 April 1999, p. 7.
5. Bradley Graham, "Joint Chiefs Doubted Air Strategy," *Washington Post* 5 April 1999, p. A1; Michael Hirsh and John Barry, "How We Stumbled Into War," *Newsweek*, 12 April 1999.
6. Admiral James O. Ellis, "A View from the Top." This undated briefing prepared in the immediate aftermath of Operation Allied Force provides lessons learned from the perspective of the officer commanding both U.S. naval forces in Europe and all NATO forces in Southern Europe.
7. John A. Tirpak, "Short's View of the Air Campaign," *Air Force* 82 (September 1999).
8. Dana Priest, "United NATO Front Was Divided Within," *Washington Post*, 21 September 1999, p. A1.
9. Steven Lee Myers and Eric Schmitt, "War's Conduct Creates Tension Among Chiefs," *New York Times* 30 May 1999, p. A1. Only on June 3 did the president even go through the motions of meeting with the Joint Chiefs as a group—a session widely interpreted as intended to provide political cover to permit Clinton to reverse his prohibition on the use of ground troops.
10. Jason DeParle, "Allies' Progress Remains Unclear as Few Details Are Made Public," *New York Times*, 6 April 1999, p. A10.
11. "Impersonal War On the Adriatic," *New York Times*, 9 April 1999, p. A10.
12. Patricia Cohen, "Ground Wars Make Strange Bedfellows," *New York Times*, 30 May 1999, p. wk5.
13. Interview with Margot Adler, "All Things Considered," National Public Radio, 29 June 1999.
14. The one breach in the Pentagon's policy of anonymity produced not empathy but embarrassment. The American public did become familiar with a specific handful of soldiers in the war zone, namely the three unfortunate G.I.s who were captured in Macedonia and incarcerated in Belgrade. The U.S. Army's

ill-advised decision to shower these soldiers with decorations upon their release provoked loud guffaws and contributed to the impression that the military was engaged in an attempt to manufacture heroes.

15. John Donnelly, "Air War Leader Greeted Coolly by Senators," *Boston Globe*, 2 July 1999, p. A1.

16. John M. Broder, "Laurels Elude President As Public Judges a War," *New York Times*, 22 June 1999, p. A22.

17. Carla Anne Robbins, "To All but Americans Kosovo War Appears A Major U.S. Victory," *Wall Street Journal*, 6 July 1999, p. A1.

18. Carl von Clausewitz, *On War* (Princeton: Princeton University Press, 1976), p. 89.

19. Quoted by Barbara Tuchman, *The American People and Military Power in an Historical Perspective*, Adelphi Papers, 173 (London: Institute for Strategic Studies), p. 6.

20. Gertrude Himmelfarb, *One Nation, Two Cultures* (New York: Alfred A. Knopf: 1999), p. 20.

21. Samuel P. Huntington, *The Clash of Civilizations and the Remaking of World Order* (New York: Simon and Schuster, 1996), pp. 301–308; James Kurth, "The Real Clash," *The National Interest* 37 (fall 1994): 3–15.

22. Bill Clinton, "American Security in a Changing World," Washington, D.C., 8 January 1997.

23. Madeleine K. Albright, "Address to the Milwaukee Business Community," Milwaukee, Wisc., 2 October 1998.

24. "Clinton's Speech on Kosovo: 'We Also Act to Prevent a Wider War,'" *New York Times*, 2 April 1999, p. A11.

25. Bill Clinton, "Remarks by the President to the Council on Foreign Relations," 14 September 1998.

26. Madeleine K. Albright, "Remarks and Q & A Session," Howard University, Washington, D.C., 14 April 1998.

27. Charles A. Beard and Mary R. Beard, *The Rise of American Civilization*, vol. 2 (New York: Macmillan, 1930), pp. 490–95; William Appleman Williams, *The Tragedy of American Diplomacy*, 2d ed., rev. (New York: Dell, 1972), *passim*.

28. Madeleine K. Albright, "Confirmation Hearing," 8 January 1997.

29. Bill Clinton, "Remarks by the President to the Council on Foreign Relations," 14 September 1998.

30. Bill Clinton, "Remarks by the President on Foreign Policy," San Francisco, Calif., 26 February 1999.

31. "Press Briefing by National Security Advisor Sandy Berger," Rio de Janeiro, Brazil, 15 October 1997.

32. Madeleine K. Albright, "Remarks and Q & A Session," Howard University, Washington, D.C., 14 April 1998.

33. Bill Clinton, "Remarks by the President in Foreign Policy Speech," Mayflower Hotel, Washington, D.C., 7 April 1999.

34. Bill Clinton, "American Security in a Changing World," Washington, D.C., 5 August 1996.

35. Bill Clinton, "Remarks by the President to American Society of Newspaper Editors," San Francisco, Calif., 15 April 1999.

36. Deputy Secretary of Defense John J. Hamre, "The Future of the U.S. Military Presence in Europe," Chicago, 4 August 1999.

37. The concept of using military power to "shape the environment" now permeates Pentagon documents. Senior military officers routinely cite it as a priority mission. See, for example, General Henry H. Shelton, "Surviving Peace," Harvard University, 11 December 1997.

38. "Clinton's Speech on Kosovo: 'We Also Act to Prevent a Wider War,'" New York Times, 2 April 1999, p. A11.

39. Bill Clinton, "Helping Write 21st Century International Rules," National Defense University, Fort McNair, Washington, D.C., 29 January 1998.

40. Stephanie Gutmann, "Sex and the Soldier," The New Republic, 24 February 1997, p. 19.

41. Elizabeth Becker, "Military Goes by the Book, but It's a Novel," New York Times, 16 August 1999, p. A15. Emphasis added. The novel is Once an Eagle by Anton Myrer.

42. By the year 2000, the U.S. Army at least had seemingly capitulated to the trend toward of individual autonomy, choosing a new recruiting slogan—"An Army of One"—in part because it conveyed the sense that military service offered an attractive avenue for "self-actualization." James Dow, "Ads Now Seek Recruits for 'An Army of One,'" New York Times, 10 January 2001, p. A1.

43. Peter D. Feaver and Christopher Gelpi, "A Look at Casualty Aversion," Washington Post, 7 November 1999, p. B3.

44. Tom Ricks, "Military Is Becoming More Conservative, Study Says," Wall Street Journal, 11 November 1997, p. A20.

45. The Republican Party already views the military as a constituency to which it lays claim. In another sign of the changing civil-military climate, the Republican National Committee now takes out ads in service-oriented newspapers attacking the commander in chief by name for having "damaged our military's readiness and hurt troop morale" and calling on soldiers to vote for the GOP. See the full-page ad entitled "Keeping the Commitment: Republicans Reverse Years of Military Neglect," Air Force Times, 13 December 1999, p. 57.

46. In the fiscal year ending in September 1999, the Marine Corps alone of the four services met its recruiting goal without compromising its standards—this despite the fact that the Pentagon is now spending $1.8 billion annually on recruiting. Andrea Stone, "Paying High Price for Preparedness," USA Today, 22 October 1999, p. 18A.

7 Revolution Deferred: Kosovo and the Transformation of War

Michael G. Vickers

I

In the decade since the Persian Gulf War, public debate over defense issues in the United States has been sporadic, diffuse, and generally desultory. To the extent that military matters have engaged the attention of citizens, discussion has tended to focus on issues such as the proper uses of force, on allegations of sagging combat readiness, and above all on social issues, especially those relating to gender and sexual orientation.

Among specialists, however, a different debate has occurred, one that has been continuous, narrowly focused, and intense. For a small but influential core of soldiers, defense analysts, and journalists, one issue above all others has dominated the defense agenda throughout the 1990s: the Revolution in Military Affairs (RMA). In the eyes of its adherents, the RMA constitutes the latest in a series of military revolutions—periods of profound change in military affairs that render obsolete existing means for conducting war. Earlier revolutions—for example, the industrialization of warfare in the nineteenth century or the emergence of naval air power and armored warfare between the world wars in the century just concluded—brought to the battlefield new technologies. The RMA promises to do so as well. But a military revolution is not exclusively a technological phenomenon nor does it occur instantaneously. The change entailed by a genuine revolution is also conceptual and social. Over a period of years or decades it transforms warfighting concepts, challenges traditional military organizations and bureaucracies, and generates radically different demands for human and material resources. In its simplest terms, the RMA is the military revolution of the information (and biotech) age, one that entails the adaptation of military institutions to the imperatives, opportunities, and dangers peculiar to that age. This essay explores the connection between the RMA debate and the war in Kosovo.

When the Cold War ended and victory in the Persian Gulf endowed the United States with the mantle of "world's only superpower," Americans found themselves in the possession of a force already exhibiting incipient RMA capabilities—stealth, precision-guided munitions (PGMs), and all-weather imaging satellites, for example. Yet the military establishment that existed in 1991 remained for the most part an artifact of the industrial age, albeit one that was magnificently trained and equipped. With the demise of the Soviet Empire, that force had both accomplished its primary purpose and largely outlived its usefulness. As even the most ardent fans of that force recognized—even General Colin Powell, then serving as the immensely influential chairman of the Joint Chiefs of Staff—the end of the Cold War demanded a "new" military.[1] America's need for military power had by no means diminished, but henceforth that power would respond to a different set of circumstances. The only questions concerned the extent and character of the change required.

In the decade that followed, a succession of high-profile commissions and study groups—beginning with the Bush administration's "Base Force" plan of 1991 and continuing through the Bottom-Up Review, the Commission on Roles and Missions, the National Defense Panel, and the first Quadrennial Defense Review—convened to chart a path toward defense reform. Along the way, each attempted to take the measure of the RMA and to assess its implications for the United States. To take Pentagon claims at face value, the result of this process was to win the military itself over to the imperative of transformation—fundamental institutional change. Senior leaders in each of the services fully embraced the need to transform Cold War–era forces. In documents such as Joint Vision 2010 and Joint Vision 2020, the imperative of "revolutionizing" the armed forces became official doctrine. Well-funded initiatives such as Army XXI—creating ground forces for a "digital battlefield"—seemingly affirmed that transformation was well underway. Indeed, those serving in uniform during the first decade of the post–Cold War era—a time of dizzying change and ceaseless activity producing an extraordinary outburst of interventionism abroad—could be forgiven for concluding that something akin to a revolution had indeed occurred.

The Kosovo war of 1999 offers an opportunity to take stock of defense reform. In that conflict, with only a handful of exceptions, U.S. forces performed to a very high standard. Yet the war against Yugoslavia shows that defense transformation has stalled. Despite a decade's worth of exertions, the process of adapting the U.S. military to the post–Cold War security environment has achieved disappointing results. If anything, the gap between actually existing capabilities and existing or emerging requirements looms larger than it did a decade ago. A decade of talk about an RMA had done remarkably little to bring it to fruition. Although Kosovo showcased some RMA-like capabilities on the part of the United States, the chief lessons of that conflict lie in what it tells us about the institutional impediments to a real transformation of the American military.

II

At one level, Operated Allied Force would seem to affirm that U.S. military dominance remains as great at the end of the 1990s as it was at the beginning of that decade. The United States and its NATO allies prevailed at minimal cost. Although the war was not without its well-publicized miscalculations and missteps—NATO underestimated Serb determination, failed to anticipate certain enemy actions, and committed egregious blunders such as bombing the Chinese embassy—these could be attributed to the fog and friction inherent to war. The fact of the matter is that NATO won and did so quite handily. A related fact of equal significance is that in conducting the war U.S. forces carried the lion's share of the burden and American air power enjoyed a near monopoly on the capabilities that finally delivered victory.

Yet if Operation Allied Force qualifies as a legitimate success, it offers little cause for complacency. Victory in this very small war against a small, backward country without powerful friends willing to act on its behalf was never seriously in doubt. A war pitting the United States and its NATO allies against the rump of Yugoslavia is the equivalent of a preseason scrimmage pitting a top NFL team against a high school squad. However scrappy and determined the high schoolers, the outcome of such a contest is foreordained, whether the NFL team is at the top of its form or merely starting to get in shape.

The security environment that is evolving in the aftermath of the Cold War confronts the United States with three, distinctive requirements, two of them glimpsed, however imperfectly, in Kosovo. The first of these involves maintaining an edge in military capability over potential peer competitors— not necessarily states of equivalent wealth and military capacity (there are none), but those like China that can, in the not too distant future, pose a serious military challenge, much as Japan did in the 1940s. This is the arena of long-term, high-technology competition in areas such as missile defense or maritime and space supremacy. By and large, Kosovo had nothing to do with this requirement.

The second requirement is the need to project superior military forces to critical regions such as Europe, the Persian Gulf, and Northeast Asia. The aim is, of course, chiefly to deter adventures such as Saddam Hussein's invasion of Kuwait in 1990, or Slobodan Milosevic's assaults on the non-Serb components of the disintegrating Yugoslav republic in the ensuing decade. But should deterrence fail—and clearly, throughout the 1990s it often did—the United States must be able to win its wars in a manner peculiar to the new international political environment, at extremely modest cost to itself in terms of military losses, and almost equally limited losses to enemy civilians. Many of these constraints have grown over time: They now seem to include, for example, a regard for the physical environment after the conduct of military operations.

The third requirement stems from the nature of conflict after the Cold War, and above all from the proliferation of ethnic and civil wars, the fraying and even collapse of fragile state structures, and the ready availability of military hardware to all kinds of substate entities. Whether it is called peacekeeping, humanitarian intervention, or (perhaps a more honest term) imperial policing, this function sets its own peculiar operational imperatives for vigilance, safety of both troops and civilians, and duration.

The three kinds of forces suggested by this analysis do not necessarily resemble one another. A space-dominance force, for example, would have little to offer a peacekeeping operation, although satellites might provide some useful support to such a force. The nonlethal munitions required to restrain crowds, or the identification technology useful in keeping track of individuals in an occupied population, might offer little for a mid-intensity conventional operation such as Kosovo. In all three cases, however, military technology, if properly fit into the right kinds of organizations and using the right kinds of operational concepts, should make modern armed forces look quite different from their predecessors of twenty or thirty years ago.

The Kosovo war shows that, despite all of the rhetoric about defense transformation in the 1990s, and despite all of the quasi-imperial experience of the same decade, the United States military lags far behind in developing the capabilities demanded by these requirements. Indeed, there is some danger that the success of the Kosovo war, inelegant though it might be, will impede rather than enhance the momentum for serious military reform.

III

As a measure of U.S. progress in perpetuating the dominance it enjoyed at the end of the Cold War, Kosovo serves, in some respects, as a classic "precursor war"—a conflict hinting at the potential of transformational change, even if it did not manifest that change fully. During Operation Allied Force, that potential was apparent in the performance of a variety of RMA-related systems, chief among them long-range precision strike weapons, advanced reconnaissance platforms, and techniques for conducting information warfare.

Thus, for example, the 49 sorties flown by the B-2 stealth bomber during Operation Allied Force constituted the first ever large-scale effort to mount a long-range, precision-strike offensive from a secure base on American soil.[2] Beginning on the first night of the war, the B-2 smashed Yugoslav command bunkers, radar installations, communications sites, bridges, arms factories, and other heavily defended targets. Continuing a practice first evident during the Persian Gulf War, for the first 58 days of Operation Allied Force only stealth aircraft—B-2s and F-117s—were used over the enemy capital.[3] Although the B-2 flew only 1 percent of all NATO sorties, it accounted for 11 percent of the bombs dropped during the campaign. The aircraft's precision targeting system produced a higher percentage of targets destroyed per target attacked than any other aircraft.[4] According to the campaign's senior air commander, Air Force Lieutenant General Michael Short, the B-2 with its all-weather satellite-guided bombing system was the "greatest technology success story of Operation Allied Force."[5] NATO Supreme Allied Commander General Wesley Clark concurred, testifying that the B-2 was "the key weapons system for continuing to bring pressure to bear on the enemy, and was an absolutely critical ingredient of success."[6]

Operation Allied Force also saw the introduction of several new PGMs, continuing the trend away from traditional "dumb" bombs. During Operation Desert Storm, PGMs had comprised a mere 7 percent of total munitions employed. For the air campaign in Kosovo that figure increased to 35 percent. Since the Gulf War, U.S. reliance on conventional PGMs to attack military and strategic targets has increased by an order of magnitude.[7] In four of the five most recent U.S. power projection operations, PGMs accounted for more than 60 percent of the total ordnance employed. (See Table 7.1.)[8]

During Operation Allied Force, cruise missiles further cemented their role, along with stealth aircraft, as weapons of first resort. U.S. forces used Global Positioning System–guided Tomahawk Land Attack Missiles (TLAMs) to attack nearly half of all government, military, and police headquarters, air defense systems, and electric power grids that were hit throughout the war. When NATO targeted the high rise that housed the Socialist Party headquarters and state-run television in Belgrade, it did so by programming eight TLAMs to strike precise aim points on the sixth floor and roof in order to disable the building's primary fire-sprinkler system. The building burned for three days. Nor were cruise missiles employed only against large fixed facilities. Twenty-six TLAMs, including 10 with sub-munitions, were also used against 18 mobile targets during the conflict. In all, U.S. surface ships and submarines fired 218 Tomahawk cruise missiles against 66 Serb targets. Approximately 181 hit their intended target.[9]

In addition, with the initial combat employment of the Joint Direct Attack Munition (JDAM), the war for Kosovo further accelerated the shift toward all-weather, GPS-guided munitions.[10] The $14,000 JDAM outperformed laser-guided bombs and cruise missiles that are 10 to 70 times more expensive, and became the weapon of choice for the most sensitive targets. For example, B-2-delivered JDAMs took out the Danube River bridges in Novi Sad that had defied laser-guided strikes.[11]

During Operation Allied Force, Unmanned Aerial Vehicles (UAVs) came of age. The near-continuous surveillance of Yugoslav field forces that they provided to NATO included extensive monitoring of the forced evacuation of ethnic Albanians. UAVs probed Serb air defenses, scouted attack and escape routes, identified targets, and performed battle damage assessment. They conducted electronic eavesdropping, served as airborne communica-

TABLE 7.1 Trends in PGM Use

Operation	TLAMs Expended	CALCMs Expended	Short Stand-Off/ Gravity PGMs Expended	Unguided Munitions Dropped	Percent Conventional Precision Strike
Deliberate Force— Bosnia, August–September 1995	13	33	662	318	69
Desert Strike— Iraq, September 1996	31	13	0	0	100
Desert Fox— Iraq, December 1998	330	90	230	250	72
Infinite Reach— Sudan/Afghanistan, August 1998	79	0	0	0	100
Allied Force— Kosovo, March–June 1999	218	111	≈7,700	≈15,000	≈35

SOURCE: Internal CSBA Research based on multiple sources

tions relays, and jammed Yugoslav communications. Had the war lasted a few days longer, the Air Force would have used UAVs mounting laser designators to pick out Yugoslav military targets.[12] The Pentagon even gave consideration to using an armed Israeli UAV to attack Yugoslav air defenses.[13]

Operational Allied Force also witnessed the first combat use of computer-network attack tools by the U.S. military. An information operations (IO) cell reportedly launched attacks against the command and control infrastructure supporting Serb air defenses. Part of the effort involved manufacturing false radar images and signal-intelligence intercepts and inserting them into the Serb air-defense system.[14] Only a small portion of the offensive information-warfare "toolbox" was apparently used, however. According to one senior U.S. commander, "Properly executed, IO could have halved the length of the campaign. . . . All the tools were in place . . . [but] only a few were used."[15]

Complementing these limited information warfare attacks, the United States for the second time in a decade employed specialized warheads to disable a nation's electrical grid. Electronic power distribution munitions containing spools of fine, electrically conductive filaments wreaked havoc on Serbia's electrical power infrastructure, to include both power generating stations and transformer yards. Conductive filaments shorted out high voltage lines and caused five power grids to fail, cutting off electricity to 70 percent of the country.[16]

Submarines played a limited role in Allied Force, but still managed to deliver 25 percent of all cruise missiles launched during the 78-day campaign—a six-fold increase over the 1991 Persian Gulf War.[17] One sub, the USS *Miami*, made history of sorts by conducting Tomahawk launches successively against Iraq in Operation Desert Fox and against Yugoslavia in Operation Allied Force.[18]

Yet if Operation Allied Force affirmed the potential of certain RMA capabilities, it also revealed the extent to which several others were in very short supply. At the time of the war for Kosovo, only nine B-2s had been outfitted to full operational ("Block 30") configuration. During the campaign, the Pentagon's total inventory of critical munitions such as the conventional air-launched cruise missile (CALCM) and the JDAM fell below one hundred. To enable U.S. forces to prosecute their war against Milosevic, the Pentagon found itself obliged to raid munitions stockpiles of commands in other regions of the world.[19] According to Duncan Hunter, chairman of the House Armed Services Committee's Subcommittee on Military Procurement, Kosovo showed that the Pentagon's procurement of PGMs is not keeping up with the growing U.S. appetite for using them.[20]

Finally, with respect to Kosovo as a test case for evaluating U.S. efforts to sustain global military dominance, what did not happen during this eleven-week precursor war is as important, if not more so, than what did occur. In contrast to any future peer competitor worthy of the name, the rump state of Yugoslavia lacked the capability of placing the American homeland at risk. It was unable to challenge U.S. access to forward bases or to outer space. It could not threaten American control of the sea. To state the matter bluntly, the Yugoslavia that managed to hang on for 11 weeks provides at best a weak surrogate for the sort of military power that the United States must be able to defeat and would prefer to overawe.

IV

Casting the war for Kosovo as a surrogate for imperial policing produces conclusions that are more troubling still. Like it or not, the lion's share of responsibility for imperial policing will fall to the service that has traditionally in U.S. history served as a military constabulary—the United States Army. Just as the army in the nineteenth century pacified the West, at the dawn of the last century governed Cuba and the Philippines, and after World War II occupied Germany and Japan, so too the army of the post–Cold War era is fated to assume similar responsibilities. Events in Somalia, Haiti, and Bosnia within the last decade, and in Kosovo itself in the war's aftermath, make that abundantly clear.

Yet the actual war over Kosovo shows how slow the army has been to grasp the full implications of its new/old role. Converting the army of the Cold War into an effective instrument for imperial policing also requires transformation, albeit of a different sort than that required to exploit the RMA. The army's embarrassing contribution to Operation Allied Force shows how far that service lags behind in effecting the necessary change.

The war over Kosovo can be viewed as an episode in imperial policing in this sense: The massive violation of international norms posed by the Yugoslav campaign of ethnic cleansing—a campaign that allied air power failed to check—required a ground presence to provide immediate, effective protection to the afflicted Kosovar Albanian population. That portion of the army agile enough to deploy on short notice to the theater of operations—

traditional light infantry—lacked survivability. Sending the 82d Airborne Division (or for that matter U.S. Marines) to the rescue would have entailed the risk of substantial U.S. casualties. Neither political nor military authorities in Washington were willing to accept that risk. Yet when the Pentagon at the urging of the Supreme Allied Commander Europe attempted to improvise a force with more muscle, the result was a full-fledged fiasco. Task Force Hawk, the army's much ridiculed effort to deploy an attack-helicopter task force to the war zone, fell victim to inadequate technology, poor operational readiness, and a long-standing institutional propensity, in the words of former Chief of Staff General Dennis Reimer, "to go in a little too heavy." The result was a mix of tragedy and farce.

To support and protect a mere 24 AH-64 Apache attack helicopters, the army determined that it was necessary to deploy a grand total of 6,200 troops. To provide this contingent with the wherewithal it required, the army shipped 26,000 tons of equipment to a staging area in Albania. Doing so consumed 550 C-17 sorties and cost $480 million. The cargo included more than a dozen 70-ton M1A1 tanks—too heavy to use on most Albanian roads—42 Bradley fighting vehicles, and 24 Multiple Launch Rocket Systems with extended-range, Army Tactical Missile System missiles. To preside over this arsenal, the army cobbled together a tactical headquarters that itself required the shipment of 20 five-ton Expando vans from Germany. The army also shipped 190 containers of ammunition, and enough repair kits to support twice the number of Apaches actually deployed. Thirty-seven other utility helicopters—Blackhawks and Chinooks—rounded out this mammoth task force.

Fabricating a base from which this force could operate posed further challenges. Transforming the tiny airfield at Rinas, Albania, into an adequate facility required 667,000 square meters of rock fill and 58 specially designed landing pads. Self-deploying the Apaches from their base in Germany alone took 12 days. When they arrived, they were not ready for combat. Sixty-five percent of the pilots had fewer than 500 flying hours under their belts.[21] None were proficient in flying with night-vision goggles.[22] With the Joint Chiefs doubting the wisdom of the operation and the army warning of heavy losses if the Apaches went into combat, it is hardly surprising that the task force assembled over a period of weeks at such great expense never got into the fight. The protection that U.S. forces offered to the hapless victims of ethnic cleansing was limited to receiving the survivors into refugee camps.

V

The limitations of the force with which the U.S. went to war in Kosovo—measured against the requirements of either global power projection or imperial policing—reflect both the lingering legacy of the Cold War and also the outcome of the post–Cold War drawdown. In this as in other respects, Operation Allied Force resembled Operation Desert Storm, the Gulf War of 1991. In both cases, the military's chief reaction to the conflict was a mixture of satisfaction at a predetermined success and irritation at not having had even more of a free hand at using the full-range of capabilities at its disposal. Although the Pentagon throughout the 1990s repeatedly touted its commitment to "revolutionary" change, and although a decade of experience with peacemaking, peacekeeping, and humanitarian intervention has reacquainted American soldiers with the demands of imperial policing, the services have clung whenever possible to the Cold War status quo. At best, the services have pursued a "revolution without pain" that leaves core platforms intact and attempts to preserve familiar organization, procedures, and war-fighting concepts. The army won't relinquish its heavy tanks. The navy won't give up its carriers. And the air force continues to insist that short-range, manned fighters constitute the real essence of air power.

Consistent with this preference for the familiar, the allocation of defense resources emphasized consumption over investment throughout the 1990s. From the peak year of the Reagan buildup (FY 1985) to the war in Kosovo, annual investment spending plummeted from $184 billion to $92.1 billion. In the meantime, funding for operations and support (which includes operations and maintenance, personnel, military construction, and family housing) declined by little more than a fifth, from $252.4 billion to $200.5 billion.[23] Making matters worse, the preponderance of research and development since the end of the Cold War has gone to completing the development of systems devised during (and for) the Cold War or to making incremental improvements to systems already fielded.

For example, the centerpiece of the Pentagon's current investment program is the planned purchase of three new tactical fighters: the Air Force F-22, the Navy F/A-18E/F, and the Joint Strike Fighter. Current plans call for the purchase of 339 F-22s, 548 F/A-18E/Fs, and 2,852 Joint Strike Fighters (1,763 for the Air Force, 480 for the Navy, and 609 for the Marine Corps).

Development and procurement costs for the three aircraft are projected to total a jaw-dropping $340 billion.[24] Other big-ticket purchases include the construction of three new aircraft carriers at a cost of some $18 billion, some 30 Virginia-class attack submarines at nearly $2 billion each, and a fleet of 458 V-22 Osprey tilt-rotor, vertical-takeoff and -landing aircraft at a cost of $35 billion. The army meanwhile plans to replace most of its existing inventory of helicopters with a fleet of 1,213 Comanche helicopters for $35 billion, and to upgrade its arsenal of heavy artillery with 480 Crusader self-propelled howitzers, bigger than the guns they replace and priced at $11 billion. Five separate theater-wide missile defense systems, expected to cost in excess of $40 billion, are also in the works.[25]

As this emphasis on short-range manned aircraft, massive aircraft carriers, and heavy artillery suggests, from both strategic and budgetary perspectives the Pentagon's actual investment plan will go further toward perpetuating the existing force structure than toward transforming it. Even at that, the total cost of the wish list assembled by the services exceeds by $40–50 billion or more *per year* the amount of funding currently projected to be available.[26]

To a remarkable extent, the RMA-relevant systems showcased over Kosovo barely managed to avoid being "crowded out" of 1990s defense budgets in favor of "legacy" modernization. The size of the B-2 fleet, a hotly debated issue since the end of the Cold War, offers a case in point. In 1981 the Reagan administration first established the projected size of the B-2 fleet at 132 aircraft.[27] A month after the fall of the Berlin Wall, Secretary of Defense Richard Cheney ordered a review of four major aircraft programs, among them the B-2. While the review classified the B-2 chiefly as a nuclear-armed bomber, Secretary Cheney also speculated that "the B-2's conventional capabilities will become increasingly important as forward forces decline and the need for rapid-decisive global power projection increases."[28] Still, in April 1990, for fiscal and political reasons, Cheney reduced the planned B-2 buy to 75 aircraft. A little over a year later, the number slipped even further. Influential members of the House of Representatives, led by Rep. Ron Dellums (D-Calif.) and Rep. John Kasich (R-Ohio), capped the B-2 program at a paltry 20 aircraft, despite a plea from President George H. W. Bush.[29]

Politics, not defense requirements, produced the decision to cut the B-2 force to 20.[30] Top military and defense officials at the time and ever since assailed the decision as ham-handed and illogical. According to former Air Combat Command commander General John Loh, "we got to 20 not because it was the right number; we got to 20 because it was the minimum number to provide an operational capability."[31] But such a capability would indeed be no more than minimal.[32]

Operation Desert Storm seemingly demonstrated the requirement for a robust force of stealthy long-range bombers. Yet studies sponsored by the Clinton administration repeatedly reaffirmed the decision to limit the B-2 fleet to 20 (now 21) aircraft. To reach their conclusion, however, these studies relied on unrealistically optimistic assumptions about warning time, American access to forward bases, and the feasibility of swinging forces between theaters. Analyses undertaken beyond the administration's aegis, it should be noted, came to sharply different conclusions. For example, the 1997 Independent Bomber Force Review chaired by former National Security Adviser Brent Scowcroft argued that in the uncertain security environment of the twenty-first century the U.S. requirement for long-range air power will, if anything, increase. The panel recommended congressional funding of at least nine additional B-2s (adding an additional squadron to the two currently in the force structure). It also suggested that Congress create an air-force command responsible for long-range strike operations.[33] The review concluded, "With no funding, no modernization plan, and no evident concern for their absence, the bomber force faces inevitable extinction."[34]

Hostility to the B-2 may well be sharpest within the air force itself. That antagonism, according to the Scowcroft Commission, stems in no small measure from bureaucratic politics. The ascendance of "fighter generals" over "bomber generals" since the 1980s has greatly weakened institutional support for long-range bombers.[35] Thus, whereas in 1950 the ratio of fighters to bombers in the U.S. inventory was 2:1, by 1995 it had grown to 16:1.[36] The ratio of fighter investment to bomber investment is projected to increase by more than an order of magnitude from FY 1998 to FY 2003 (3.5:1 to 37.5:1). Development of a follow-on to the B-2 is not scheduled to begin until 2019, with procurement deferred until 2034.[37]

As with the B-2 bomber, the tale of UAV development by the Department of Defense is one of half-hearted support and squandered opportunity. The United States currently has two promising UAV programs under development: the Global Hawk high-altitude, long-endurance UAV and the Unmanned Combat Air Vehicle. The RQ-4A Global Hawk is to replace the U-2, a manned long-range, high-altitude reconnaissance aircraft now four decades old.[38] Global Hawk is expected to have a range of 14,000 miles and to fly at an altitude of more than 65,000 feet, transmitting images of ground targets via satellite. Global Hawk is currently projected to cost $15.3 million each, far less than a U-2.[39] The spy plane demonstrated its potential in a recent exercise, flying a 28-hour, trans-Atlantic mission and transmitting imagery directly to U.S. forces in the field.[40] The non-stealthy Global Hawk, however, cannot penetrate denied air space. In short, it is susceptible to being shot down. Yet a high-altitude, long-endurance UAV with a stealthy design, the "Tier III," died at the hands of budget cutters early in the Clinton administration.

The only other surviving major UAV initiative is the Unmanned Combat Air Vehicle (UCAV), a stealthy, 26-foot-long, boomerang-shaped craft being developed by Boeing.[41] UCAV will have a range of 1,000 miles, be able to fly 550 miles per hour, and carry up to a dozen 250-pound bombs. It will be controllable either via AWACS aircraft or ground station. At $10 million per plane, it is projected to cost about two-thirds *less* than the Joint Strike Fighter while possessing comparable strike capabilities.[42] Development costs are projected to be orders of magnitude less.[43] Initial fielding of the UCAV is currently projected after 2010.[44]

But if UCAV survives that long the credit will go less to the Pentagon than to the system's congressional promoters. In the year 2000, the chairman of the Senate Armed Services Committee, Senator John Warner, proposed a goal of making one-third of operational deep-strike aircraft unmanned within ten years.[45] Warner has his work cut out for him. As a senior defense official noted, "assimilating new technologies is very difficult for a very structured organization, especially if those technologies are somewhat threatening to the organization."[46] To an air force whose founding identity revolves around manned flight, UAVs and UCAVs pose such a threat.

The submarine offers a third case demonstrating the obstacles impeding defense transformation. In one sense, of course, the sub is an unlikely symbol of revolutionary change: It has formed an essential part of the fleet for decades. Yet if reconfigured to perform new roles, this familiar type of warship offers a readily available means to improve RMA capabilities—especially for long-range attack of land-based targets. One promising idea entails the conversion of four Ohio-class, Trident nuclear ballistic missile submarines (SSBNs)—designed to deliver strategic nuclear weapons—into SSGNs or platforms for delivering conventional munitions. The START II Treaty already requires the United States to reduce its Trident fleet from 18 to 14 boats. When the navy begins decommissioning these submarines beginning in FY 2003, they will each have 20 years of operational life left. Converting the boats to SSGNs would entail retrofitting their 24 ballistic missile launch tubes to accommodate 154 cruise missiles (22 tubes with 7 missiles each) and up to 66 Navy SEALs or other commandos. The net cost of conversion would be between $500 million and $1 billion per boat.[47]

The SSGN would carry more Tomahawks than any other currently existing platform. It would also deliver them far more economically than other platforms. With a total of four SSGNs available, two would be deployed at any given time. The unknown presence of an SSGN might help catch an enemy unawares, and the SSGN's ability to "ripple fire" all 154 missiles in six minutes would have potentially devastating effects. The SSGN would also facilitate large-scale special operations. Having a stealthy platform capable of firing several dozen Tomahawks, according to Clinton administration Secretary of the Navy Richard Danzig, would, in turn, free up attack subs and other assets from the hard-pressed surface fleet for other missions.

Nevertheless, as with the B-2 and UAV, the SSGN faces significant opposition. Within the Navy's surface warfare community, many see it as a threat to the next generation of destroyer, the DD-21. Whether or not the SSGN ever makes the leap from concept to reality stands as another measure of the Pentagon's ability to distance itself from the status quo.

VI

The point is not that building more B-2s instead of new types of short-range fighters, favoring unmanned over manned aircraft, or transforming a handful of SSBNs into SSGNs will alone secure long-term U.S. military dominance. Indeed, as expressions of the RMA, these particular systems represent at best the preliminary outlines of a revolution still very much in the making. Rather, the point is that the shilly-shallying, hesitancy, and niggardliness that have characterized the Pentagon's embrace of even these readily available RMA capabilities testifies to the larger obstacles to genuine defense transformation. If the United States fails to overcome those obstacles, it risks forfeiting to others—powers less wedded to industrial-age conceptions of warfare—advantages that the RMA offers.

Although the dimensions of a fully mature RMA are at present only dimly seen, it holds the promise of capabilities that within a decade or two will make even the most advanced, cutting-edge weaponry of the 1990s seem out of date. Those capabilities include: space-based radar satellites that can track moving ground targets; ground- and air-based radars that can "see through walls"; sophisticated information warfare tools; non-lethal weapons based on directed energy (e.g., high-power microwaves) or biotechnology; advances in miniaturization leading to micro-UAVs and micro-satellites; stealthy, information-intensive ground forces that rely heavily on robotics; and the development of sea-control techniques employing extended-range, anti-ship missiles, stealthy, weaponized UAVs, land-based over-the-horizon radars, and ocean-surveillance satellites. The continued evolution of the RMA and the diffusion of RMA capabilities can no more be averted than could the nuclear arms race following Hiroshima. Barely recognized by most Americans, a competition to exploit the RMA's military potential for political advantage is now well underway.

The record of reform in the 1990s—and, more particularly, the way that the military has chosen to interpret the "lessons" of Kosovo—underscores the reality that it is by no means a foregone conclusion that the United States will prevail in this competition. For the most part, the Pentagon concluded that Operation Allied Force produced few lessons worth noting, certainly none that required any rethinking of service-procurement plans. Victory over Milosevic affirmed the Pentagon's sense of complacency. It reinforced the military's conviction that all would be well if only a post-Clinton presidency would bump up the aggregate level of defense spending, thereby permitting the services to follow through on plans to restock their arsenals with next-generation aircraft carriers and fighter planes.

There is one exception to that statement. Coming out of Kosovo, the United States Army found itself face-to-face with irrelevance and declared that it had "gotten the message." In short order, the army jettisoned its ill-advised Army XXI project—little more than an effort to add a gloss of information technology to a conception of mechanized warfare dating back to the 1930s —and embarked on a new initiative to create lighter, more-mobile forces. This marked a radical change of course for the army. It remains to be seen whether this new initiative will produce forces able to satisfy the full range of high-end power-projection challenges and imperial policing burdens facing the army. Still, this one service at least deserves credit for its willingness to reexamine hitherto sacrosanct assumptions. Absent such willingness, defense transformation will remain a chimera.

Why should Americans care? Do not the easy triumphs of Operations Desert Storm and Allied Force, bookends on the decade of the 1990s, indicate that all is well? One might respond that, in war, smugness sooner or later gets its comeuppance: In 1870, a highly professional French army, armed with a superior rifle and prototypical machine guns, was soundly whipped by a German army that had achieved unprecedented standards of operational excellence; in 1942, American and British pilots were amazed to find themselves pitted against a Japanese air force qualitatively superior to their own; in 1973, cocky Israeli tankers paid a heavy price at the hands of semi-literate Egyptian peasants whom they had crushed with ease only six years earlier. History is replete with such surprises.

In the case of present-day America, the potential outlines of such a surprise are already visible. These include a China investing heavily in weapons aimed at neutralizing American aircraft carriers and surface warships; lesser antagonists looking to weapons of mass destruction or relatively primitive missiles to deter U.S. intervention or intimidate American allies; and guerrillas and terrorists becoming ever more skillful at operating in urban and semi-urban environments. These antagonists understand America's strengths and weaknesses — its impatience, its open if complex decision-making system, its reluctance to suffer or inflict heavy losses. Only the most sanguine temperament would assume that no opponent, or collection of opponents, will figure out ways to bypass America's strengths and capitalize on its weaknesses.

In the end, the impetus for challenging old assumptions about defense may have to come from outside the armed services. Based on a very preliminary reading of events, the administration of President George W. Bush, especially Bush's secretary of defense, Donald Rumsfeld, seems to appreciate that point. Shortly after taking office, the new Bush administration dashed the hopes of military leaders (and many Republican supporters) by announcing that it had no intention of requesting an immediate boost in defense spending. Rumsfeld insisted that before entertaining requests for a possible budget increase he would conduct a comprehensive review of strategic requirements, a review driven from the top rather than cobbled together so as to satisfy the niceties of interservice consensus. This approach offers cause for hope that Rumsfeld is aiming for more than cosmetic change. But the actual conclusions reached by that review, and Rumsfeld's capacity to implement them, remain to be seen. Neither the services nor their allies in Congress and within the defense industrial sector are likely to relinquish their hold on the past without a fight. But if the United States continues to defer the transformation required both for global dominance and imperial policing, it may well find that the war over Kosovo ends up being the last "easy win" it enjoys for some time.

Notes

1. Colin Powell, *My American Journey: An Autobiography* (New York: Random House, 1995), pp. 435–58.

2. The aircraft were refueled in the air twice on the way to Kosovo, and an additional two times on the return leg.

3. Bill Sweetman, "B-2 Is Maturing Into A Fine Spirit," *Jane's International Defense Review*, May 2000. While pilot error appears to have been the principal cause of the F-117 shootdown—the bomb door was reportedly left open between target runs, causing the aircraft's radar cross section to increase substantially—the plane's "first generation" stealth technology, now some twenty years old, is increasingly vulnerable to long-wave, early-warning radars.

4. Frank Wolfe, "Pentagon Report Lauds B-2; Notes Shortfalls," *Defense Daily*, 16 February 2000, p. 6.

5. Paul Richter, "B-2 Drops Its Bad PR In The Air War," *Los Angeles Times*, 8 July 1999, p. 1.

6. Tony Capaccio, "U.S. Won't Order More Northrop B-2s, Stevens Says," *Fort Worth Star-Telegram*, 2 July 1999.

7. On PGM trends and information operations, see Andrew Krepinevich and Robert Martinage, "Transforming Strategic Strike Operations" (Washington, D.C.: Center for Strategic and Budgetary Assessments, 2001).

8. Totals exclude PGMs used in Operations Southern and Northern Watch, which are still ongoing. As of summer 1999, PGMs comprised 86 percent of the weapons used in Northern Watch and 100 percent of those used in Southern Watch.

9. Bryan Bender, "Tomahawk Achieves New Effects In Kosovo," *Jane's Defence Weekly*, 19 July 2000, p. 3.

10. B-2 stealth bombers were the only aircraft configured at the time to drop the new bombs. A total of 656 JDAMs were expended during Allied Force.

11. Patrick Ryan, "The Bargain Basement Bomb," (Long Island) *Newsday*, 14 November 1999, p. 23. JDAM development was spurred by failures during the Persian Gulf War, where sandstorms and smoke from oil fires foiled some laser-guided bomb strikes, and by the desire to reduce costs. JDAMs also permit bomb release from much higher altitudes, enhancing aircraft and pilot survivability. Alas, not all JDAM achievements during the Kosovo war fell on the positive side of the ledger. It was a JDAM that took out the Chinese embassy in downtown Belgrade.

12. David Fulghum, "Kosovo Conflict Spurred New Airborne Technology Use," *Aviation Week & Space Technology*, 23 August 1999, p. 30.

13. Bryan Bender, "Cold War Treaty Could Block Future US Weapons," *Jane's Defence Weekly*, 20 October 1999. The United States refrained from using a

bomb-dropping UAV—the "Harpy" on loan from Israel—because of concerns that doing so might violate the Intermediate Nuclear Forces Treaty with the former Soviet Union. The State Department subsequently determined that weaponized, *reuseable* UAVs are not cruise missiles and, as such, would not violate the treaty.

14. David Fulghum, "Yugoslavia Successfully Attacked by Computers," *Aviation Week & Space Technology*, 23 August 1999, pp. 31, 34. See also David Fulghum, "Telecom Links Provide Cyber-Attack Route," *Aviation Week & Space Technology*, 8 November 1999, p. 81, and Bob Brewin, "Kosovo Ushered in Cyberwar," *Federal Computer Week*, 27 September 1999, p. 1.

15. Andrew Rathmell, "Information Operations—Coming of Age?," *Jane's Intelligence Review*, May 2000, p. 52.

16. See David Fulghum, "Electronic Bombs Darken Belgrade," *Aviation Week & Space Technology*, 10 May 1999, pp. 34–36, and "Russians Analyze U.S. Blackout Bomb," *Aviation Week & Space Technology*, 14 February 2000, p. 59.

17. Andrea Stone, "Request For Subs Could Spark Defense Battle," *USA Today*, 8 March 2000, p. 22A. The 25-percent figure includes British as well as U.S. attack submarines.

18. Richard Newman, "The Navy Weighs A Potent New Weapon," *U.S. News & World Report*, 28 February 2000.

19. Bryan Bender, "US Weapon Shortages Risked Success In Kosovo," *Jane's Defence Weekly*, 6 October 1999. Laser-guided bombs and the AGM-130 television and infrared-guided missile were among the weapons transferred from other commands.

20. Sheila Foote, "Services Reviewing Requirements For Preferred Munitions," *Defense Daily*, 20 October 1999, p. 1.

21. "Army Hunts For Answers As Apaches Fail In Kosovo," *Baltimore Sun*, 16 July 1999.

22. Dana Priest, "Army's Apache Helicopter Rendered Impotent In Kosovo," *The Washington Post*, 29 December 1999, p. 1. During the three weeks of training with night-vision goggles to prepare for operations in mountainous terrain, accidents killed two Apache pilots.

23. Steven M. Kosiak, *Analysis of the FY 2001 Defense Budget* (Washington, D.C: Center for Strategic and Budgetary Assessments, February 2000), Appendix: Table 4. All figures are in FY 2001 dollars.

24. Steven M. Kosiak, *Options for U.S. Fighter Modernization* (Washington, D.C: Center for Strategic and Budgetary Assessments, September 1999), p. 4.

25. Cost estimates are derived from DoD Selected Acquisition Reports and other sources. Theater-wide missile-defense programs include a Patriot upgrade (PAC 3), Navy Area Defense, Navy Theater-Wide, Theater High Altitude Air Defense (THAAD), and the Airborne Laser.

26. For additional details, see Michael G. Vickers and Steven M. Kosiak, *The Quadrennial Defense Review: An Assessment* (Washington, D.C.: Center for Strategic and Budgetary Assessments, December 1997).

27. President Ronald Reagan, Remarks and a Question-and-Answer Session with Reporters on the Announcement of the United States Strategic Weapons Program, 2 October 1981, in *Public Papers of the Presidents: The Administration of Ronald Reagan, 1981* (Washington, D.C.: U.S. Government Printing Office, 1982), p. 879.

28. Richard Cheney, in House Armed Services Committee, Hearings, *National Defense Authorization Act for Fiscal Year 1991—H.R. 4739*, HASC No. 101-45, 101ˢᵗ Cong., 2ⁿᵈ sess., p. 790.

29. President George Bush, Address to the American Defense Preparedness Association, 9 July 1991.

30. A test-flight vehicle was later upgraded by the Clinton administration, bringing total force size to 21 aircraft—16 in operational units and 5 for attrition reserve and training.

31. General John Loh in House National Security Committee Hearings, *National Defense Authorization Act for Fiscal Year 1996—S.1124 (H.R. 1530)*, HNSC No. 104-4, p. 1219. The House Armed Services Committee had originally tried to cap the B-2 fleet at 15 aircraft, which would have yielded just one squadron of no more than 11 combat-ready aircraft—enough, according to General Loh, for a limited operation like the 1986 raid against Libya, but little else.

32. Secretary of the Air Force Donald Rice in House Armed Services Committee Hearings, *National Defense Authorization Act for Fiscal Year 1993*, HASC 102-41, p. 235.

33. *Scowcroft Independent Bomber Force Review*, p. 17, reproduced in *Congressional Record—House*, 23 June 1997.

34. Ibid., p. 3.

35. A 1995 survey of 283 serving air-force generals revealed that nearly 60 percent had some background in tactical aviation, while a little more than 10 percent had an association with the bomber force. Among the 10 four-star generals, none had a bomber background, while 9 had experience in tactical aviation. Cited in Andrew Krepinevich, *The Air Force of 2016* (Washington, D.C.: Center for Strategic and Budgetary Assessments, 1996), p. 19.

36. Barry Watts, "The Air Force in the Twenty-First Century," in *The Emerging Strategic Environment*, ed. Williamson Murray (Westport, Conn.: Praeger, 1999), pp. 183–217.

37. U.S. Air Force, "Air Force White Paper on Long-Range Bombers," 1 March 1999, p. 10.

38. Among the payloads the Global Hawk will carry is an advanced synthetic-aperture radar system, capable of 1-ft. resolution. A Global Hawk flying over

Philadelphia will be able to take targetable images of the Pentagon. Global Hawk's radar will also have a ground moving-target indicator capability. See David Fulghum, "UAV To Carry U-2 Recce Unit," *Aviation Week & Space Technology*, 15 May 2000, pp. 28–30.

39. Christian Lowe, "Global Hawk Costs Soaring," *Defense Week*, May 1, 2000, p. 6.

40. Timothy Gaffney, "Pilotless Spy Plane, Crosses Ocean," *Dayton Daily News*, 18 May 2000, p. 1E.

41. The UCAV has been unofficially dubbed the "Uncounted Air Vehicle." Airforce officials are wrestling with ways of forming two UCAV squadrons without having them count against the service's authorized limit of 20 fighter wings.

42. Dave Moniz, "Air Force's Pilotless Bombers To Be Tested Next Year," *USA Today*, 21 August 2000, p. 8A.

43. The UCAV is currently a $110-million technology-development program. Cost savings would also accrue from operations. The air force currently spends about $2 million for initial training of each pilot, and about $1 billion a year to keep 2,000 F-16 pilots trained and ready for their job. See Paul Richter, "Pilotless Plane Pushes Envelope For U.S. Defense," *Los Angeles Times*, 14 May 2000, p. 1.

44. Boeing, the prime contractor, estimates that engineering and manufacturing development would take six years and would involve eight flight-test vehicles. Production of 202 UCAVs (enough for nine squadrons) could begin as early as 2013. At any given time, 80 percent of the UCAVs would be in storage, with the other 20 percent undergoing maintenance or training. Mark Hewish, "Coming Soon: Attack of the Killer UAVs, *Jane's International Defense Review*, September 1999, p. 36.

45. "Warner: Speed Development of Unmanned Combat Systems," *Defense Daily*, 9 February 2000, p. 1. The air force is conducting experiments to adapt Predator as a weapons carrier—in part, it seems, to head off congressional pressure for more spending on UCAVs. "Air Force Plans Demonstration Of Predator's Ability To Drop Bombs," *Inside the Air Force*, 26 May 2000, p. 1.

46. Christian Lowe, "Pentagon Drafting Master Plan For UAVs," *Defense Week*, 17 July 2000, p. 1.

47. Rick Newman, "Navy Sizes Up Tomahawk Tridents," *Defense Week*, 28 February 2000, p. 1.

Index